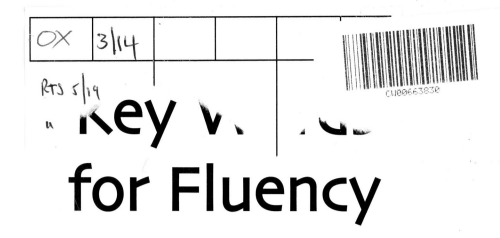

Key Words
for Fluency

Intermediate
collocation practice

learning and practising the
most useful words of English

George Woolard

HEINLE

Australia • B   om • United States

3302919060

Key Words for Fluency Intermediate
George Wollard

Publisher: Christopher Wenger

Director of Development: Anita Raducanu

Development Editor: Jimmie Hill

Director of Marketing: Amy Mabley

Intl. Marketing Manager: Eric Bredenberg

Production Manager: Sally Giangrande

Sr. Print Buyer: Mary Beth Hennebury

Illustrator: Bill Scott

Cover/Text design: Anna Macleod

ISBN: 978-0-7593-9628-9

Heinle, Cengage Learning EMEA
Cheriton House, North Way, Andover, Hampshire, SP10 5BE
United Kingdom

Cengage Learning is a leading provider of customised learning solutions with office locations around the globe, including Singapore, the United Kingdom, Australia, Mexico, Brazil and Japan. Locate our local office at **international.cengage.com/region**

Cengage Learning products are represented in Canada by Nelson Education Ltd.

Visit Heinle at **http://elt.heinle.com**
Visit our corporate website at **www.cengage.com**

The author

George Woolard is an experienced ELT teacher and trainer who has worked in Greece, Malaysia and the UK. He now teaches at Stevenson College, Edinburgh. His publications include Lessons with Laughter and Grammar with Laughter (Thomson ELT).

Acknowledgements

I am grateful to Michael Lewis for his comments in the early stages of the development of the Key Word approach that underpins this book. should also like to thank those colleagues and students at Stevenson College, Edinburgh, whose feedback proved invaluable during the development and writing of this material. Lastly, I am particularly grateful to my editor, Jimmie Hill, for his meticulous comments and guidance in shaping this book. George Woolard

Printed in China by RR Donnelley
3 4 5 6 7 8 9 10 – 13 12 11

To the student

Dear Student

Words have friends!

You have probably spent a long time learning new words. However, it is not enough to know only a word and its meaning. You also need to know what other words it combines with to make natural expressions in English. Words have friends, and you need to know who they are! We call this relationship between words 'collocation'. This is a very important part of learning vocabulary.

Key words

This book practises the collocations of some of the most useful words in English. These 'key words' are the nouns we use to talk about particular topics. For example, nouns like *trip, flight, passport* are key words if you want to talk or write about travelling.

How is the book organised?

This book is organised into topics, divided into 22 sections. Each section consists of a number of one-page units. Each unit consists of a box at the top of the page, which lists the most common collocations of the key word. This is followed by exercises which help you to notice and practise the collocations of that key word in natural expressions and sentences.

How to use this book

There is simply not enough time to learn all these collocations in class, so this book is designed for self-study, and will help you to develop your vocabulary quickly and independently.

If you do one unit of this book every day, in under a year you will have learned over 3,000 expressions. That will make an enormous difference to your English!

This book can also help you with your work in class. For example, if the topic in your coursebook is about jobs, then it would be a good idea to look at Unit 4 – Work.

Lastly, collocation practice is one of the best ways to prepare for the FCE and similar examinations, especially for the speaking and writing sections.

Keep this book!

This is a book for life. When you have completed the exercises, it becomes your personal vocabulary reference book – a resource book that you can return to again and again.

George Woolard
Edinburgh 2005

Contents

Before you begin   6

Section 1: A place to live
world   10
country   11
home   12
building   13
accommodation and rent   14

Section 2: The environment
environment   16
pollution, fumes, waste and rubbish   17
earthquake and flood   18
storm   19
damage   20

Section 3: The natural world
weather   22
heat and temperature   23
air   24
light   25
fire   26
water   27
noise and silence   28

Section 4: Work
job   30
career   31
staff and duty   32
qualification and interview   33
skill   34
training   35
wage, salary and pay   36

Section 5: Travel
trip   38
holiday   39
flight   40
delay and destination   41
passenger   42
passport and visa   43
luggage and fare   44

Section 6: Traffic
traffic   46
street   47
route and map   48
accident   49
injury   50

Section 7: Education
education   52
course   53
lesson   54
practice and homework   55
exam and mark   56

Section 8: Sport and fitness
sport   58
team   59
game   60
race, competition and match   61
victory   62
defeat   63
prize   64
strength   65
energy and exercise   66

Section 9: Health
health   68
illness   69
disease and infection   70
stress   71
smoking and drugs (illegal)   72
pain   73
appointment, symptom and test   74
treatment and cure   75
operation and drug   76

Section 10: Money
money and cash   78
savings, fortune and debt   79
price   80
fee and charge   81
expense   82

Section 11: Food
food   84
drink   85
meal and dish   86
diet and appetite   87
party   88

Section 12: Fun and entertainment
fun and entertainment   90
joke   91
television and programme   92
concert   93

fan and audience   94

film   95

music and song   96

Section 13: People

life   98

death   99

age   100

character   101

clothes and fashion   102

appearance   103

habit and routine   104

Section 14: Relationships

friend   106

enemy   107

marriage   108

divorce   109

love   110

respect   111

family   112

Section 15: The body and the senses

head   114

hand   115

heart   116

eye   117

sight   118

view   119

smell   120

taste   121

voice   122

breath   123

sleep and dream   124

Section 16: Feeling and mood

feeling   126

mood   127

happiness and pleasure   128

anger   129

fear and anxiety   130

worry   131

confidence   132

disappointment and relief   133

surprise and shock   134

Section 17: Society

government and election   136

vote   137

society   138

justice   139

law   140

Section 18: Crime and punishment

crime and criminal   142

offence, offender and victim   143

arrest and charge (criminal)   144

evidence   145

trial and verdict   146

sentence and fine   147

punishment and prison   148

Section 19: Conflict

war   150

peace   151

attack   152

defence   153

bomb and explosion   154

casualty   155

weapon and gun   156

dispute and strike   157

campaign and demonstration   158

Section 20: Communication

language   160

conversation   161

discussion   162

speech   163

secret, rumour and lie   164

Section 21: Information

news   166

message   167

document   168

article   169

letter   170

mail   171

advert, publicity and reputation   172

Section 22: Technology

machine   174

equipment   175

computer and internet   176

fault   177

repair   178

Answer Key   179

Alphabetical List of Words   196

Before you begin

1. What are key words?

'Key words' are the most common and most useful words in English. They are the most important words to learn. The main reason they are important is because they can combine with lots of other words in short expressions. We call these expressions 'collocations'.

2. What are collocations?

Collocation is 'the grammar of words' – how words go together with other words. Collocation tells us which words can come before or after other words. Here are some examples from this book:

> • verbs with money
> You can earn money, save money, lend money, and inherit money.
> • adjective with price
> You can pay the full price for something. Perhaps you only paid half-price.
> • verbs with food
> You can prepare, serve, eat and waste food.

These are just a few of the collocations you will learn in this book.

3. Why are all the key words in this book nouns?

Nouns are the most important words we know. All the other parts of speech – adjectives, pronouns, adverbs, verbs, and prepositions – are important too, but they don't tell us as much as nouns do. Nouns tell us WHAT we are talking about:

> a language

Verbs then tell us what we can do with a language:

> learn it, acquire it, speak it or translate it.

Adjectives can then tell us what kind of language:

> our first language, a foreign language, body language, bad language.

But the most important idea is to start with ideas or things which we express with nouns. If you are having a meal and you would like the salt, you could simply say:

> salt

Everybody knows that you want the salt. So you could have said:

> the salt
> or   the salt, please
> or   pass the salt, please
> or   Could you pass the salt, please?

We know that the last sentence is the best way of saying what we want. If we had said:

> Could you pass the X, please?

nobody would know what we wanted! In this situation, the noun 'salt' carries 99% of our meaning.

4. Why is it important to learn the collocations of the most important nouns?

If we know 100 of the most important nouns, and we learn 10 verbs or adjectives which can go with them, we will then know 1,000 expressions. Every time we learn 100 nouns with 10 collocations of each, we add another 1,000 expressions to our vocabulary. Quite simply, learning to use more words along with the words we already know is the most useful way to expand our English. If you study all three books in this Key Words for Fluency series, you will learn over 10,000 expressions.

5. Who chose the words in this book?

These words chose themselves! In all the modern databases of English, the key words in this book are among the most commonly used. The best way for you to improve your English is to learn the most common collocations of these most common words. This intermediate book contains around 15 collocations of over 200 of the most useful words at this level. That means you will practise over 3,000 useful expressions if you study this book. Dictionaries contain thousands of words and expressions, but they cannot tell you which ones to learn or how to use them.

"He makes too many silly mistakes!"

The 3,000 expressions in this book will help you to improve and help you to pass your examinations.

6. Why is this book called Key Words for Fluency?

Fluency is the ability to speak naturally, listen efficiently, read quickly, and write well. What does this mean?

1. Speaking naturally means NOT making everything up one word at a time, but speaking in whole expressions at normal speed.
2. Listening efficiently means understanding people at the speed at which they speak. This means that when you hear the first word of an expression or the first few words of a sentence, you know how it is going to end.
3. Reading quickly means that your eye is ahead of your brain! You are able to predict what the author has written.
4. Good writing is writing which expresses exactly what you want to say in natural ways which the reader will immediately understand.

All those skills depend on having a large store of words and expressions which you don't need to think about or construct every time you use English. The more collocations you know, the less you need to think! And the more fluent your English becomes.

7. Test yourself!

Here are eight common situations. You should be able to guess the missing words immediately.

1. I need to work harder at my English. I make too many silly . . . .
    The answer is 'mistakes'. Although people would understand what you meant if you said 'faults', it is not the word we use in this situation. Again, 'make a mistake' or 'make mistakes' is a fixed expression – a collocation.

2. Look, we've got plenty of time. I'd like to see what the countryside round here is like. Let's take the scenic . . . . home.
    The answer is 'route'. You wouldn't say 'scenic road' or 'scenic way'. The collocation is 'scenic route'. If you used 'way' or 'road', people would understand, but 'scenic route' is the natural choice.

3. If your television breaks down in the first three months, we promise to replace it free of . . . .

   The answer is 'charge'. You might have guessed 'cost'. Again, your meaning is clear, but the collocation used in this situation is 'free of charge'.

4. Not only did she win the marathon, she also set a new world . . . .

   The answer is 'record'. In fact, the whole collocation is 'set a new world record'. This is a good example of a verb + adjective + noun collocation. Most of the collocations in this book are two or three words:
   verb + noun   or   adjective + noun   or   noun + preposition + noun
   This example shows that collocations can be quite long. It is really important that you learn the whole expression.

5. There's been a coup and the president and his family have fled the . . . .

   The answer is 'country'. You 'flee a country' if you are a politician and you want to get out fast! We don't 'flee the nation' – always the country.

6. On the way to Athens last week, we flew through an electric storm. The plane was struck by

   . . . .

   The answer is 'lightning'. You are 'struck by lightning'. You can't be 'struck by thunder'. The collocation 'struck by lightning' is fixed. You never need to think about it! Just learn it and remember it!

7. It's so stuffy in here. I just want to get out into the fresh . . . .

   The answer is 'air'. You might think of saying: I just want to get outside. Because we have this ready-made collocation 'get out into the fresh air', that's the natural thing to say!

8. Sorry, I'm late. The traffic was terrible. My taxi got stuck in a traffic . . . .

   The answer is 'jam'. The collocation 'traffic jam' is so common, it's difficult to think of it as two words! However, it is important that you notice and learn the whole expression 'got stuck in a traffic jam'. And it is equally important that you make yourself use the expression. Practise by changing the pronoun, the tense, and the context. For example:
   We got stuck in a huge traffic jam on the way to the airport and missed our flight.
   I try to avoid the rush hour because I hate getting stuck in traffic jams.

Finally

I hope that these 8 examples help you understand why noticing and learning collocation is so important:

- The more collocations you know and can use, the more fluently you will be able to speak. It means you won't have to make up everything new all the time – you can just remember whole expressions.
- The more collocations you know, the easier it will be to understand people who speak quickly – particularly native speakers.
- The more collocations you know, the easier it will be to read because you won't have to read every word.
- The more collocations you know, the easier it will be to write well and accurately. You won't need to translate from your own language into English as much.

Section 1

A place to live

world   10

country   11

home   12

building   13

accommodation and rent   14

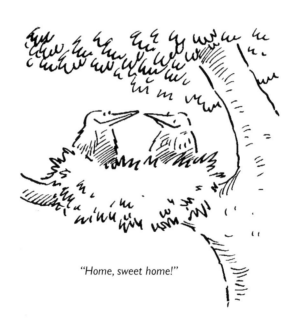

"Home, sweet home!"

world

Verb + world	Adjective + world	World + noun
change the world	a changing world	world affairs
destroy the world	an ideal world	world peace
take over the world	the outside world	a world authority
see the world	a safer world	a world record
	the whole world	

1. Verb + world

Complete the sentences with the correct form of the above verbs:

1. As a young man I wanted to . . . . the world before I settled down. That's why I went off to Australia and New Zealand.
2. Like many young people, my son is very idealistic and he wants to . . . . the world and make it a better place.
3. Man is the only creature capable of . . . . the world.
4. Fast food outlets seem to have . . . . over the world. You'll find burgers and fries in almost every corner of the planet.

2. Adjective + world

Complete these sentences with the above adjectives:

1. As the only survivor of the crash, I felt I was the luckiest man in the . . . . world.
2. We must get rid of nuclear weapons to guarantee our children a . . . . world.
3. We live in a rapidly . . . . world and must learn to adapt if we are to succeed.
4. In an . . . . world, no one would go hungry.
5. The people on this small island have no telephones or radios – they are completely cut off from the . . . . world.

3. World + noun

Complete these sentences with the above nouns:

1. Dr Voits, a world . . . . on UFOs, will be giving a talk in the main lecture theatre this evening.
2. Maurice Green broke his own world . . . . when he won the 100 metres at the Olympics.
3. If you want to broaden your knowledge of world . . . . , you should read a newspaper every day.
4. The recent increase in terrorism is a real threat to world . . . .

Notes

1. Note these prepositional expressions:
   The ceremony was watched by millions around the world / throughout the world / the world over.
2. Note these expressions:
   There's nothing in the world we can do about it. (nothing at all)
   There's no need to rush, we've got all the time in the world. (have plenty of time)
   He carried on, without a care in the world. (not worried about anything at all)
   The food was out of this world! (fantastic)
   Thanks for coming. It means the world to me. (very important to me)
3. Note that if you break a world record, you become the world record holder.

Key Words for Fluency – Intermediate

country

Verb + country	Adjective + country	Common expressions
enter a country	a foreign country	countries break off relations
flee a country	a free country	countries go to war
paralyse a country	a neighbouring country	countries gain independence
represent a country	an underdeveloped country	countries host sporting events
run a country	a wealthy country	countries sign agreements

1. Verb + country

Complete the sentences with the correct form of the above verbs:

1. He .... the country to escape arrest for the murder of his wife.
2. A rail, air and bus strike has .... the country. Most offices and factories have had to shut down.
3. You'll need a visa to .... the country.
4. Many people are unhappy with the way the government is .... the country.
5. She was proud to .... her country at the recent Olympics.

2. Adjective + country

Complete these sentences with the above adjectives:

1. It's hard to believe that, in such a .... country, some people don't have enough food.
2. It's difficult to live in a .... country if you don't speak the language.
3. Don't tell me what to do! It's a .... country and I can do what I like!
4. The UN is often involved in settling border disputes between .... countries.
5. The developed world should provide more aid to .... countries.

3. Common expressions

Match the halves:

1. Which country will host
2. Twenty countries signed
3. The country gained
4. Our country has broken off
5. The two countries are in danger of

a. independence from the UK in 1967.
b. going to war over oil.
c. diplomatic relations with the UK.
d. an agreement to stop whaling.
e. the next Olympic Games?

"She was so proud to represent her country!"

Note

Note these verb + preposition expressions:
We are here today to honour those who fought and died for their country in two World Wars.
Thirty illegal immigrants have been deported back to the country they came from.
All vehicles are checked at the border to prevent drugs being smuggled into the country.

home

Verb + home	Home + noun	Verb + noun + home	Preposition + home
get home	home address	take a taxi home	at home
head home	home cooking	see (you) home	away from home
leave home	home delivery	send (you) home	from home
return home	home town	welcome (you) home	on the way home
call home			
own your home			

1. Verb + home

Complete the sentences with the correct form of the above verbs:

1. He . . . . home at the age of 18 and joined the army.
2. I think we should . . . . home now, before it gets too dark.
3. I might be able to go – it depends on what time I . . . . home from work.
4. Some people want to . . . . their home, while others are quite happy to rent.
5. I . . . . home once a week on my mobile to see how my parents are keeping.
6. We became increasingly worried when our daughter failed to . . . . home.

2. Home + noun

Choose the correct collocation:

1. When I went away to university I missed my mother's home cooking / meals.
2. Please remember to write your home address / street at the top of the letter.
3. The price of the dishwasher includes free home transport / delivery and installation.
4. When she dies, she wants to be buried in her home city / town.

3. Verb + noun + home

Complete the sentences with the correct form of the above verbs:

1. The teacher . . . . him home from school for bad behaviour.
2. One of my colleagues . . . . me home safely after the party.
3. If you miss the last bus, you can always . . . . a taxi home.
4. Hundreds of fans went to the airport to . . . . their team home.

4. Preposition + home

Match the two halves:

1. My job involves a lot of travel so I'm
2. There was nobody
3. I stopped at the supermarket
4. The internet makes it possible

a. on the way home from work.
b. to work from home.
c. at home when I called.
d. away from home for weeks at a time.

Notes

1. Note these adjective collocations:
   My ideal home would have an indoor swimming pool and it would overlook the sea.
   He's from a broken home. His parents separated when he was only four.
   They spend the summer in their holiday home in the French Alps.

2. Note the expressions 'home-grown' and 'home-made':
   We had home-grown vegetables and home-made bread for lunch.

building

Verb + building	Adjective + building	Noun + prep + building
construct a building	a derelict building	appearance of a building
demolish a building	an empty building	damage to the building
convert a building	a fine building	entry to the building
evacuate a building	a high-rise building	a floor of the building
restore a building	the main building	the tenants of a building
	a public building	

1. Verb + building

Complete the sentences with the correct form of the above verbs:

1. Our company has the contract to design and . . . . the new parliament building.
2. This beautiful old building has been painstakingly . . . . to its former glory.
3. Within minutes of receiving the bomb threat, we had . . . . the building.
4. There are plans to . . . . the old school building into homes for the elderly.
5. Engineers say that the building is unsafe and that it will have to be . . . .

2. Adjective + building

Complete the sentences with the above adjectives:

1. Our footsteps echoed through the . . . . building.
2. New York has . . . . buildings everywhere.
3. On the day of the King's funeral, flags flew at half mast on all . . . . buildings.
4. Many homeless people end up sleeping rough in parks and . . . . buildings.
5. My department isn't in the town centre, but the . . . . building of the university is right in the middle of town.
6. Prague is a beautiful city with lots of . . . . buildings.

"It's nothing but high-rise buildings everywhere!"

3. Noun + preposition + building

Complete the sentences with the above nouns:

1. . . . . to the building has been estimated at £60,000.
2. By law, there has to be a fire exit on each . . . . of the building.
3. The burglars gained . . . . to the building through the back door.
4. All the . . . . of the building are unhappy about the increase in rents.
5. The interior of the hotel has been extensively renovated, but the outward . . . . of the building hasn't changed for over 100 years.

Notes

1. Note how we say we like a building:
   It is an attractive building with beautiful gardens.
   The castle is an impressive building with its high walls and huge gate.
   The Blue Mosque in Istanbul is a truly magnificent building.
2. A 'listed building' is one which cannot be changed without permission from the government. It is usually an important building because of its history or design.

accommodation and rent

Verb + accommodation	Adjective + accommodation	Verb + rent
find accommodation	free accommodation	afford the rent
provide accommodation	furnished accommodation	owe rent
live in accommodation	self-catering accommodation	pay the rent
guarantee accommodation	temporary accommodation	put up the rent
		withhold the rent

1. Verb + accommodation

Complete the sentences with the correct form of the above verbs:

1. We help new employees to . . . . suitable accommodation in the city. Most find something they like within a week or two.
2. Students are . . . . accommodation in the halls of residence for their first year. We're lucky we have plenty of student flats and rooms.
3 It's a small hotel but it can . . . . accommodation for up to thirty people.
4. My Uncle Paul is disabled and . . . . in sheltered accommodation, where there is a warden on call to provide help if needed.

2. Adjective + accommodation

Complete the sentences with the above adjectives:

1. The council is using the local school hall as . . . . accommodation for the families made homeless by the recent floods.
2. We're in . . . . accommodation, so we'll be doing all our own cooking.
3. The flat had a bed and a chair! That's not what I call . . . . accommodation!
4. In return for . . . . accommodation and food, I tidy the house and look after the two kids while the parents are at work.

3. Verb + rent

Complete the sentences with the correct form of the above verbs:

1. I . . . . a slightly higher rent than the other tenants in the flat because my room is the biggest.
2. The landlord wants to . . . . up the rent by £25 a month, but I'm refusing to pay any more.
3. We're . . . . the rent until the landlord agrees to get the central heating fixed.
4. We need a bigger house for our large family, but we can't . . . . the rent.
5. The landlord is threatening to evict the tenants if they don't pay the rent they . . . . by the end of the week.

Notes

1. Note these expressions with 'accommodation':
   There's a shortage of / a lack of cheap rented accommodation for students in London.
2. Note these expressions with 'rent':
   Since losing my job, I've fallen behind with the rent. (not able to pay it)
   The rent is due one month in advance. (pay for the month ahead)
   Most of my salary goes on rent. I've very little left for food and entertainment.
   I have a spare room to let at a monthly rent of £55.
   What's the rent on the house?

Section 2

The environment

environment   16
pollution, fumes, waste and rubbish   17
earthquake and flood   18
storm   19
damage   20

"Now, Carol, don't you think you're taking this a bit too far?"

environment

Verb + environment	Adj + environment	Noun + prep + ...
respect the environment	a hostile environment	damage to the environment
harm the environment	a male environment	effect on the environment
pollute the environment	a pleasant environment	a threat to the environment
protect the environment	a safe environment	in harmony with the ...
	a stress-free environment	the destruction of the ...

1. Verb + environment

Complete these sentences with the correct form of the above verbs:

1. Many of the town's factories continue to . . . . the environment. The local rivers have all been ruined by the chemicals from some of them.
2. I always try to buy eco-friendly products that don't . . . . the environment.
3. The government hopes to teach children to . . . . the environment through new projects in schools.
4. Acid rain produced by factories is killing trees across the country. The government must introduce new policies to . . . . the environment.

2. Adjective + environment

We use 'environment' to describe the conditions that we learn and work in. Complete the sentences with the above adjectives:

1. My office is quite bright and spacious. It's a . . . . working environment. Unlike some people, I actually like coming to work!
2. No working environment is entirely . . . . There are always pressures.
3. As a deep-sea diver I have to work in a dangerous and . . . . environment.
4. I work in a predominantly . . . . environment. I'm the only woman in the office!
5. Employers should provide a . . . . working environment for their employees so that accidents are avoided as far as possible.

3. Noun + preposition + environment

Complete these sentences with the above nouns:

1. Many chemicals used in industry have a damaging . . . . on the environment. Some of them take a very long time to disappear.
2. Overpopulation is probably the greatest . . . . to the environment today.
3. It's important that tourism develops in . . . . with the environment.
4. Every day large areas of forest disappear to make paper for newspapers. Few of us take the time to think about this large scale . . . . of the environment.
5. We are causing serious . . . . to the environment by using up the Earth's natural resources.

Notes

1. An 'environmentalist' is someone who wants to protect the environment.
The Green Party is a political organisation whose main aim is to protect the environment.
Greenpeace is an international organisation which organises protests around the world to protect the environment.
2. We talk about 'environmentally-friendly products'.

　　　　　　　Key Words for Fluency – Intermediate

pollution, fumes, waste and rubbish

Verb + pollution	Verb + fumes	Verb + waste	Verb + rubbish
reduce pollution	inhale fumes	create waste	clear up rubbish
pollution destroys	fumes pour out	dispose of waste	collect rubbish
pollution threatens	be overcome by	dump waste	pick up rubbish
pollution rises	fumes	recycle waste	recycle rubbish

1. Verb + pollution

Complete these sentences with the correct form of the above verbs:

1. Most cars now have a catalytic converter to help . . . . pollution.
2. Air pollution has . . . . to unacceptable levels in some areas of the city.
3. Scientists have warned that pollution is . . . . the ozone layer.
4. Pollution from the oil tanker is . . . . fish farms all along the coast.

2. Verb + fumes

Complete these sentences with the above verbs:

1. Thick black exhaust fumes were . . . .
   out of the back of the old bus.
2. Three firemen needed hospital treatment
   after . . . . poisonous fumes.
3. A number of workers were . . . .
   by toxic fumes from the burning factory and
   had to be carried out of the building by firefighters.

"You should've seen the black exhaust fumes pouring out of the bus!"

3. Verb + waste

Complete these sentences with the above verbs:

1. We have a compost bin which we use to
   . . . . our household waste.
2. The company was fined for . . . .
   untreated industrial waste into the river.
3. We use too much packaging on food.
   It . . . . a lot of unnecessary waste.
4. Is there a safe way to . . . . of nuclear waste?

4. Verb + rubbish

Complete these sentences with the correct form of the above verbs:

1. The rubbish is . . . . on Mondays, but I put the bin out on Sunday night.
2. Who's responsible for . . . . up the rubbish after the carnival?
3 Please . . . . up your rubbish when you leave, and put it into the bins.
4. Why not . . . . your household rubbish instead of throwing it away?

Note

Note these expressions:
The government lays down strict guidelines for the disposal of hazardous waste.
There should be an international ban on the dumping of radioactive waste at sea.
After the match the stadium was littered with rubbish.

earthquake and flood

Verb + earthquake	Flood + verb	Flood + noun
predict an earthquake	floods cause damage	flood damage
survive an earthquake	floods cut the area off	flood victim
set off an earthquake	floods hit the area	flood warning
withstand an earthquake	floods sweep things away	flood water
earthquakes hit		
earthquakes devastate		
earthquakes shake buildings		

1. Verb + earthquake

Complete these sentences with the correct form of the above verbs:

1. Most of the tall buildings in Tokyo have been designed to . . . . earthquakes. It's always the older buildings which sustain the most damage.
2. A major earthquake will probably . . . . Los Angeles within the next 50 years.
3. In the future, scientists hope to become more accurate in . . . . earthquakes. But persuading people to leave their homes is another matter!
4. A huge earthquake, measuring 7.5 on the Richter scale, ... the whole region. There are only a few buildings left standing in the whole area.
5. The earthquake . . . . many buildings in the area, but the tremors were not powerful enough to cause any of them to collapse.
6. Few buildings . . . . the earthquake intact. Most suffered damage of some kind or other.
7. There are fears that the slight tremors we have experienced in recent months may . . . . off a full-scale earthquake.

2. Flood + verb

Complete these sentences with the correct form of the above verbs:

1. The floods have . . . . off a number of villages in the area. Rescue services are using boats to get food and drinking water through to the flood victims.
2. The region was . . . . by a series of flash floods. There was no time to issue flood warnings and hundreds were drowned as a result.
3. Heavy floods have . . . . away homes and roads in the south of Bangladesh. Villagers will have to wait until the flood waters recede before they can return.
4. These severe floods have . . . . widespread destruction. It'll be months before the flood damage is cleared up.

Now underline the flood + noun expressions in the sentences.

Notes

1. Note these expressions with 'earthquake':
   The west coast of America is prone to earthquakes. (likely to be affected by them)
   It's an earthquake-prone region.
   Hundreds of people were buried alive in the earthquake.
   Places like Naples and Los Angeles are in earthquake zones.

2. Note these expressions with 'flood':
   People living in low-lying areas were evacuated to higher ground because of the floods.
   After the catastrophic floods the government declared a state of emergency.
   The floods have left thousands of people homeless.

storm

Verb + storm	Common expressions
storms break	badly damaged in a storm
storms strike	blown down in a storm
storms destroy	blown off in a storm
storms rage	struck by lightning in a storm
storms die down	wrecked in a storm
be caught in a storm	uprooted in a storm
sleep through a storm	

1. Verb + storm

Complete these sentences with the correct form of the above verbs:

1. Hundreds of people were made homeless when severe storms . . . . the east coast of America.
2. A violent storm . . . . just as we reached the beach, and we had to run for shelter.
3. A terrible storm . . . . for two whole days. We couldn't leave our hotel till it had . . . . down. It was terrifying!
4. The old church was completely . . . . in the great storm of 1954.

Complete the verb phrases with the correct preposition:

5. We were caught . . . . . . a heavy storm on the way home last night.
6. I don't know how you managed to sleep . . . . . . the thunderstorm.

2. Common expressions

Match the halves:

1. Two ships were driven onto rocks and
2. A number of roofs were
3. One of the town's oldest buildings was badly
4. Thousands of trees were
5. Several people were struck by lightning

a. blown off during the violent storms.
b. during yesterday's electrical storm.
c. uprooted in the great storm.
d. wrecked in the storm.
e. damaged in the storm.

"Thousands of trees were uprooted in the storm."

Notes

1. Note these expressions with 'storm':
   We took shelter from the storm in a bus shelter.
   The storm left 10,000 homes without power or water.
   The storm caused widespread damage.
   It was the worst storm in living memory.
2. Note this expression:
   It was the storm of the century! Nobody has seen anything like it!
3. 'It was a storm in a teacup' means there was a lot of argument, or worry about something unimportant.

damage

Verb + damage	Noun + of + damage
cause damage	the cost of the damage
insure against damage	the extent of the damage
prevent damage	a risk of damage
suffer damage	signs of damage
repair damage	(£200) worth of damage

1. Verb + damage

Complete these sentences with the correct form of the above verbs:

1. Please help us to .... damage to the forest by keeping to the paths.
2. The storm .... damage to property estimated at £100 million.
3. Your house doesn't seem to have .... much damage in the gales.
4. All our household products are .... against theft and accidental damage.
5. It'll cost about £50,000 to .... the damage caused by the fire.

2. How much damage?

Mark the sentences (LOT) if they mean a lot of damage, and (LIT) for little damage:

1. The volcanic eruption caused considerable damage to buildings. It will take millions of dollars to repair them.
2. When the river floods, it causes extensive damage to the surrounding villages.
3. It was a relatively small earthquake. It caused only minor damage to buildings.
4. Fortunately, there were no injuries, and the damage to my car was minimal.
5. The oil spill has killed fish and caused incalculable damage to the coastline.
6. The house only suffered superficial damage from the high winds. Only a few slates were missing from the roof.
7. If we don't reduce pollution, we will cause serious damage to the environment.

3. Noun + of + damage

Complete these sentences with the above nouns:

1. Storms cause thousands of pounds' .... of damage to property every year.
2. It was difficult to appreciate the full .... of the damage at the time. It was not until the morning after that the sheer scale of the damage could be seen.
3. The .... of the damage caused by the oil spill will be around £200 million.
4. Although we hit a rock, there were no obvious .... of damage to the boat.
5. Unless we can lower the levels of air pollution, there is a serious .... of damage to some of the old buildings and monuments in the city centre.

Notes

1. Note the adjectives we use to describe damage that can't be repaired:
   If we can't stop the oil leaking from the tanker, irreparable damage will be done to the coastline.
   De-forestation has caused irreversible damage to the soil. Nothing will ever grow in it again.
   The small amounts of toxic chemicals in these fish can cause permanent brain damage in children.
2. Note this expression:
   Don't worry. No damage has been done.
3. Note that in 3-2 'extent of the damage' and 'scale of the damage' are similar in meaning.

Section 3

The natural world

weather   22
heat and temperature   23
air   24
light   25
fire   26
water   27
noise and silence   28

"Typical!"

weather

Verb + weather	Adjective + weather	Noun + prep + weather
the weather changes	(boiling) hot weather	the best of the weather
the weather holds	(bitterly) cold weather	a break in the weather
the cold weather sets in	dry weather	a pleasant spell of weather
dress for the weather	wet weather	a sudden change in the
the weather turns hot or	glorious weather	weather
cold	unpredictable weather	

1. Verb + weather

Complete these sentences with the correct form of the above verbs:

1. You're not properly . . . . for this sort of weather. Put a coat on!
2. If the fine weather . . . . until the weekend, we'll go camping.
3. After a cool bright day, the weather . . . . warm and thundery last night.
4. There's a chill in the air. It looks like the weather is . . . . for the worse.
5. We'll need to paint the outside of the house before the cold weather . . . . in.

2. Adjective + weather

Complete these sentences with the above adjectives:

1. It's 35°C today. We don't usually have such boiling . . . . weather in Britain,
   but the summers have become warmer in recent years.
2. Bring plenty of warm clothes with you. In January the weather is bitterly . . . .
3. Be careful. The path down to the beach can be quite slippery in . . . . weather.
4. Exceptionally . . . . weather over the past year has led to a shortage of water.
5. My parents had two weeks of . . . . weather, but it rained all the time here.
6. Scotland is a beautiful country, but it has notoriously . . . . weather. It can be
   pouring with rain one minute and brilliant sunshine the next!

3. Noun + preposition + weather

Match the two halves:

1. A lot of us were caught out by the sudden change in weather.
2. It's been an unusually long period of dry and settled weather.
3. I think we got the best of the weather in the north today.
4. We're hoping for a break in the weather.

a. London certainly seems to have got the worst of the weather, with rain all day.
b. Few of us had bothered to bring an umbrella.
c. We won't be able to take the boat out if this wind continues.
d. We haven't had such a pleasant spell of weather for a long time.

Notes

1. Note these expressions:
   After a good start we ran into some bad weather and had to travel more slowly.
   We'll have your birthday party outside, weather permitting. (if the weather is suitable)
   He goes out jogging in all weathers. (even when it is raining, snowing etc)
2. The 'weather forecast' is a statement of what the weather is likely to be:
   The weather forecast said it would rain all day tomorrow.

Key Words for Fluency – Intermediate

temperature and heat

Verb + temperature	Adjective + temperature	Verb + heat
control the temperature	the average temperature	escape from the heat
take somebody's ...	a constant temperature	feel the heat
the ... rises / increases	a high temperature	generate heat
the ... falls / drops	freezing temperatures	lose heat
temperatures reach 40°C		withstand heat

1. Verb + temperature

Complete these sentences with the correct form of the above verbs:

1. The temperature will drop sharply tonight. it is expected to . . . . to minus 10.
2. Tomorrow the temperature will . . . . steadily to a maximum of about 22°C.
3. When I was in hospital, a nurse . . . . my temperature every two hours.
4. In some areas temperatures can . . . . 40°C in the summer.
5. You can . . . . the temperature in this room by adjusting the thermostat on the radiators.

2. Adjective + temperature

Complete these sentences with the above adjectives:

1. . . . . temperatures have turned the lake into a skating rink.
2. The art gallery's heating system maintains a . . . . temperature to protect the paintings.
3. Make sure you heat the food to a . . . . temperature to kill any harmful bacteria.
4. What's the . . . . temperature in Cairo in July?

3. Verb + heat

Complete the sentences below with the correct form of the above verbs:

1. I could . . . . the heat of the sun on my back as I walked through the park.
2. Rubbing your hands together will . . . . heat and keep them warm.
3. Houses . . . . a lot of heat through their windows.
4. In summer, we leave the city for the seaside to . . . . from the oppressive heat.
5. The Space Shuttle uses special tiles to help it . . . . the extreme heat of re-entry into the Earth's atmosphere.

Notes

1. Note the following expressions with 'temperature':
   Red wine is best served at room temperature.
   Temperatures soared into the 40s.
   On holiday it took me a few days to get used to the change in temperature.
2. Note the adjectives we use to describe extreme heat:
   The bonfire gave out a fierce heat and I had to move away.
   The firefighters were driven back by the intense heat of the burning car.
3. Note the following ways of describing high temperatures:
   Only tourists are silly enough to wander about in the heat of the day!
   I don't know how they manage to work in this heat without air conditioning.

"Oh, nurse, I just love it when you take my temperature!"

air

Verb + air	Adjective + air	Preposition + air
need air	cold air	by air
pollute the air	fresh air	into the air
breathe air	thin air	through the air
gasp for air	polluted air	on air
put air into a tyre	stale air	
	still air	

1. Verb + air

Complete the sentences below with the correct form of the above verbs:

1. I'm going outside for a moment – I feel a little sick. I . . . . some air.
2. After two minutes under water, he came to the surface, ... for air.
3. The quality of the air we . . . . is not as good as it was a hundred years ago.
4. You should . . . . some air into your tyres – they look flat to me.
5. Smokers . . . . the air for other people, and that's why I think smoking should be banned in public places such as restaurants and pubs.

2. Adjective + air

Complete these sentences with the above adjectives:

1. It's stuffy in here. We need some . . . . air, so let's open the windows.
2. We often go into the countryside to escape from the . . . . air of the city.
3. At high altitudes it is difficult to breathe because of the . . . . air.
4. The windows had been shut all week, so the air was rather . . . .
5. Nothing moved in the . . . . air. There wasn't a breath of wind.
6. I felt an icy blast of . . . . air against my legs when she opened the door.

3. Preposition + air

Match the halves:

1. The delighted fans threw their hats high
2. I love to watch birds flying
3. Our goods are sent all over Europe
4. This programme first went

a. through the air.
b. by air.
c. on air 20 years ago. (on radio or TV)
d. into the air.

"We threw our hats into the air!"

Notes

1. Note the following expressions:
   For a week after the fire at the tyre factory, the smell of burning rubber filled the air.
   She seems to have vanished into thin air. I can't find her anywhere.
   The air was thick with smoke. Almost everybody in the bar was smoking.
2. The expression 'open air' means outside:
   The farmers' market is held in the open air in the town centre. (outside)
   We ate in an open-air restaurant / swam in an open-air pool / went to an open-air concert.

Key Words for Fluency – Intermediate

light

Verb + light	Adjective + light	Noun + of + light	Expressions with
get light	artificial light	a flash of light	prepositions
need light	poor light	a glimmer of light	up to the light
let in the light	a bright light	a source of light	by the light of
block out the light	a soft light		in my light
light fades	the fading light		

1. Verb + light

Complete the sentences with the correct form of the above verbs:

1. I pulled the blinds down to . . . . out the light so I could watch television.
2. I'm afraid it's a north-facing room, so it doesn't . . . . much light.
3. Put the plant near a window. It . . . . a lot of light.
4. I opened the curtains to . . . . in the light.
5. The light was . . . . , so we had to stop playing. It was difficult to see the ball.

2. Adjective + light

Choose the correct collocation:

1. The light was so bright / sharp that I had to cover my eyes with my hands.
2. Modern farmers use both natural and artificial / unnatural light to grow tomatoes
   – especially in the winter.
3. The harsh light emitted by fluorescent tubes hurts my eyes. I much prefer the milder /
   softer light of a light bulb.
4. Reading in little / poor light can strain your eyes, and could even damage them.
5. It was difficult to read the signposts in the disappearing / fading light.

3. Noun + of + light

Complete the sentences with the above nouns:

1. A tiny window was the only . . . . of light in the prison cell.
2. We saw a . . . . of light in the distance, and hoped it was our hotel.
3. A witness said there was a blinding . . . . of light, followed by an explosion.

4. Expressions with prepositions

Match the halves:

1. When I'm camping I like to read
2. Move to the side – you're in my light
3. The shop assistant held the bank note

a. up to the light to see if it was genuine.
b. by the light of a candle.
c. and I can't see what I'm doing.

Note   Note these expressions:
> When we left the building we were momentarily blinded by the sunlight.
> Light from the street lamps outside was shining through a small gap in the curtains.
> The light reflecting off the surface of the water dazzled me, and I had to put on my sunglasses.
> There's light coming from under the door so somebody must be in.
> The light wasn't good enough to take photographs.
> In the failing light, I could just make out the figure of John in front of me.
> In summer, the days are very long in Scandinavia. It is light all night in the far north.

fire

Verb + fire	Fire + verb	Fire + noun
start a fire	a fire burns	a fire alarm
light a fire	a fire goes out	a fire drill
put out a fire	a fire breaks out	a fire escape
cause a fire	a fire destroys	a fire extinguisher
fight a fire	a fire spreads	a fire risk
catch fire		

1. Verb + fire

Complete the sentences with the correct form of the above verbs:

1. The car . . . . fire in the crash, but the driver managed to get out safely.
2. Police believe that the fire at the castle was . . . . by an electrical fault.
3. 50 firemen . . . . the fire at the factory. It took 3 hours to . . . . it out.
4. It's very cold in here. Shall I . . . . the fire?
5. We are treating the fire as suspicious. We believe it was . . . . deliberately.

"Where's the fire extinguisher?"

2. Fire + verb

Complete the sentences with the correct form of the above verbs:

1. The cinema was . . . . by fire. The whole building was completely gutted.
2. Fire . . . . out during the night, but all the hotel guests managed to escape.
3. The fire swept through the museum, then . . . . rapidly to adjoining buildings.
4. When we arrived at the hotel, a coal fire was . . . . brightly in the fireplace.
5. Remember to put some logs on the fire. Don't let the fire . . . . out!

3. Fire + noun

Complete the sentences with the above nouns:

1. Smouldering cigarettes are dangerous and are a well-known fire . . . .
2. When you hear the fire . . . ., make for the nearest exit.
3. We climbed out of the window and used the fire . . . . to leave the building.
4. The kitchen is on fire! Where's the fire . . . .?
5. We have regular fire . . . . so staff know how to leave the building safely.

Notes

1. Note that we use 'start a fire' to describe somebody who wishes to cause damage, whereas we use 'light a fire' to describe making a fire for comfort. We also use 'set fire' to describe starting a fire:
The young boy was playing with matches and he accidentally set his bed on fire / set fire to his bed.

2. Note that we talk about 'electric, gas, coal, and log fires'.
We've got an old electric fire in the bedroom, which doesn't give out much heat.
Sometimes we refer to a coal or log fire as an 'open fire'.
We don't have an open fire any more. It just made too much mess.

water

Verb + water	Adjective + water	Verb + preposition + water	Noun + of + water
boil water	fresh water	dilute with water	a drop of water
drink water	mineral water	dive into water	a shortage of water
pour water	boiling water	fill with water	a supply of water
spill water	drinking water	float on water	
water flows		splash with water	
water drips		wade through water	

1. Verb + water

Complete the sentences with the correct form of the above verbs:

1. You'll get dehydrated quickly in this heat, if you don't . . . . lots of water.
2. Make sure you . . . . the water before adding the pasta to the pot.
3. I accidentally knocked the glass over and . . . . water all over my book.
4. After washing the dishes, he . . . . the dirty water down the sink.
5. There's water . . . . onto the floor. There must be a leak in a pipe somewhere.
6. In a central heating system, hot water . . . . from the boiler, through the pipes to the radiators.

2. Adjective + water

Complete the sentences with the above adjectives:

1. Bacteria in . . . . water is a major cause of disease in poor countries.
2. While making tea he dropped a kettle of . . . . water and scalded his leg.
3. The water was dirty, so we drained the pond and filled it with . . . . water.
4. Would you like some . . . . water? Still or sparkling?

3. Verb + preposition + water

Complete the sentences with the above prepositions:

1. I thought the box would float . . . . water, but it sank to the bottom of the pond.
2. The fisherman waded . . . . the water to reach his boat.
3. I splashed my face . . . . cold water in order to wake myself up.
4. Dilute the juice . . . . plenty of water.
5. The policeman dived fully clothed . . . . the water to rescue the drowning boy.
6. He filled the basin . . . . hot water and washed himself with a cloth.

4. Noun + of + water

Match the two halves:

1. Nuclear power stations are usually situated near
2. We drank bottled water when there was
3. I always have

   a. a shortage of drinking water.
   b. a drop of water in my whisky.
   c. a good supply of water.

Note   Note these expressions:
Water boils at a temperature of 100°C and freezes at a temperature of 0°C.
Water gushed out of the broken pipe and flooded the road.
Due to the long spell of dry weather, water supplies are dangerously low.

noise and silence

Verb + noise	Adjective + noise	Adjective + silence
make a noise	an awful noise	complete / total silence
sleep through noise	a deafening noise	a long silence
shut out noise	a funny noise	a stunned silence
can't stand the noise	a piercing noise	an awkward silence
	background noise	
	a squeaking noise	

1. Verb + noise

Complete the sentences with the correct form of the above verbs:

1. Keep the noise down. I can't work when you're . . . . so much noise.
2. I tried unsuccessfully to . . . . out the noise of the roadworks outside my house. In the end, I had to turn up my hi-fi to drown it out.
3. I can't . . . . the noise of a door banging. It drives me up the wall.
4. I just don't know how the baby manages to . . . . through all that noise.

2. Adjective + noise

Complete the sentences with the above adjectives:

1. The engine's making a . . . . noise. I need to get the garage to look at it. I've got a feeling it's going to cost me a lot of money!
2. The noise of the disco was . . . . I had a headache after an hour.
3. I can't make out what he's saying on the tape. There's too much . . . . noise.
4. One wheel on the trolley is making a horrible . . . . noise. It needs some oil.
5. Will you stop that . . . . noise this instant! I can't hear myself think.
6. The fire alarm gave out a . . . . noise which made me jump out of my skin.

3. Adjective + silence

Choose the correct collocation:

1. After eight months a letter arrived from her daughter, ending her big / long silence.
2. I wasn't relaxed, so our conversation was full of awkward / awful silences.
3. When they told us we had won a million pounds in the prize draw, we just sat there in surprised / stunned silence. We just couldn't believe it.
4. I've been getting nuisance phone calls recently. Every time I answer the phone there is complete / full silence. Nobody speaks, but I know someone is there.

Notes

1. Note these expressions with 'noise':
   We had to shout above the noise of the traffic to hear each other.
   It's absolutely impossible to work with all this noise going on!
   I'm a very light sleeper. The slightest noise wakes me up.
   We're finding it difficult to get used to the constant noise of the traffic.
2. Note the kind of things we do 'in silence':
   They drove home in silence. (they didn't talk)
   If you're not happy, you should complain. Don't just suffer in silence.
3. It's quite common nowadays to 'observe a minute's silence' as a mark of respect after some terrible disaster.

Section 4

Work

job	30
career	31
staff and duty	32
qualification and interview	33
skill	34
training	35
wage, salary and pay	36

"Miss Ramsbottom, I'm sure your dog was the best-behaved in its class four years running, but it's your qualifications I'm interested in!"

job

Verb + job	Adjective + job	Noun + preposition + job
apply for a job	a challenging job	the perks of the job
get a job	a boring job	the pressures of the job
hold down a job	a rewarding job	qualifications for the job
look for a job	a responsible job	
lose your job	a stressful job	

1. Verb + job

Complete the sentences with the correct form of the above verbs:

1. Max had better be careful. If he's late
   for work again, he might .... his job.
2. I've been .... for a job for 3 months,
   but I haven't had much success so far.
3. I've .... for a job with a company in Berlin.
   The interview is next week.
4. Brian left after only a week. He never manages
   to .... down a job for long.
5. I finally .... a temporary job, washing
   dishes in a hotel, but it's only for a month.

"It's very well-paid, but it's also a very stressful job."

2. Adjective + job

Choose the correct collocation:

1. I don't think doctors are paid enough for doing such a high / responsible job.
2. Pilots are well-paid, but it's a very stressful / nervous job. I'd rather have my health.
3. Helping sick people is very satisfying. For me, it's a very rewarding / thankful job.
4. My job is so routine that I hate it. Filing papers all day is such a boring / flat job.
5. The job isn't difficult / challenging enough for me – I want something more creative.

3. Noun + preposition + job

Complete the sentences with the above nouns:

1. I get five free flights a year. It's one of the .... of the job.
2. Well, there's no doubt that you've got the right .... for the job, but your
   lack of experience might count against you.
3. He resigned when he realised that the .... of the job were making him ill.

Notes
1. We talk about 'full-time' and 'part-time' jobs, 'temporary' and 'permanent' jobs:
   While studying at university I also had a part-time job in a supermarket.
   After years of temporary employment he landed a permanent job with a local newspaper.
2. Note the different verbs that we use to describe jobs:
   What exactly does the job entail? Does it involve a lot of paperwork?
3. Note the way we describe the qualities needed for a job:
   This job requires good mental skills.
   The job demands good eyesight and a high level of concentration.
4. Note these job + noun phrases:
   Lots of people are more interested in job satisfaction than in earning high salaries.
   There's hardly any job security in acting. You are only employed for short periods of time.

Key Words for Fluency – Intermediate

career

Verb + career	Adjective + career	Noun + preposition + career
begin a career	a brilliant career	a change of career
choose a career	a promising career	a turning point in your career
pursue a career	a worthwhile career	your choice of career
further your career		the height / pinnacle of your career
wreck your career		the greatest performance of your ...

1. Verb + career

Complete the sentences with the correct form of the above verbs:

1. This scandal has . . . . his career as a politician. It's now in ruins.
2. He's the owner of a chain of hotels, but he . . . . his career as a porter.
3. Getting more qualifications is probably the best way to . . . . your career.
4. I think money is a big factor for most people when it comes to . . . . a career.
5. I graduate from university soon and I'm hoping to . . . . a career in business.

2. Adjective + career

Complete the sentences below with the above adjectives:

1. She considers teaching a . . . . career. It is very satisfying to feel that you are helping people to develop.
2. He had a . . . . career in politics, becoming Prime Minster at the young age of 46.
3. He had a . . . . career ahead of him in football until a knee injury put him out of the game at the age of 21.

3. Noun + preposition + career

Match the two halves:

1. She is now the managing director of the organisation.
2. At 50 he felt like a change of career.
3. Parents should advise and support their children in their choice of career.
4. At a concert in front of 40,000 people,
5. Moving to a new company marked a turning point in my career.

a. Gabrielle gave the greatest performance of her career so far.
b. So he gave up his job as a lawyer and went into teaching.
c. I'm much happier in my new job.
d. However, it's important that they don't try to influence their choice.
e. At the age of only thirty, she has reached the height of her career.

Notes
1. Note the following career + verb collocations:
   Her singing career took off after her appearance on the Chris Evans Show. (became successful)
   George Mackay played more than 700 games in a career spanning 20 years.
2. Note these expressions:
   Most working women manage to successfully combine family life with a career.
   She wants to get ahead in her career. She's eager to climb the career ladder.
3. Note these two ways of saying the same thing:
   Have you ever thought of teaching as a career / a career in teaching?

staff and duty

Verb + staff	Noun + prep + staff	Verb + duty
employ staff	the dedication of the staff	carry out your duties
recruit / take on staff	a member of staff	fail in your duties
train staff	the turnover of staff	report for duty
lay off staff	vacancies for staff	be suspended from duty
		your duties include (tasks)

1. Verb + staff

Choose the correct collocation:

1. Because of falling orders, the company has been forced to decrease / lay off staff. At least 50 will have to go.
2. All our sales staff are educated / trained to handle difficult customers.
3. Our embassy in Paris employs / uses around twenty full-time staff.
4. I hear the bank is recruiting / starting staff at the moment. I believe they are taking on about a hundred people.

2. Noun + preposition + staff

Complete the sentences with the above nouns:

1. There are always plenty of . . . . for staff in bars and hotels.
2. This project has been a great success, thanks to the . . . . of the staff. I'd like to thank you for all the hard work you've put into it.
3. There is a high . . . . of staff in the catering trade. Most restaurants find it difficult to hold on to staff.
4. The police suspect that a . . . . of staff tipped off the thieves who stole the computers last night.

3. Verb + duty

Complete the sentences with the correct form of the above verbs:

1. You should . . . . for duty at seven o'clock on Monday morning.
2. She is a hard-working employee who . . . . out all her duties conscientiously.
3. The police officer has been . . . . from duty until the claims of corruption against him have been investigated.
4. Your duties will . . . . opening and answering the mail every morning.
5. The social worker is accused of . . . . in her professional duties and she is facing dismissal as a result.

Notes

1. Note these adjective collocations with 'staff':
   The company has a large workforce of permanent and temporary staff.
   Our hard-working and dedicated staff provide an excellent service to our customers.
   We only have a skeleton staff over the Christmas period so service will be slower than usual.
2. Note these expressions with 'duty':
   What time are you on duty / off duty? (when do you start work / when do you finish work?)
   Firefighters worked above and beyond the call of duty during the disaster.
   Two police officers were killed in the line of duty. (while doing their job)

qualification and interview

Verb + qualification	Verb + interview
have a qualification	be invited to an interview
get / obtain a qualification	have an interview
study for a qualification	dread the interview
courses lead to a qualification	prepare for the interview
Adjective + qualification	hold an interview
an academic qualification	**Expressions with interview**
a further qualification	make a good impression at the interview
a recognised qualification	don't do yourself justice at the interview
	come across badly at the interview

1. Verb + qualification

Complete the sentences with the correct form of the above verbs:

1. The course . . . . to a professional qualification in business administration.
2. Sadly, some children leave without . . . . a single qualification.
3. You'll never get a good job if you don't . . . . any qualifications.
4. . . . . for further qualifications is one way of getting promotion.

2. Adjective + qualification

Complete the sentences below with the above adjectives:

1. For employers, practical experience is as important as . . . . qualifications.
2. You must have a university degree or a . . . . qualification of equal status.
3. Some graduates go on to take . . . . qualifications – e.g. a master's degree.

3. Verb + interview

Complete these sentences with the above verbs:

1. I've . . . . a lot of job interviews since I graduated, but not one job offer yet.
2. Candidates who are successful in the written test will be . . . . to an interview.
3. The best way to . . . . for an interview is to find out all you can about the job.
4. Interviews will be . . . . in London next week.
5. I'm . . . . my interview later today. I'm already a bundle of nerves.

4. Expressions with interview

Match the halves:

1. He made a good impression at the interview.
2. He came across very badly in the interview.
3. He didn't do himself justice in the interview.

a. He never looked at them!
b. They want to interview him again.
c. They offered him a job straightaway!

Notes

1. Note that 'qualification' is often followed by 'in':
   She has qualifications in mathematics and chemistry.
2. Note these expressions with 'interview':
   Initial interviews will be conducted by telephone.
   They gave me a really hard time at the interview.
   My whole future is riding on this interview.
   I blew my chances of getting the job by arriving late for the interview.

skill

Verb + skill	Adjective + skill	Noun + of + skill
learn a skill	basic skills	use of your skills
hand down skills	communication skills	test of your skills
test skills	computer skills	degree of skill
update your skills	practical skills	
equip someone with skills	social skills	

1. Verb + skill

Choose the correct collocation:

1. The aim of the examination is to investigate / test your problem-solving skills.
2. The company is looking for staff who are willing to learn / train new skills.
3. This weekend refresher course is designed for staff wishing to lift / update their computer skills.
4. These traditional skills have been given / handed down from generation to generation.
5. The introductory course aims to equip / educate students with good study skills.

2. Adjective + skill

Complete the sentences below with the above adjectives:

1. In schools, all children are taught the . . . . skills of reading, writing and arithmetic.
2. At present, there is a shortage of people with . . . . skills like joinery and bricklaying.
3. To be an effective teacher, you must have good . . . . skills.
4. Nowadays, you need basic . . . . skills for most office jobs.
5. The job involves organising and attending receptions and conferences. We're looking for someone with good . . . . skills – the sort of person who is equally at home talking to a duchess or a refuse collector.

3. Noun + of + skill

Complete the sentences with the above nouns:

1. Keeping control of the car on the ice was a real . . . . of my skill as a driver.
2. Brain operations are complicated and the surgeon needs a high . . . . of skill.
3. Nurses used to complain that they are given menial tasks to do, which made little . . . . of their professional skills.

Notes

1. Note the verbs we use to describe the skill needed to do something:
   It takes great skill to build one of these tiny machines.
   The job requires / demands / calls for great skill and an eye for detail.
2. Note the following prepositional phrases:
   He performed the task with great skill.
   She has excellent / no skills in map-reading.
3. Note these expressions:
   The staff development programme provides opportunities for you to acquire new skills.
   A good manager requires a number of highly specialised skills.
   These exercises will develop the students' speaking and listening skills.

Key Words for Fluency – Intermediate

✗ training

Verb + training	Adjective + training
complete your training	basic training
provide training	formal training
receive training	intensive training
require training	proper training
	regular training

1. Verb + training

Complete the sentences with the correct form of the above verbs:

1. We . . . . on-line training and support in the use of all our software packages.
2. Please note that operation of this equipment . . . . special training.
3. All employees of this bank . . . . special training in dealing with armed robbers.
4. Although my sister has . . . . her medical training, she has no intention of becoming a doctor. What a waste of time, effort and money!

2. Adjective + training

Complete the sentences below with the above adjectives:

1. All new recruits undergo six weeks' . . . . training at the army camp.
2. No one must operate this machine without . . . . training.
3. His paintings sell for thousands of pounds, but he's had no . . . . training as an artist. He's completely self-taught.
4. As technology changes so quickly these days, it is essential that all employees receive . . . . training.
5. Last year I took a course in learning how to fly, and after a period of three months' . . . . training, I qualified as a pilot.

"I'll never forget my basic training!"

Notes

1. Note the prepositions that follow 'training':
   We received training in several different teaching methods.
   We'll need to provide training for the new members of staff.
2. Note that 'in-service training' is training that you do while you have a job.
   The college runs a number of academic courses and also provides in-service training for secretaries, chefs and mechanics.
3. Note these noun expressions:
   All our advisors have completed a comprehensive training programme.
   Training sessions will be held on Mondays at 9am.
   I have to go on a training course to learn new sales techniques.
   The shop opens late on Mondays for staff training.

wage, salary and pay

Verb + wage / salary	Common expressions with pay
earn a wage / salary	receive equal pay
live on / survive on your ...	award a pay rise to someone
demand a higher ...	accept a pay cut
my ... goes on / is spent on (rent)	get full pay
tax is deducted from your ...	qualify for sick pay
	reject a pay offer

pay: the money you get for doing your job, paid as a weekly wage or as a salary

wage: usually paid weekly – the pay of manual workers

salary: usually paid monthly – the pay of non-manual workers

1. Verb + wage / salary

Complete the sentences with the correct form of the above verbs:

1. She . . . . a good salary, but nothing compared to what her boss gets.
2. Most of my wages . . . . on the rent and bills.
3. He lost his job so they have to . . . . on one wage now.
4. In the UK, tax is automatically . . . . from your salary.
5. Angry teachers are . . . . higher salaries and better conditions.

2. Wage or salary?

Choose wage or salary:

1. The government plans to raise the minimum wage / salary from £4.50 to £5 per hour.
2. He was offered a six-figure wage / salary to move to a rival company.
3. The owner of the restaurant only pays the waiters a weekly wage / salary of £90.
4. He earns a good wage / salary as a doctor, but not as much as a consultant gets.
5. My wage / salary goes directly into the bank on the last Wednesday of each month.
6. The basic wage / salary is low, so I'll have to do overtime to make enough money.

3. Common expressions with pay

Only pay is possible in these sentences. Match the halves:

1. Nurses have been awarded	a. a 5% pay cut.
2. As a temporary employee I don't qualify for	b. equal pay for the same work.
3. Men and women should receive	c. a 5% pay rise.
4. The unions have rejected	d. sick pay.
5. Women employees get 18 weeks' maternity leave	e. the latest pay offer.
6. In order to save the company, the staff accepted	f. on full pay.

Notes

1. Note the expression 'on my wage / salary / pay':
   How can they possibly support their families on such a low wage / salary?
   I can't afford to run a car on my wage / salary / pay.
2. Note the following expressions:
   She asked for an advance on her salary so that she could pay her medical bills. (get paid early)
   There are two wage earners in our family, so we live quite comfortably.
   What's the pay / salary like? What are the wages like?
3. A 'living wage' is one which provides enough for your basic needs:
   Teaching no longer pays a living wage and I have to give private lessons to get by.

Key Words for Fluency – Intermediate

Section 5

Travel

trip	38
holiday	39
flight	40
delay and destination	41
passenger	42
passport and visa	43
luggage and fare	44

"Travelling light!"

trip

Verb + trip	Adjective + trip	Noun + of + trip
afford a trip	a free trip	the highlight of the trip
cancel a trip	a good trip	the length of the trip
go on a trip	a long trip	a souvenir of the trip
plan a trip	a round trip	the cost of the trip
make a trip	a trip abroad / overseas	
ruin a trip		

1. Verb + trip

Complete the sentences with the correct form of the above verbs:

1. You need your parents' permission if you want to . . . . on the school trip.
2. A friend is going to lend me the money. Otherwise, I couldn't . . . . the trip.
3. Unfortunately, the trip's been called off. It was . . . . due to lack of interest.
4. I've . . . . the same trip by car so often, I could do it with my eyes shut.
5. Our camping trip was . . . . by heavy rain. We ended up wet and miserable.
6. I hear you're . . . . a shopping trip to France? Do you mind if I come?

2. Adjective + trip

Complete the sentences below with the above adjectives:

1. Children always get restless on . . . . trips by car.
2. There are three . . . . trips to America to be won in today's competition.
3. Did you have a . . . . trip?
   > No, it was a disaster from start to finish.
4. I have to go to Oxford and back. It's about a 60-mile . . . . trip.
5. I'm planning my first trip . . . . I'm off to Greece in the summer.

3. Noun + of + trip

Complete the sentences with the above noun phrases:

1. The . . . . of our trip to India was the visit to the Taj Mahal.
2. The full . . . . of the trip, including insurance, will be around £600.
3. I have a piece of volcanic rock as a . . . . of my trip to Mount Vesuvius.
4. I'm not very happy with the . . . . of the trip. I think two weeks is long enough!

Notes

1. Note the trip + verb collocations:
   The trip cost £1,200 and involved four flights. It also included an overnight stay in Singapore.
2. We name trips according to how we travel:
   It's only a 30-minute bus trip.   Do you fancy going on a boat trip this afternoon?
   or according to the purpose of the trip:
   a fishing / camping / shopping / sightseeing / business trip.
3. A 'day trip' is when you go somewhere and come back on the same day.
   A 'trip of a lifetime' is the kind of trip most of us can only dream about.
4. Note these expressions:
   Thanks for posting that letter for me – it saved me a trip.
   I could have spared myself an unnecessary trip by phoning to see if the library was open.
5. Note that 'trip' refers to travelling somewhere, staying there and travelling back, whereas 'journey' refers only to travelling in one direction.

holiday

Verb + holiday	Adjective + holiday	Holiday + noun
book a holiday	a package holiday	a holiday brochure
cancel your holiday	a public holiday	a holiday job
enjoy your holiday	a relaxing holiday	a holiday resort
spend a holiday	a paid holiday	a holiday weekend
take a holiday	a dream holiday	
ruin your holiday		

1. Verb + holiday

Complete the sentences with the correct form of the above verbs:

1. They always .... their summer holidays in the Canary Islands.
2. Our holiday was .... by bad weather. It rained nearly every day.
3. The boss works all the time. He never .... a holiday.
4. Well, ... your holiday. I hope you have a great time.
5. I don't .... my holiday till the last minute, in the hope of getting a bargain.
6. Always take out holiday insurance in case you have to .... it.

2. Adjective + holiday

Complete the sentences with the above adjectives:

1. All permanent staff are entitled to four weeks'.......... holiday each year.
2. I spent a .... holiday on the beach, reading and sunbathing.
3. A cruise round the world on a luxury liner would be my .... holiday.
4. The 1st of May is now a .... holiday in many countries.
5. We went on a cheap .... holiday to Majorca.

3. Holiday + noun

Match the two halves:

1. I took a holiday job
2. It's a holiday weekend,
3. Rimini is a popular holiday resort
4. We plan our summer holidays in December

a. on the Adriatic coast.
b. so the roads will be crowded with holiday traffic.
c. by looking through all the holiday brochures.
d. as a waiter when I was a student.

"It's only a holiday job."

Notes

1. Note the multi-word verbs in the following sentences:
   I'm afraid Mr Smith is away on holiday until the end of the week. Can I help you?
   Our holiday fell through at the last minute because the travel company went bankrupt.
   Give me a ring when you get back from holiday.
   We had to cut short our holiday because Richard became ill.
2. Note that we name holidays according to when we have them: *the Christmas / summer holidays;* and according to the type of holiday: *a golfing / skiing / walking holiday.*
3. A 'bank holiday' is when shops, businesses, and banks are closed. (US English: a national holiday)

flight

Verb + flight	Adjective + flight	Noun + prep + flight
catch a flight	a bumpy flight	arrival of the flight
miss a flight	a connecting flight	cancellation of the flight
flights are called	a direct flight	the duration of the flight
flights are delayed	a long-haul flight	final / last call for the flight
flights are diverted	a scheduled flight	on standby for a flight
flights are cancelled	a smooth flight	
flights get into airports	a short flight	

1. Verb + flight

Complete the sentences with the correct form of the above verbs:

1. We checked out of our hotel at 6am in order to . . . . the early flight to Paris.
2. When your flight is . . . . , please make your way to the departure lounge.
3. The flight leaves from Rome at 2pm and . . . . into Boston at 6pm local time.
4. Unfortunately, our flight to Minorca was . . . . We took off 4 hours late.
5. Get a move on! We need to hurry or we'll . . . . our flight.
6. All flights from Newcastle have been . . . . due to heavy snow.
   Meanwhile, all Newcastle-bound flights are being . . . . to Edinburgh.

2. Adjective + flight

Choose the correct collocation:

1. I've never been on a long-haul / long-distance flight before. I've only flown in Europe.
2. There's no direct / straight flight to Geneva, but you can fly to Luton and catch a joining / connecting flight from there.
3. It's only a small / short flight from London to Paris.
4. Charter flights are generally much cheaper than scheduled / timetabled flights.
5. There was a lot of turbulence, so we had a pretty bumpy / shaky flight. It wasn't quite as level / smooth as we had expected.

3. Noun + preposition + flight

Complete the sentences with the above nouns:

1. This is the final . . . . for flight EJ121 to Geneva.
2. Passengers are requested not to smoke for the . . . . of the flight.
3. Air France apologises for the late . . . . of this flight.
4. He was put on . . . . for the flight to New York because it was fully-booked.
5. British Airways regret to announce the . . . . of flight BA033 to London.

Notes

1. 'Domestic flights' are within a country; 'international flights' are between countries:
   The number of international flights has increased dramatically in recent years.
   There is no in-flight entertainment on our domestic flights.
2. Note these expressions:
   The Australian airline, Qantas, operates regular flights to the Far East.
   British Airways offers non-stop flights from London to Singapore.
   Many people suffer from jet-lag after long flights.
   Flight T232 to Cairo is now boarding at Gate 15.

delay and destination

Verb + delay	Noun + prep + delay	Adjective + destination
apologise for a delay	apologies for the delay	an exotic destination
avoid a delay	a series of delays	your intended destination
expect a delay	liability for the delay	a new destination
cause delays	the reason for the delay	a popular destination
face delays		the top destination

1. Verb + delay

Complete the sentences with the correct form of the above verbs:

1. Roadworks are causing heavy congestion in the city centre, so long delays can be . . . .
2. Air passengers . . . . long delays this weekend due to the strike by air traffic controllers.
3. We . . . . for the delay in getting your luggage to you, and for any inconvenience this may have caused.
4. The accident has . . . . some delays in train services in and out of York.
5. Please check in early to . . . . delays.

2. Noun + preposition + delay

Complete the sentences with the above nouns:

1. What's the . . . . for the delay? We've been standing here for over 3 hours.
2. We would like to offer our . . . . for the slight delay to your flight today.
3. After a . . . . of delays, we finally reached our hotel two days late.
4. The airline accepts no . . . . for delays caused by bad weather.

"18 hours is not a slight delay!"

3. Adjective + destination

Complete the sentences with the above adjectives:

1. Spain is still the most . . . . holiday destination for the British.
2. At customs, you'll be asked your . . . . destination and how long you plan to stay.
3. Machu Picchu is the . . . . tourist destination in Peru.
4. Virgin Airlines are adding . . . . destinations to their world-wide network.
5. E-flight.com offers tickets to . . . . destinations like Bali at great prices.

Notes
1. Note the verbs in this sentence:
   According to the programme, we should reach / arrive at / get to our destination about midday.
2. Note the following expressions with 'delay':
   My train should get in at eight o'clock, if there are no unexpected delays.
   It should take me about an hour to get there, allowing for traffic delays.
   Flights are subject to delay because of bad weather.
   Unnecessary delays are caused by passengers not appearing when their flights are called.

passenger

Passenger + verb	Adjective + passenger	Common expressions
passengers travel	an angry passenger	Passengers are:
passengers board (planes)	a drunken passenger	required to
passengers can be stranded	a business class passenger	asked to
passengers can be killed	a nervous passenger	requested to
passengers proceed to	a terrified passenger	reminded that
gates		

1. Passenger + verb

Complete the sentences with the correct form of the above verbs:

1. Flight LK 03 is now boarding. Will passengers please . . . . to gate 34.
2. Passengers . . . . the ferry at 7am and disembark at Zeebrugge at 5pm.
3. Many passengers flying into London are . . . . on to other destinations.
4. The driver and all four passengers were . . . . outright in the accident.
5. Thousands of passengers were . . . . at Orly Airport last night following a lightning strike by air traffic controllers.

2. Adjective + passenger

Complete the sentences with the above adjectives:

1. An . . . . passenger demanded to know why his flight had been overbooked.
2. The cabin crew smile frequently to reassure . . . . passengers that all is well.
3. . . . . passengers held onto their seats as the plane hit some severe turbulence.
4. Economy class passengers are packed in like sardines at the back of the plane, while the . . . . passengers at the front have fully reclining seats and lots of legroom.
5. The cabin crew are trained to restrain . . . . passengers who become violent.

3. Common expressions

Match the two halves:

1. Passengers are reminded that
2. Due to increased security measures, passengers are asked to
3. Once the plane has landed, passengers are requested to
4. To avoid delays, passengers are required to

a. arrive at least two hours before their flight.
b. remain seated until the plane has come to a complete standstill.
c. smoking is not permitted on this aircraft at any time.
d. show their boarding passes as they enter the plane.

Notes

1. Note the verbs we use to describe taking passengers somewhere:
   The ship carries both freight and passengers between Hong Kong and Singapore.
   The high-speed rail link transports air passengers to the city centre in just 20 minutes.
   Passengers were ferried to the island in small boats.
2. Note the verbs we use with taxis and buses:
   The taxi picked up a passenger outside the hotel and dropped him (off) at the airport.
   The bus stopped to let a passenger off.
   Passengers must not get on or off the bus while it is moving.

Key Words for Fluency – Intermediate

passport and visa

Verb + passport	Adjective + passport	Verb + visa
renew your passport	a forged passport	apply for a visa
show your passport	a new passport	extend your visa
surrender your passport	a valid passport	need a visa
stamp a passport		obtain a visa
steal a passport		overstay your visa
a passport expires		refuse somebody a visa
		a visa can expire

1. Verb + passport

Complete the sentences with the correct form of the above verbs:

1. My passport . . . . this month. I'll have to . . . . it before my holiday.
2. You don't have to . . . . your passport at the border. We're all in the EU.
3. If your passport is lost or . . . . , inform your embassy immediately.
4. He had to . . . . his passport to the police to prevent him leaving the country.
5. The immigration official . . . . my passport and handed it back to me.

2. Adjective + passport

Complete the sentences with the above adjectives:

1. Travellers are reminded that for a holiday abroad they need a . . . . passport.
2. I need to get a . . . . passport – my old one's expired.
3. During the raid on the house, the police found drugs and . . . . passports.

3. Verb + visa

Match the two halves:

1. I need to stay longer in the UK to finish my studies
2. There are long delays in obtaining visas to the region,
3. I have to leave the country by the end of June
4. If you overstay your visa, you will be deported.
5. He was refused an entry visa to the US
6. You don't need a visa

a. because my visa expires then.
b. because of his criminal record.
c. so apply early.
d. to visit Japan for a stay of under six months.
e. so I will need to extend my visa.
f. You should make arrangements to have your visa renewed before it runs out.

"I overstayed my visa, so they deported me. They were really nice about it!"

Notes

1. Note the following passport + noun collocations:
   You will need to provide a passport photo for your membership card.
   What a nightmare! It took us nearly two hours to get through passport control.
2. Note these expressions with 'visa':
   I entered the country on a tourist visa / on a study visa. It is valid for six months.
   You won't be allowed to enter Tibet without a visa.

luggage and fare

Verb + luggage	Adjective + fare	Expressions with fares
pack your luggage	the exact fare	fares rise / increase /go
insure your luggage	a flat fare	up / shoot up
lose your luggage	full fare	fares are cut / reduced /
weigh your luggage	half-fare	slashed
screen luggage	a return fare	
search luggage		

1. Verb + luggage

Complete the sentences with the correct form of the above verbs:

1. Please . . . . your hand luggage and make sure it's not more than 5kg.
2. They were furious when they learned that the airline had . . . . their luggage.
3. X-ray machines are used at airports to . . . . luggage for weapons and bombs.
4. Things often go missing, so we strongly recommend you . . . . your luggage.
5. When flying, make sure you . . . . your luggage yourself.
6. All our luggage was . . . . for illegal drugs.

2. Adjective + fare

Complete the sentences with the above adjectives:

1. You'll have to pay the . . . . fare. There's no concessionary fare for students.
2. The . . . . fare depends on when you are coming back.
3. There's a . . . . fare of £1 on all buses. You can go anywhere for that price.
4. Children travel . . . . on all our trains.
5. Please have the . . . . fare ready when you enter the bus. No change is given.

3. Expressions with fares

Match the halves:

1. Starting next month, taxi fares		a. by a massive 50%.
2. Bus fares are to rise by an average of 10 per cent		b. will be going up.
3. A lot more people would use public transport		c. because of increased fuel costs.
4. Air fares to the US have been slashed		d. shot up by 30% in the last year.
5. Due to increased running costs train fares have		e. if fares were cut.

Notes

1. Note these expressions:
   Please do not leave your luggage unattended.
   Only one piece of hand luggage may be taken onto the aircraft.
   All hand luggage must be stowed under the seat in front or in the overhead lockers.

2. We use 'baggage' rather than 'luggage' in these expressions:
   You'll have to pay extra if you exceed your baggage allowance.
   Excess baggage is charged at the rate of £20 per kilo.
   Baggage reclaim is the place at an airport where you collect your luggage after a flight.

3. Note these verb + fare collocations:
   I save on fares by walking to work.
   Ticket inspectors are necessary in order to stop people trying to dodge fares.

Section 6

Traffic

traffic 46
street 47
route and map 48
accident 49
injury 50

"Oh, were you the one who gave me a parking ticket last week? I'm terribly sorry. I didn't realise!"

traffic

Verb + traffic	Noun + prep + traffic	Traffic + noun
direct traffic	a break in the traffic	traffic congestion
divert traffic	a build-up of traffic	traffic accident
hold up traffic	the noise of traffic	a traffic jam
reduce traffic	a queue of traffic	a traffic warden
traffic builds up	the volume of traffic	
traffic thins out		

1. Verb + traffic

Complete the sentences with the correct form of the above verbs:

1. Traffic will be .... through side streets while the road is being resurfaced.
2. Traffic on the motorway was .... up for three hours by a serious accident.
3. A policeman with white gloves was .... traffic from the middle of the road.
4. The town council is examining ways of .... traffic in the city. One extreme proposal is to close the city centre to all traffic except buses and taxis.
5. The usual pattern on weekdays is that traffic .... up during the late afternoon and begins to .... out after 7pm.

2. Noun + preposition + traffic

Complete the sentences with the above nouns:

1. The roads are quiet now, but there is a steady .... of traffic in the evening.
2. We waited ages for a .... in the traffic so that we could cross the road.
3. We need new motorways to cope with the increased .... of traffic on our roads.
4. There was a long .... of traffic waiting to turn right at the lights.
5. Our house is on a main road, so we are always aware of the constant .... of traffic.

3. Traffic + noun

Match the two halves:

1. Twenty people died
2. There are plans to relieve
3. When I got back to my car
4. I was stuck in

a. a traffic warden was putting a ticket on it.
b. a traffic jam for over an hour yesterday.
c. in traffic accidents in the first month of this year.
d. traffic congestion in the city centre.

Notes

1. Note these adjective collocations:
   For your own safety, always walk facing oncoming traffic on country roads.
   If you leave before 4pm, you should manage to avoid the rush-hour traffic.
   We've had an awful journey – there was heavy traffic all the way.
   The traffic was quite light, so we got through Leeds quicker than we expected.
2. Note these expressions:
   The holiday traffic heading for the coast has ground to a halt on the M4. Police are reporting tailbacks of up to ten miles.
3. Note these other types of traffic:
   Air traffic has increased 50% in the last five years.
   Rail traffic was severely disrupted by last night's heavy snowstorms.

street

Verb + street	Adjective + street	Common expressions
clean up the streets	a crowded street	beg in the street
patrol the streets	a deserted street	live in the same street
wander through the streets	the High Street	come up to you in the street
cross over the street	a one-way street	stop someone in the street
go down the street	a side street	bump into her in the street
parade through the streets		

1. Verb + street

Complete the sentences with the correct form of the above verbs:

1. Thousands of tourists . . . . through the streets of Rome every day.
2. It's a very secure area because the police . . . . the streets night and day.
3. We'll have to . . . . over to the other side of the street to get to the market.
4. Thousands of soldiers . . . . through the streets to celebrate the end of the war.
5. . . . . down the High Street and turn left. The post office is on your left.
6. The local council has launched a campaign to . . . . up the city's streets.

2. Adjective + street

Complete the sentences with the above adjectives:

1. My brother was fined for driving the wrong way down a . . . . street.
2. At 3 in the morning the streets were . . . . There wasn't a soul to be seen.
3. Boots is a big company. There's a branch of the store in every . . . . Street.
4. A bomb went off in a . . . . street, killing 20 people and injuring many more.
5. We left the busy main street and found a quiet bar in one of the . . . . streets.

3. Common expressions

Match the halves:

1. He was reduced to begging in the street
2. Strangers come up to us in the street and
3. I stopped someone in the street
4. We work in the same area
5. As kids, we used to live in

a. to ask for directions.
b. in order to get something to eat.
c. say how much they enjoy our television show.
d. the same street.
e. so we often bump into each other in the street.

"He was reduced to begging – in the street!"

Notes

1. Note these expressions:
   In summer the streets of Brighton are filled with tourists.
   Many of the streets are lined with tall trees.
2. We use the verb 'roam' if we want to suggest somebody is looking for trouble.
   After the match gangs of football hooligans roamed the streets looking for a fight.
3. The 'High Street' is the main shopping street in the centre of a town.

route and map

Verb + route	Adjective + route	Verb + map
take a route	an alternative route	bring a map
mark the route	a direct route	draw a map
plan a route	an escape route	read a map
people line a route	a popular route	study a map
	a roundabout route	maps show things
	a scenic route	

1. Verb + route

Complete the sentences with the correct form of the above verbs:

1. It's always a good idea to . . . . your route before you leave.
2. Here, take this map. I've . . . . the shortest route to the college in red.
3. I'd . . . . the longer route via the bypass – it'll be quicker in the long run.
4. Crowds of well-wishers . . . . the route, waving flags as the Queen passed.

2. Adjective + route

Complete the sentences with the above adjectives:

1. We had plenty of time, so we took the . . . . route through the mountains and enjoyed the magnificent views.
2. I don't know why it took us so long. I must have taken a really . . . . route.
3. Motorists are advised to find an . . . . route during repairs to the bridge.
4. Make sure you are aware of all the possible . . . . routes from the plane.
5. The coastal path between Dover and Hastings is a . . . . route for walkers. There's some amazing wildlife.
6. The most . . . . route from the house to the stadium is through the town centre. It's shorter, but it isn't any quicker.

3. Verb + map

Complete the sentences with the correct form of the above verbs:

1. Look! I can't . . . . the map and drive at the same time!
2. All members receive a detailed map . . . . all the major tourist attractions.
3. Francis . . . . a map on how to get to her house on the back of an envelope.
4. We forgot to . . . . a map of the area, but it doesn't matter as I know the way.
5. We . . . . the map carefully to see if we had enough time to reach the next hostel before it got dark.

Notes
1. Note these expressions with 'route':
I live on a busy bus route, so I can get to work more quickly.
Accommodation won't be a problem. There are plenty of B&Bs along the route / en route.
We travelled by motorway to the match, but we returned home by a different route.
2. Note these expressions with 'map':
Can you show me where you live on this map?
The guide pointed out the best beaches on the map.
It's not on the map!
Never go walking in these hills without a map and compass.

Key Words for Fluency – Intermediate

accident

Verb + accident	Adjective + accident	Noun + of + accident
avoid an accident	a freak accident	the cause of the accident
cause an accident	a fatal accident	in the event of an accident
have an accident	a minor accident	the scene of the accident
reduce accidents	a serious accident	a series of accidents
witness an accident	a tragic accident	
accidents happen		

1. Verb + accident

Complete the sentences with the correct form of the above verbs:

1. This accident could have been . . . . if safety procedures had been followed.
2. The campaign against drinking and driving has . . . . road accidents by 20%.
3. The police would like to hear from anyone who . . . . the accident.
4. I've been driving for 30 years and I've never . . . . an accident of any kind.
5. It was the kind of accident that could have . . . . to almost anyone.
6. It's hard to say what . . . . the accident, but police think the driver fell asleep.

2. Adjective + accident

Match the two halves:

1. There was only a million and one chance of this happening.
2. Make sure you always check for head injuries,
3. If you hadn't acted so quickly,
4. The boy drowned when he fell through the ice.
5. Three motorists died

a. It was such a tragic accident.
b. even if it is only a minor accident.
c. It was a freak accident.
d. in a fatal accident late last night.
e. there could have been a serious accident.

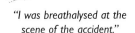

"I was breathalysed at the scene of the accident."

3. Noun + of + accident

Complete the sentences with the above nouns:

1. After two months experts are still trying to establish the . . . . of the accident.
2. In the . . . . of an accident, call this number – 01122 54637770.
3. After a . . . . of accidents in the fog, the police warned drivers to slow down.
4. Both drivers were breathalysed at the . . . . of the accident.

Notes

1. Note these expressions:
   Careless / reckless driving was to blame for the accident.
   I walked away from the accident without a scratch.
   It was an accident waiting to happen. (likely to happen)
   This junction is a notorious accident black spot. (a lot of accidents have happened here)
2. Note the verbs we use to describe the effects of an accident:
   Remarkably, no one was seriously hurt in the accident.
   Twenty people died and over a hundred were injured in the accident.
   The accident left him paralysed from the waist down / scarred for life / partially blind.

injury

Verb + injury	Noun + of + injury	Common expressions
prevent injury	the pain of an injury	because of injury
cause an injury	reports of injuries	due to / owing to injury
suffer an injury	the risk of injury	through injury
recover from an injury	a series of injuries	as a result of injury
be treated for injuries	the full extent of the ...	following injury
escape with only minor injuries		

1. Verb + injury

Complete the sentences with the correct form of the above verbs:

1. The people nearest the explosion . . . . horrific injuries from flying glass.
2. Always wear protective footwear on the site to . . . . injuries to your feet.
3. Survivors of the plane crash were . . . . for injuries at local hospitals.
4. A man died in the accident, but I was lucky to . . . . with only minor injuries.
5. His appalling injuries had been . . . . by a blunt instrument such as a hammer.
6. She has now fully . . . . from the horrendous injuries she received to her hands and hopes to return to her work as a secretary soon.

2. Noun + of + injury

Complete the sentences with the above nouns:

1. Unfortunately, he's had a . . . . of injuries since he joined the team.
2. The bomb exploded outside a café, but there are no . . . . of serious injuries.
3. Cyclists are advised to wear helmets to reduce the . . . . of head injury.
4. Morphine is used by doctors to deaden the . . . . of serious injuries.
5. The ambulance is on its way to the hospital. We don't know the full . . . . of the casualty's injuries yet, but we don't believe they are life-threatening.

3. Common expressions:

Match the halves:

1. He had to give up his football career
2. The driver of the car died
3. The British boxer Ali Ahmed
4. Henman won't be playing
5. He had to pull out of the tournament

a. as a result of the injuries she received.
b. may never fight again following his injury.
c. at the last minute through injury.
d. because of a crippling ankle injury.
e. in today's match due to a shoulder injury.

Now go through the exercises and notes, and find adjectives that describe a serious injury:

1. . . . .   2. . . . .   3. . . . .   4. . . . .   5. . . . .

and one adjective for an injury which isn't serious:

6. . . . .

Note   Note the following expressions:
     Don't try to lift these books by yourself. You'll do yourself an injury.
     There is little doubt that a seat belt would have prevented his injuries.
     The murder victim had died from multiple injuries and stab wounds.
     A post-mortem examination revealed that he had suffered terrible internal injuries.

Section 7

Education

education   52
course   53
lesson   54
practice and homework   55
exam and mark   56

"Can you explain, Smithers, how it is possible to get no marks
– zero, nothing, zilch – in your biology examination?
That's quite an achievement!"

education

Verb + education	Adjective + education	Noun + preposition + education
get an education	a good education	access to education
give you an education	higher education	the aim of education
invest in education	nursery education	standard of education
return to education	private education	the right to education
pay for your education	religious education	
	secondary education	
	sex education	

1. Verb + education

Complete the sentences with the correct form of the above verbs:

1. My parents . . . . me the best education that money could buy.
2. Parents must make sure that their children . . . . a proper education.
3. A growing number of adults are . . . . to full-time education.
4. We put some money aside every month to . . . . for our daughter's education.
5. The Prime Minister said that his government will continue to . . . . in education. An extra £100 million will be spent next year on school buildings.

2. Adjective + education

Complete the sentences below with the above adjectives:

1. There will be free . . . . education for all three-year-olds within five years.
2. Some people think that . . . . education is unfair and that we should all have the same educational opportunities.
3. The number of students in . . . . education has doubled in the last 10 years. The government is now thinking of building several new universities.
4. I'm against . . . . education in schools. I think it should be done at home.
5. In the UK, most young people receive . . . . education in primary school. They learn the facts of life early.
6. Like most parents, I just want my children to have a . . . . education.
7. The government wants to make . . . . education compulsory up to the age of 18.

3. Noun + preposition + education

Complete the sentences with the above nouns:

1. The cuts in funding will have an effect on the . . . . of education in schools.
2. By law all children in the country have the . . . . to a free education.
3. One . . . . of education must be to teach children to think for themselves.
4. . . . . to higher education has improved, with more students now at university.

Notes

1. In the UK a 'public' school is a private or fee-paying school. Government schools, where education is free, are called 'state' schools. Education is compulsory in the UK between the ages of 5 and 16.
2. 'Further education' is for adults who have left school. The classes are usually at a college and not at a university. 'Special education' is provided for children who have physical problems or learning difficulties.
3. Note these expressions:
   The new government has announced its education policy / an increase in spending on education.

course

Verb + course	Adjective + course	Noun + prep + course
do a course	a crash course	completion of a course
complete a course	a demanding course	a guide to a course
drop out of a course	an introductory course	a place on a course
schools run courses	an on-line course	the entry requirements for
courses consist of (lectures)	a vocational course	a course
courses deal with (subjects)		

1. Verb + course

Complete the sentences with the correct form of the above verbs:

1. This language school . . . . English courses for complete beginners.
2. Older people are returning to school to . . . . courses in using computers.
3. If you . . . . the course successfully, you will be awarded a certificate.
4. The course . . . . with the fundamentals of car maintenance.
5. It's a difficult course. 50% of the students usually . . . . out within 3 weeks.
6. The course . . . . of a series of lectures with a written exam at the end.

2. Adjective + course

Choose the correct collocation:

1. It was a very tough and heavy / demanding course, but we managed to complete it.
2. I'm going to Japan to work soon, so I'm taking a crash / fast course in Japanese.
3. I studied art, but most of my friends did vacation / vocational courses, like nursing.
4. The college runs on-line / internet courses where a lot of the teaching is done through the internet and e-mail.
5. The introductory / primary course is for those people who have no knowledge or experience of teaching.

3. Noun + preposition + course

Complete the sentences with the above nouns:

1. Make sure you fulfil the entry . . . . for the course before you send off the application form.
2. I have a conditional offer of a . . . . on a nursing course. I have to pass all my exams this year to be accepted on the course.
3. Our website provides a comprehensive . . . . to courses at UK universities.
4. Students are given a certificate on successful . . . . of the course.

Notes

1. Note the verbs we use to describe taking a course:
   A total of 48 students enrolled for / signed up for the course in photography.
2. Note the verbs we use to describe the aims of a course:
   This course is designed to give students a grounding in car maintenance.
   This course prepares graduates for careers in the tourist industry.
3. 'Undergraduate' and 'postgraduate' courses are taken at university:
   I'm doing a three-year undergraduate course in computing at Leeds University.
4. A 'crash course' teaches you a lot about a particular subject in a short period of time.
5. Note this expression:
   I was forced to withdraw from the course due to illness.

lesson

Verb + lesson	Preposition + lesson	Noun + of + lesson
have lessons	a lesson about something	the aims of the lesson
skip a lesson	a lesson with someone	the point of a lesson
prepare a lesson	during a lesson	the start of the lesson
begin / start a lesson	in a 40-minute lesson	the main points of the
give lessons		lesson
catch up with your lessons		

1. Verb + lesson

Complete the sentences with the correct form of the above verbs:

1. Teachers' salaries are very low, so I'm . . . . private lessons at weekends.
2. The teacher is terrible. I don't think he . . . . his lessons carefully enough.
3. I got into trouble when my father found out that I had been . . . . lessons.
4. My English teacher always . . . . his lessons with a warm-up exercise.
5. My brother is determined to be an actor so he's . . . . lessons in drama.
6. I was off school for 5 weeks, so I have quite a few lessons to . . . . up with.

2. Preposition + lesson

Complete the following sentences with the above prepositions:

1. We've got a lesson . . . . Mr Humphreys this afternoon.
2. You can't expect to learn everything about computing . . . . a one-hour lesson.
3. The lesson was . . . . the rise and fall of the Roman Empire.
4. No talking is allowed . . . . the lesson.

3. Lesson or class

Put a line through a word if it is not possible and try to think of a reason why it isn't:

1. I'm having driving classes / lessons from my uncle.
2. The school runs evening lessons / classes throughout the year.
3. I think Jack is going to need some private classes / lessons if he's going to have any chance of passing A level maths!
4. The teacher dismissed the lesson / class early because she had a meeting.

4. Noun + of + lesson

Match the halves:

1. The teacher started by going over the main
2. I just don't see
3. It always takes the students a while to settle down
4. The main aim of my lesson was

a. the point of this lesson!
b. at the start of the lesson.
c. to get the students talking.
d. points of yesterday's lesson.

Notes

1. Note these expressions:
   We spent the whole lesson copying from the blackboard / looking out of the window.
   I hope these lessons will improve my pronunciation / my communication skills.
2. If you are very angry with someone, the following expression can be useful:
   I'm going to teach him a lesson!
   Somebody needs to teach Dave a lesson in how to be polite to customers!

practice and homework

Verb + practice	Expressions with practice	Verb + homework
need practice	It takes (years) of practice.	give homework
have practice	be out of practice	get some homework
improve with practice	It's just a question of practice.	do your homework
learn through practice	Practice makes perfect.	correct homework
come with practice		hand in your homework
give you practice		help you with your ...

1. Verb + practice

Complete the sentences with the correct form of the above verbs:

1. Using a mouse is the easiest thing in the world once you've . . . . some practice.
2. This exercise . . . . students practice in using the past tense.
3. Most trainee teachers . . . . practice in writing on a blackboard.
4. Don't worry. Your English will . . . . with practice.
5. Playing the piano is the kind of skill that only . . . . with years of practice.
6. You get knowledge from books, but skills can only be . . . . through practice.

2. Expressions with practice

Match the halves:

1. Your English will improve if you work hard.
2. I'll try to use my French,
3. Don't give up.
4. If you want to learn to play the piano,

a. Driving's just a question of practice.
b. it'll take years of practice.
c. Speak as much as you can. Practice makes perfect.
d. but I'm a bit out of practice.

"It's just a question of practice, Wolfgang!"

3. Verb + homework

Complete the sentences with the correct form of the above verbs:

1. You can't watch TV until you've . . . . all your homework.
2. He never manages to . . . . in his homework on time.
3. You . . . . more homework at secondary school than at primary school.
4. The English teacher . . . . the whole class extra homework for misbehaving.
5. My brother used to . . . . me with my homework, but he's gone to university.
6. Our teacher . . . . our homework during the lunch hour, then gave it back to us.

Notes
1. Note these expressions:
   I'm afraid he can't come out just now. He's busy with his homework.
   Why do you always leave your homework to the very last moment?
2. An 'assignment' is an individual piece of work that a student has to do:
   I stayed up late last night to complete a class assignment.
   This is a really tough assignment.
3. We can use 'assignment' and 'piece of work' in these sentences:
   Do you actually fail the course if you don't hand in a piece of work?
   I've had an 'A' for every assignment I've done this year.

exam and mark

Verb + exam	Verb + mark
revise for an exam	get a mark
sit an exam	lose marks
mark an exam	give a mark
pass / fail an exam	deduct marks
scrape through an exam	**Adjective + mark**
Expressions with exam	your final mark
make a mess of an exam	full marks
pass an exam with flying colours	a good mark
a really stiff / hard exam	a low mark
How did you do in your exams?	the top mark

1. Verb + exam

Complete the sentences with the correct form of the above verbs:

1. I spent the whole weekend . . . . for my final exams. I didn't go out once.
2. Do we have to . . . . an exam at the end of the course?
3. She's exceptionally bright and she . . . . all her exams easily.
4. I almost failed the exam. I just managed to . . . . through with 51%.
5. I don't know what grade I got because the teacher hasn't . . . . our exam yet.

2. Expressions with exam

Match the halves:

1. How did you do in your exams?	a. I think he got nearly 100%.
2. I made a complete mess of the exam.	b. I don't think many of us will pass.
3. He passed the exam with flying colours.	c. I mucked the whole thing up.
4. It was a really stiff exam.	d. Badly. I failed three of them.

3. Verb + mark

Complete the sentences with the correct form of the above verbs:

1. I'm hoping to . . . . a good mark in the exam tomorrow.
2. Please remember that marks will be . . . . for bad spelling.
3. The teacher . . . . the highest mark to Mandy.
4. She would've got 100%, but she . . . . four marks for poor handwriting.

4. Adjective + mark

Complete the sentences below with the above adjectives:

1. He did no revision for the maths exam, but he still got a . . . . mark.
2. Nobody got . . . . marks in the spelling test, but I got nearly all the answers right.
3. Harry scored the . . . . mark in the English test. He's always first in the class.
4. Project work accounts for 50% of your . . . . mark for this course.
5. If you get . . . . marks in the test, you'll have to take the test again.

Notes

1. At school a 'test' is often something less formal than an exam, e.g. a reading test.
2. Note this expression with 'mark':
   You have to give him full marks for trying. (He didn't succeed, but tried very hard.)

Section 8

Sport and fitness

sport	58
team	59
game	60
race, competition and match	61
victory	62
defeat	63
prize	64
strength	65
energy and exercise	66

"Not a fair match!"

sport

Verb + sport	Adjective + sport	Sports + noun
watch sports	a contact sport	a sports centre
play a sport	a dangerous sport	sports coverage
take up a sport	an indoor sport	sports equipment
hate sport	a popular sport	sports events
	a spectator sport	sports facilities
	a team sport	

1. Verb + sport

Complete the sentences with the correct form of the above verbs:

1. Do you . . . . any other sports besides tennis and golf?
2. I . . . . sport when I was at school. I just couldn't do anything well.
3. You're not getting enough exercise. Why don't you . . . . up a sport?
4. I prefer . . . . sport to taking part.

2. Adjective + sport

Choose the correct collocation:

1. Baseball is a common / popular sport in Japan.
2. There's a high risk of injury with contact / touch sports like rugby.
3. Motor racing is an exciting but highly dangerous / unsafe sport.
4. Squash is an indoor / inside sport.
5. Basketball is a spectator / viewer sport, but fishing isn't. Who would pay money to watch somebody fish!
6. The Olympic Games include group / team sports like football and hockey, and individual ones such as the discus and the javelin.

3. Sports + noun

Complete the sentences with the above nouns:

1. Sports . . . . are often sponsored by big companies, like Nike and Adidas.
2. I work in a large sports . . . . I'm a swimming instructor.
3. Our sports shop stocks a wide range of sports . . . . and sportswear.
4. Sports . . . . in the local newspaper is good.
5. The council is hoping to find extra money to improve sports . . . . for youngsters living in inner-city areas.

Notes
1. Note these expressions:
   The school is keen to involve more young people in sport.
   I believe that killing animals for sport is morally wrong, and should be banned.
2. Note these noun + preposition + sport expressions:
   My husband is a sports fanatic, but I'm afraid I don't share his love of sport.
   My brother is very athletic. He seems to have a natural talent for sport.
3. Note these expressions:
   Banning boxing would only drive the sport underground. (people would do it illegally)
   Golf is a sport with a very clean image. (players do not behave badly or take drugs)
4. Skiing and ice-skating are referred to as 'winter sports', but we don't talk about 'summer sports'.

team

Verb + team	Team + verb	Adjective + team	Team + noun
play in / for a team	teams celebrate	the winning team	team effort
support a team	teams win / lose	the defeated team	team captain
make the team	teams take part in	a strong team	team mates
be dropped from a team	competitions	teams are evenly-matched	team spirit
			team sports

1. Verb collocations

Complete the sentences with the correct form of the above verbs:

1. Smith . . . . in the first team for eight years, and captained it for two years.
2. He's been picked for the Olympics. It's the third time he's . . . . the team.
3. He wasn't playing very well, so the manager . . . . him from the team.
4. Which football team do you . . . . ?
5. Sixteen teams will . . . . part, but only four will go through to the second round.
6. My team . . . . in the final – they were easily beaten.
7. The team . . . . their victory by opening bottles of champagne.

2. Adjective + team

Complete the sentences with the above adjectives:

1. We have a . . . . team and therefore a good chance of winning the game.
2. Some of the players from the . . . . team were in tears at the end of the game.
3. The two teams are evenly- . . . . I think it's going to be a very close game.
4. The delighted supporters of the . . . . team ran onto the pitch at the end of the match.

3. Team + noun

Complete the sentences with the above nouns:

1. Hussain, the team . . . . , was injured in the game against Australia.
2. They've got real team . . . . – a real desire to work together.
3. I much prefer to play team . . . . like football and basketball.
4. The goalkeeper apologised to his team . . . . for the mistake that lost them the game.
5. It was a real team . . . . Everyone contributed to the success of the event.

Notes

1. Note these expressions:
   He was a member of the British Olympic team.
   Ferguson coached the team to their second league championship in three years.
2. When a team plays in their own stadium, they are the 'home team'. The other team is the 'away team'.
3. We talk about teams in areas other than sport:
   Medical teams are travelling to the disaster area to care for the wounded.
   Rescue teams are still working to free those trapped in the collapsed building.
   Mr Jones will be joining our sales team as from next Monday.
   A team of experts has been called in to investigate the cause of the accident.
   I'm part of a team of scientists involved in cancer research.

game

Verb + game	Adjective + game	Noun + prep. + ...	Types of game
abandon a game	a clean game	coverage of a ...	a board game
make up a game	a physical game	the object of a ...	a card game
play a game	a tiring game	preparation for a ...	a computer game
win or lose a game	a quick game	the result of a ...	a party game
miss a game		the rules of a ...	a team game

1. Verb + game

Complete the sentences with the correct form of the above verbs:

1. It's important that you .... the game according to the rules.
2. If we .... this game, we're out of the championship.
3. He's always .... up new language games for his students to play in class.
4. Roberto Carlos is still injured and will .... tonight's game.
5. When the rain started we had to .... the game.

2. Adjective + game

Complete the sentences with the above adjectives:

1. There's time for a .... game of cards before the train leaves.
2. American football is a very .... game, so injuries are quite common.
3. It was a tough but .... game. There was no dirty play.
4. Squash is a .... game which requires high levels of fitness and stamina.

3. Noun + preposition + game

Complete the sentences with the above nouns:

1. The .... of the game is to get rid of all your cards before your opponent does.
2. You can see live .... of the game against Sweden on Channel 2.
3. The referee is the person who should know all the .... of the game.
4. With both teams playing well, it is difficult to predict the .... of the game.
5. They've been training hard in .... for tonight's big game.

4. Types of game

Complete the sentences with the types of game:

1. I hated .... games like football when I was at school.
2. .... games like chess keep children amused when the weather is bad.
3. Musical Chairs is a well-known .... game.
4. I won £500 in a .... game, but lost it all at the roulette wheel.
5. The problem with .... games like Tetris is they can be highly addictive.

Note
Note these expressions:
The game ended in a draw.
Computer games provide endless hours of fun.
The game involves throwing metal horse shoes at a stick.
Roulette is a game of chance, whereas chess is a game of skill.
I can't seem to get the hang of this game. (be able to play it)
Don't take it so seriously! It's just a game!

race, competition and match

Verb + race	Noun + race	Expressions with
watch a race	a horse race or boat race	**competition**
take part in a race	a 10-km race	a knockout competition
finish a race	**Verb + competition**	a round of a competition
win or lose a race	hold / run a competition	**Expressions with match**
withdraw from a race	enter a competition	play a match
be disqualified from a race	be knocked out of a	a football match
	competition	a tennis match
		a qualifying match

competition:	people compete against each other for a prize
race:	people or animals run, or drive faster than each other
match:	two teams or individuals try to defeat each other

1. Verb + race

Complete the sentences with the correct form of the above verbs:

1. Lewis is in top form. He has . . . . his last 10 races.
2. Two British athletes had to . . . . from the race because of injury.
3. More than 45 horses are expected to . . . . part in this year's big race.
4. Not all the participants are expected to . . . . the race. It's over 35kms long.
5. Thousands of spectators turned up to . . . . the race.
6. He was . . . . from the race for using drugs and banned from all competitions.

2. Verb + competition

Complete the sentences with the correct form of the above verbs:

1. . . . . our free competition and you could walk away with £500,000.
2. All the German teams were . . . . out of the competition in the early stages.
3. A magazine is . . . . a competition to find Britain's most intelligent person.

3. Race, competition or match?

Only one choice is possible in the following sentences. Circle the correct collocation:

1. My team was eliminated in the second round of the race / competition / match.
2. Highlights of England's qualifying race / competition / match will be shown at 10.30 pm.
3. Tennis tournaments like Wimbledon are knockout races / competitions / matches.
4. He spent all his money gambling on horse races / competitions / matches.
5. The girls challenged us to a football race / competition / match.
6. It's a 10-kilometre race / competition / match from the harbour to the city centre.

Notes
1. Note these expressions:
   The race / competition is open to anyone over the age of sixteen.
   There's only a week left until the big race / match.
2. We also use 'competition' in talking about business and employment:
   There's fierce competition for jobs. There are too many people chasing too few jobs.
   There is now keen competition between universities to attract overseas students.
   We are facing stiff / intense competition from factories in the Far East.
   In the face of strong competition from big supermarkets, many small shops are going out of business.

victory

Verb + victory	Adjective + victory
sweep to victory	a dramatic victory
celebrate a victory	a decisive victory
lead (a team) to victory	an easy victory
rob (someone) of victory	a narrow victory
	a surprise victory
	a well-earned victory

1. Verb + victory

Complete the sentences with the correct form of the above verbs:

1. Champagne bottles were opened as the team . . . . their impressive victory over last year's champions.
2. We were winning, but a couple of last-minute goals . . . . our team of certain victory. In the end we lost 3-2.
3. Bobby Moore . . . . the English team to victory in the 1966 World Cup.
4. The Social Democrats . . . . to victory in the recent elections. They won by a huge margin.

2. Adjective + victory

Match the halves:

1. Brazil reached the final of the championship
2. Manchester United snatched a dramatic victory
3. Owen's third goal
4. It was a surprisingly easy victory,
5. The newcomer pulled off a surprise victory
6. It was a narrow victory,

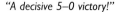

"A decisive 5–0 victory!"

a. against last year's champion in the semi-final.
b. but that final goal secured our place in the final.
c. given the fantastic reputation of the other team.
d. secured a well-earned victory for England.
e. over Bayern Munich in the closing seconds of the match.
f. with a decisive 5-0 victory over Italy.

Notes

1. Note the following adjective + preposition + victory expressions:
   The team is now certain of victory. I can't see them losing the match now.
   The fans were jubilant at / over France's victory in the final.
   We have prepared well for the match and are quietly confident of victory.
2. Note these ways of talking about winning easily:
   It was a pretty comfortable victory. The team didn't have to work very hard.
   Scotland cruised to victory in the second half of the match.
3. Note these useful phrases:
   Our new player should improve our chances of victory against Spurs in next week's match.
   The victory was sweet revenge for our defeat last season.

defeat

Verb + defeat	Adjective + defeat	Noun + preposition + defeat
suffer a defeat	a heavy / crushing defeat	the jaws of defeat
accept defeat	a humiliating defeat	the possibility of defeat
avoid defeat	a narrow defeat	revenge for your defeat
avenge a defeat	a shock defeat	a string of defeats
		the disappointment of ...

1. Verb + defeat

Complete the sentences with the correct form of the above verbs:

1. Borg . . . . defeat gracefully and shook hands with McEnroe.
2. In next week's match, the English hope to . . . . their defeat by Wales in the same competition this time last year.
3. Without their best players the team . . . . a heavy defeat in the cup final. The final score was 4-1.
4. We narrowly . . . . defeat in the semi-final when the referee disallowed a French goal in the last minute of the game.

2. Adjective + defeat

Choose the correct collocation:

1. Glasgow Rangers suffered a big / heavy defeat at the hands of their oldest rivals, Celtic. They lost 5-1.
2. The English team are still trying to recover from their sudden / shock defeat by Monaco.
3. It was such a narrow / tight defeat. We lost the competition by just three points!
4. The manager offered no excuses for his team's shaming / humiliating defeat.

3. Noun + preposition + defeat

Complete the sentences with the above nouns:

1. The Swedish team are seeking . . . . for their defeat in last year's final.
2. The manager refuses to entertain the . . . . of defeat. He expects his players to win the match easily.
3. We were losing, but our fans still hoped we could seize victory from the . . . . of defeat.
4. The recent . . . . of defeats has led to calls for the manager's resignation.
5. The team have clearly shrugged off the . . . . of last week's defeat.

Notes
1. Note these expressions:
   The team's defeat in the first round of the competition came as a big shock to many of its supporters.
   The humiliating defeat by a third division team led to the resignation of the manager.
   The manager blamed the referee for his team's defeat in the final.
2. Note these useful expressions:
   I thought I could fix the radio myself, but I've finally had to admit defeat. (give up trying to do something)
   We'll be back. We aren't going to take defeat lying down. (won't accept it easily)

prize

Verb + prize	Adjective + prize	Prize + noun
accept a prize	first prize	a prize draw
award a prize	the booby prize	prize money
claim a prize	a major / top prize	prize winners
present a prize	a consolation prize	
share a prize	a fabulous prize	
win a prize	the Nobel Prize for ...	

1. Verb + prize

Complete the sentences with the correct form of the above verbs:

1. Did you . . . . a prize in the competition?
2. Mr Liu can't be here tonight, so his wife will be . . . . the prize on his behalf.
3. There's more than one winner so the prize will have to be . . . .
4. The local Mayor will . . . . the prizes at the school sports day.
5. The winning numbers of the lottery were announced a week ago, but no one has yet stepped forward to . . . . the £1 million prize.
6. The Hamilton prize is . . . . every year to the student who has shown most progress in mathematics.

2. Adjective + prize

Complete the sentences with the above adjectives:

1. The roses I entered in the gardening show took . . . . prize in the flower section.
2. At the Oscars, the film *Gladiator* carried off nearly all the . . . . prizes.
3. I was last in the competition, so I got the . . . . prize.
4. There are . . . . prizes to be won in this week's competition – luxury cars, Mediterranean cruises and many more.
5. £300 goes to the winner, and five runners-up receive a T-shirt as a . . . . prize.
6. The . . . . Prize for Science was awarded to Dr Wilson for his outstanding work in genetics.

3. Prize + noun

Complete the sentences with the above nouns:

1. The prize . . . . each receive a year's free admission to the leisure centre.
2. Win a holiday for two in the Bahamas in our grand prize . . . . !
3. The tennis tournament offers nearly £5 million in prize . . . .

Notes
1. Note these expressions:
   There are hundreds of prizes up for grabs in our competition. (to be won)
   There are cash prizes of up to £500.
2. Note this common expression:
   There are no prizes for guessing who he is taking to the dance. (you can easily guess)
3. In the following sentences we use 'reward' and not 'prize'.
   The salary rise was a fitting reward for all his hard work.
   You deserve a reward for being so helpful. Take the rest of the day off!
   I got no reward for all the extra hard work I did.
   You 'win' a prize, but you 'get' a reward.

strength

Verb + strength	Adjective + strength	Noun + of + strength
build up your strength	full strength	a feat of strength
use your strength	inner strength	a lack of strength
save your strength	physical strength	reserves of strength
underestimate (his) strength	superhuman strength	
gather / recover your ...	superior strength	

1. Verb + strength

Complete the sentences with the correct form of the above verbs:

1. By . . . . all of his strength he managed to move the heavy wardrobe.
2. He might be small, but don't . . . . his strength. He's tougher than he looks.
3. He's on a special training programme to help him . . . . up his strength.
4. He's running slowly because he's . . . . his strength for the last 100 metres.
5. I had to sit down to . . . . my strength before I felt able to continue. I think I should go to the doctor. I don't understand why I'm so short of breath these days.

2. Adjective + strength

Choose the best collocation:

1. After an hour Sampras' better / superior strength began to tell and he won the match quite comfortably.
2. The operation will leave you feeling weak, but you should be back to full / top strength in a month or so.
3. Asterix is a cartoon character who gets his gigantic / superhuman strength from drinking a magic potion.
4. It's not his body / physical strength that makes him such a great champion, but his inside / inner strength that separates him from the other players.

3. Noun + of + strength

Complete the sentences below with the nouns above:

1. For a rugby player, he is quite small, but he uses speed to compensate for his . . . . of strength.
2. My grandfather was a circus strong man. He used to entertain people with his amazing . . . . of strength.
3. She called up her last . . . . of strength in an effort to get to the top of the mountain.

"Don't underestimate his strength!"

Notes

1. Note these expressions:
   It took all my strength to open the door.
   I hit him with all my strength.
2. Note how we describe finding the strength to do something:
   I'm finding it difficult to summon up the strength to do the housework.
   He will have to call on all his strength if he is to break Edwards' world record.

energy and exercise

Verb + energy	**Adjective + exercise**
have energy	light exercise
save your energy	regular exercise
use up energy	strenuous exercise
run out of energy	warm-up exercises
give you energy	
sap your energy	**Noun + of + exercise**
Noun + of + energy	lack of exercise
a great deal of energy	a form of exercise
a burst of energy	the effect of exercise
a source of energy	

1. Verb + energy

Complete the sentences with the correct form of the above verbs:

1. Children seem to . . . . boundless energy. I don't know where they get it from!
2. You should go to the gym. You'll . . . . up energy – AND you'll lose weight!
3. Running up the steep hill . . . . my energy and I had to stop for a rest.
4. I'm not being lazy. I'm just . . . . my energy for later.
5. Bananas . . . . you lots of energy. I always carry two or three in my bag.
6. After ten kilometres I was . . . . out of energy fast and badly needed a rest.

2. Noun + of + energy

Complete the sentences with the above nouns:

1. Chocolate is a good . . . . of energy.
2. Bringing up a young family requires a great . . . . of energy.
3. With a sudden . . . . of energy, he ran up the stairs to the top floor.

3. Adjective + exercise

Choose the correct collocation:

1. Avoid strong / strenuous exercise immediately after a meal. Wait at least an hour.
2. You can pull a muscle if you don't do some gentle preparation / warm-up exercises.
3. I go jogging every day – the doctor told me that I needed constant / regular exercise.
4. After my injury, I can do a bit of light / soft exercise such as walking, but I must avoid vigorous exercise such as running.

4. Noun + of + exercise

Match the halves:

1. Lack of exercise
2. Walking is probably
3. We've been keen cyclists since we

a. read about the beneficial effects of exercise.
b. can lead to ill-health.
c. the most popular form of exercise.

Notes
1. 'Energies' means the interest and effort that we use to do things:
   She put / threw / channelled all of her energies into her work and has no social life as a result.
   She devoted all her energies to the care of her sick mother.
2. Swimming is considered the 'best all-round exercise'.

Section 9

Health

health   68
illness   69
disease and infection   70
stress   71
smoking and drugs (illegal)   72
pain   73
appointment, symptom and test   74
treatment and cure   75
operation and drug   76

"I think we'd better do some more tests."

health

Health + verb	Health + noun	Common expressions
look after your health	a health hazard	bad for your health
nurse back to health	health reasons	essential for good health
your health improves	a health risk	harmful to your health
your health deteriorates	a health warning	do wonders for your health
your health causes concern	the health service	

1. Health + verb

Complete the sentences with the correct form of the above verbs:

1. My aunt's health . . . . rapidly last year and she died in December.
2. Remember to . . . . after your health, and it will look after you!
3. After his illness, his wife . . . . him back to health.
4. My daughter's health has . . . . a lot since she stopped eating dairy products.
5. The President's health is . . . . great concern. The doctors are not sure if he will survive the night.

2. Health + noun

Match the two halves:

1. I gave up smoking for	a. health warning.
2. In the 1980s, the British were not aware of the	b. health service.
3. This country has an excellent	c. health risks of eating meat.
4. Increasing levels of pollution are becoming a major	d. health reasons.
5. In most countries cigarette packets carry a	e. health hazard.

3. Common expressions:

Complete the sentences with a word from the above common expressions:

1. Smoking is . . . . for your health. So give up now!
2. A high fat diet is . . . . to your health, so cut down on butter!
3. Vitamins and minerals are . . . . for good health.
4. Did you know that keeping a pet can do . . . . for your health? It is a fact that people with cats and dogs visit the doctor less often than those who don't have pets.

Notes

1. Note the verbs we use to describe a loss of health:
   He was fine when I last saw him, but since then his health has taken a turn for the worse.
   My grandfather has been a fit man all his life, but at 96 his health is failing.

2. Note the following ways of describing good health and bad health:
   At the age of seventy-three she is still enjoying good health.
   My father is 91 and he's blessed with excellent health. He's never ill.
   The baby was in perfect health and weighed 4.1 kilograms at birth.
   He had been dogged by bad health all his life. He's never been well.
   He wanted to continue working, but he was forced to resign because of ill health.
   It is a well-known fact that poverty and poor health go hand in hand.
   My mother is now 88 and her health is fragile.

3. Note these noun + of + health expressions:
   Regular exercise can make a big difference to your state of health.
   After a series of tests and examinations the doctors have given him a clean bill of health.

illness

Verb + illness	Adjective + illness	Noun + preposition + illness
have an illness	a chronic illness	the cause of an illness
cause an illness	a long illness	the extent of an illness
diagnose an illness	a serious illness	a symptom of an illness
suffer from an illness	a sudden illness	a recurrence of an illness
recover from an illness		(make) a full recovery from an illness
treat an illness		

1. Verb + illness

Complete the sentences with the correct form of the above verbs:

1. One in four people will . . . . from some kind of mental illness at some point in their lives.
2. She's having some tests done to find out what's . . . . her illness.
3. There is no cure for diabetes, but the illness can be . . . . with insulin.
4. My sister hasn't fully . . . . from her illness. She's still off work.
5. I've . . . . all the normal childhood illnesses – measles, mumps, chickenpox, etc.
6. They're having difficulty . . . . my illness. I'm having more tests next week.

2. Adjective + illness

Match the halves:

1. The night before the 100-metre final, Christie was struck down by a sudden illness.
2. Elvin Moon has died after a long illness.
3. TB used to be a really serious illness,
4. Older people with a chronic illness, like arthritis,

a. can easily become depressed and exhausted.
b. As a result he had to withdraw from the race.
c. He battled for years against throat cancer.
d. but now it can be cured relatively easily.

"We're having difficulty diagnosing your illness!"

3. Noun + preposition + illness

Complete the sentences with the above nouns:

1. At the moment, it's impossible to say whether she'll make a full . . . . from her illness or not.
2. The doctors have attributed the . . . . of her illness to an unknown virus.
3. A persistent cough is one of the . . . . of the illness.
4. He's fine now and he's back at work but he's afraid of a . . . . of the illness.
5. I think he's keeping the true . . . . of his illness from me. I know it's far more serious than he has told me.

Note   Note the following:
He missed three days of work through illness. (because he was ill)

disease and infection

Verb + disease	Noun + preposition + disease
contract / get a disease	an outbreak of a disease
suffer from / have a disease	the spread of a disease
prevent disease	a cure for a disease
eradicate diseases	resistance to a disease
	the risk of disease
Adjective + disease	
an infectious disease	**Verb + infection**
a fatal disease	clear up an infection
an incurable disease	prevent infection
a rare disease	suffer from an infection
	an infection spreads

1. Verb + disease

Complete the sentences with the correct form of the above verbs:

1. We all know that regular exercise helps to . . . . heart disease.
2. My son . . . . from motor neurone disease and needs 24-hour care.
3. Almost all the people who . . . . the disease make a complete recovery.
4. Advances in medicine have . . . . many of the terrible diseases of the past, such as smallpox.

2. Adjective + disease

Complete the sentences with the above adjectives:

1. Hepatitis is a potentially . . . . disease. If you're not treated early, you could die.
2. The disease is so . . . . that the doctors have isolated him from other patients.
3. My uncle suffers from a . . . . blood disease. Only one in a million have it.
4. She has an . . . . disease. She will just have to learn to cope with it.

3. Noun + preposition + disease

Match the halves:

1. The government must act quickly to halt	a. a cure for this new disease.
2. A good diet helps the body to build up	b. a sudden outbreak of the disease.
3. Eating too much sugar and fat increases	c. the spread of the disease.
4. The race has begun to find	d. the risk of heart disease.
5. Doctors were sent to the area after	e. resistance to disease.

4. Verb + infection

Complete the sentences with the correct form of the above verbs:

1. He's having trouble breathing. He's . . . . from a serious chest infection.
2. Always apply antiseptic cream to minor cuts to . . . . infection.
3. The doctor prescribed some drops to . . . . up my ear infection.
4. If the skin infection isn't treated, it could . . . . from your legs to your body.

Note   Note these noun + preposition + infection expressions:
   I'm afraid these masks offer very little protection against infection.
   The doctor examined the cut on his leg for signs of infection.

stress

Verb + stress	Noun + of + stress
suffer from stress	the effects of stress
cope with stress	levels of stress
relieve stress	in moments of stress
thrive on stress	a sign of stress
place stress on you	a source of stress

1. Verb + stress

Complete the sentences with the correct form of the above verbs:

1. Massage can help to . . . . headaches, stress and pains. It is a relaxation technique which has been used for centuries.
2. Worried by a number of recent suicides, the university has set up a new service to help students who are . . . . from stress.
3. I don't know how she . . . . with the stress of bringing up two disabled children on her own. I certainly couldn't handle it.
4. I work better when things are difficult. I think I . . . . on stress.
5. Decisions about who should look after a sick child often . . . . considerable stress on working couples.

"A classic sign of stress!"

2. Noun + of + stress

Complete the sentences with the above noun phrases:

1. In . . . . of great stress, I close my eyes and imagine I'm on a sunny beach.
2. A common . . . . of stress in the workplace is having to do the work of colleagues who are off sick.
3. Nowadays people are more aware of the damaging . . . . of stress on the body.
4. Not being able to relax and sleep is often a . . . . of stress.
5. High . . . . of stress are a common feature of modern life. People today are more wound up and tense than they were in previous generations.

Notes

1. Note the common expressions with 'under stress':
   People under a lot of stress may experience headaches, fatigue and sleeping problems.
   Considering the amount of stress she's under, it's not surprising she gets angry so easily.
   I think the stress I was under at the time affected my judgement, and that was why I made some of these mistakes.
2. Note the following expressions:
   Because of the rapid increase in stress-related illnesses in recent years, many companies have started providing courses in stress management for all their staff.
3. Note these expressions, then think of other ways of completing them:
   One way of dealing with stress is to think positively.
   You can escape from the stresses and strains of life by going for a long walk in the countryside.

smoking and drugs (illegal)

Verb + smoking	Verb + drugs	Drug + noun
take up smoking	take / use drugs	drug abuse
approve of smoking	come off drugs	drug addict
cut down on smoking	legalise drugs	drug dealer
give up smoking	seize drugs	drug habit
refrain from smoking	supply drugs	drug overdose
	smuggle drugs	drug trafficking

1. Verb + smoking

Complete the sentences with the correct preposition:

1. I had to give . . . . smoking for health reasons. It's now two years since I quit.
2. I used to be a heavy smoker but I've managed to cut . . . . in recent months.
3. The sign on the wall said, 'Please refrain . . . . smoking in the waiting room'.
4. I don't approve . . . . smoking in restaurants. I think it should be banned.
5. I took . . . . smoking when I was 12 and I've been a heavy smoker ever since.

2. Verb + drugs

Complete the sentences with the correct form of the above verbs:

1. I don't do drugs. I've never . . . . drugs at any time in my life.
2. I think the crime rate would decrease if soft drugs like cannabis were . . . .
3. He says he's now clean. He . . . . off drugs a year ago.
4. It was his best friend who . . . . him with the drugs that killed him.
5. UK customs officials have just . . . . drugs with a street value of $2 million.
6. Anyone caught . . . . drugs into the country faces the death penalty.

3. Drug + noun

Complete the sentences with the above nouns:

1. AIDS can be spread by drug . . . . sharing needles.
2. He's a known drug . . . . who's often seen pushing drugs outside the local café.
3. The rock star, Lentrix, died of a drug . . . . in a New York hotel in 1969.
4. All parents should be aware of the early signs of drug . . . .
5. Many addicts are forced to turn to crime in order to support their drug . . . .
6. Drug . . . . is an international problem. Police forces around the world are now working together in an effort to stop it.

Notes

1. Note the verbs we use to describe the effects of smoking:
   Smoking can seriously damage your health.
   Passive smoking kills thousands of people every year.
   It is now an accepted fact that smoking causes lung cancer.
2. Note the following ways of saying that you can't smoke in a particular place:
   In the interest of safety, smoking is forbidden / prohibited in this building.
   Passengers are reminded that smoking is not allowed / not permitted on this aircraft.
3. Note these expressions with 'drugs':
   He always looks as though he's on drugs. (using drugs regularly)
   For years he was dependent on drugs, but he has finally managed to overcome his addiction.
   The President denied that he had experimented with drugs while he was a student.

pain

Verb + pain	Adjective + pain	Common expressions
bear the pain	a burning pain	alleviate pain
cause pain	a dull pain	ease the pain
complain of a pain	a throbbing pain	deaden the pain
pain passes	a sudden pain	kill the pain
pain gets worse	constant pain	relieve pain
	unbearable pain	soothe the pain

1. Verb + pain

Complete the sentences with the correct form of the above verbs:

1. An old sports injury is . . . . him a lot of pain at the moment.
2. I couldn't . . . . the pain any longer, so I took some painkillers.
3. The tablets might help, but if the pain persists or . . . . worse, see your doctor.
4. The pain was so severe that I had to hold on to a chair until it . . . .
5. She's been . . . . of pains in her chest for a few days. I've called the doctor.

2. Adjective + pain

Complete the sentences with the above adjectives:

1. I've had terrible toothache all night long – just a constant . . . . pain. I'm ringing the dentist.
2. I just bent over to pick up my suitcase and I got this . . . . pain in my back. I think I've done something!
3. I was cleaning some paint brushes and I put my hand up to my eye. I must've got some paint in it. I suddenly got this . . . . pain in my left eye. That's why I came straight round to the hospital.
4. My poor grandmother was in the most . . . . pain for the last few months of her life.
5. This pain never goes away. It's just . . . . – night and day.
6. What's the pain like? Is it a sharp pain or more of a . . . . pain?

3. Common expressions

We use a number of verbs to describe reducing pain. Match the halves:

1. Unfortunately the drugs did	a. to deaden or kill pain quickly.
2. Antacids relieve pain by neutralising acid	b. soothe the pain and stop her crying.
3. After a tiring day at work, a hot bath can	c. nothing to alleviate the pain.
4. Rub this gel onto the baby's gums and it will	d. ease all your aches and pains.
5. Morphine is given to accident victims	e. in the contents of the stomach.

Notes

1. Note these expressions:
   He was in a lot of pain.
   I had a few minor aches and pains, but nothing serious.
2. Note these ways of describing someone in pain:
   The patient was screaming with pain.
   Stomach ulcers cause great distress. The patient is often bent double with pain.
3. We talk of back pain, chest pains and growing pains (in children).

appointment, symptom and test

Verb + appointment	Verb + symptoms	Verb + test
make an appointment	show symptoms	do a test
get an appointment	doctors treat symptoms	repeat a test
have an appointment	symptoms go away	take a test
wait for an appointment	symptoms persist	have to have some
keep an appointment	symptoms include headaches	tests
miss an appointment	and a high temperature	
cancel an appointment		

1. Verb + appointment

Complete the sentences with the correct form of the above verbs:

1. Can I . . . . an appointment to see Dr Wilkins, please?
2. I'll ring the surgery, but I don't think I'll . . . . an appointment at such short notice.
3. I . . . . my appointment at the clinic today. I forgot all about it.
4. I had a sore throat, so I had to phone up and . . . . my dental appointment.
5. Unfortunately, you may have to . . . . up to six months for an appointment.
6. I won't be at work tomorrow morning. I . . . . an appointment with the dentist.
7. A lot of valuable time is lost when patients fail to . . . . their appointments.

2. Verb + symptoms

Complete the sentences with the correct form of the above verbs:

1. Keep taking the medicine until your symptoms . . . . away.
2. It is often said that western medicine . . . . the symptoms and not the cause.
3. The symptoms of the disease . . . . a high temperature and vomiting.
4. If these symptoms . . . . or get worse, consult your doctor.
5. My father is beginning to . . . . the classic symptoms of Parkinson's disease.

3. Verb + test

Complete the sentences with the correct form of the above verbs:

1. I'm afraid the blood tests were inconclusive, so we will need to . . . . them.
2. He says he's willing to . . . . a paternity test to prove he isn't the child's father.
3. We'll need to . . . . some tests to find out what's causing your headaches.
4. The specialist said that I have to . . . . some blood tests to see what's wrong.

Notes

1. Note the prepositions in these sentences:
   Consultation is by appointment only.
   I have an appointment with Dr Andrews tomorrow afternoon.
   I've got an appointment at the antenatal clinic this afternoon.
2. Note these expressions:
   The tests came back positive / negative.
   Her latest tests show that she is in the clear. (no longer has the medical problem)
3. We talk about 'blood, eye, hearing and pregnancy tests', and we 'get our eyes and blood tested'.
4. Tests are specific whereas an examination is more general, so we use 'examination' and not 'test' in the following sentence:
   A doctor will need to give you a full examination, and then he may decide he needs to do some tests.

treatment and cure

Verb + treatment	Adjective + treatment	Adjective + cure
begin treatment	an effective treatment	a complete cure
give treatment	a new treatment	an instant cure
undergo treatment	free treatment	no known cure
need treatment	urgent treatment	
respond to treatment	various treatments	

1. Verb + treatment

Complete the sentences with the correct form of the above verbs:

1. The driver was . . . . emergency treatment at the scene of the accident.
2. My mother is . . . . well to treatment and should soon be able to walk again.
3. Some cancer patients prefer to continue working while . . . . treatment.
4. Ten prisoners . . . . medical treatment after a riot at the prison.
5. There's a better chance of success if we . . . . the treatment as soon as possible.

2. Adjective + treatment

Complete the sentences with the above adjectives:

1. Doctors are trying out a . . . . treatment for asthma which involves special breathing exercises.
2. A daily dose of aspirin is a simple but highly . . . . treatment for certain heart conditions.
3. There are . . . . treatments for this complaint – surgery is just one option, but so much depends on the individual patient.
4. Three firefighters needed . . . . medical treatment after breathing in toxic fumes.
5. You get . . . . dental treatment if you are under 18 or if you are pregnant.

3. Adjective + cure

Complete the sentences with the above adjectives:

1. There is no . . . . cure for the common cold.
2. The treatment won't provide a . . . . cure for your back pain, but it will help to reduce it significantly.
3. I'm afraid there isn't an . . . . cure for this condition. It will take three months of treatment with creams before your skin returns to normal.

"I'm afraid, Mr Higginbottom, that there is no instant cure!"

Notes

1. Note this expression:
   Thanks to the treatment, her condition has improved significantly. (as a result of the treatment)
2. Note these expressions with 'cure':
   Scientists are hoping for a breakthrough in the search for a cure for Alzheimer's disease.
   Prevention is better than cure, so make sure you look after your health.
   I think it's possible that a cure for cancer will be found in my lifetime.

operation and drug

Verb + operation	Verb + drugs	Adjective + drug
have an operation	take drugs	a fast-acting drug
go through with an operation	inject drugs	a powerful drug
need an operation	test drugs	a safe drug
survive the operation	prescribe drugs	a wonder drug
perform an operation	drugs are approved	
an operation goes well or badly	drugs are withdrawn	

1. Verb + operation

Complete the sentences with the correct form of the above verbs:

1. Don't worry. A very experienced brain surgeon will be . . . . the operation.
2. My mother . . . . an operation on her eye last month.
3. I . . . . a hip replacement operation, but the waiting list is over nine months.
4. The surgeon said that I only have a fifty-fifty chance of . . . . the operation.
5. I couldn't . . . . through with the operation – I was too scared.
6. The early indications are that the life-saving operation has . . . . well. Doctors expect the patient to make a full recovery.

2. Verb + drugs

Complete the sentences with the correct form of the above verbs:

1. I have to . . . . drugs daily for high blood pressure.
2. Your doctor may . . . . pain-killing drugs to make you more comfortable.
3. The drug works more effectively if it is . . . . directly into the bloodstream.
4. The drug had to be . . . . after a number of people suffered serious side-effects.
5. The painkiller, Nohex, is not available in the UK. It hasn't been . . . . for use.
6. New drugs are not allowed into the shops until they have been thoroughly . . . .

3. Adjective + drug

Complete the sentences with the above adjectives:

1. . . . . drugs are used to treat cancer and these can have unpleasant side-effects.
2. It's a . . . . drug. It only takes a few minutes for the drug to begin to work.
3. The drug company claims that the drug is completely . . . . It has been successfully tested on thousands of patients.
4. Prozac has been hailed as a . . . . drug – a cure for lots of mental problems.

Notes

1. Note these useful expressions:
   The patient was fully conscious throughout the operation.
   The operation is performed under general anaesthetic.
   Recovery from this type of operation is a slow and painful process.
2. Note these drug + verb collocations:
   The drug may affect your vision, so avoid driving while taking it.
   The effects of the drug will wear off in a couple of hours and you'll be back to normal.
3. Note these expressions:
   This drug is not available over the counter. It is only available on prescription.
   I had an allergic reaction to the drug and had to stop taking it.

Section 10

Money

money and cash   78
savings, fortune and debt   79
price   80
fee and charge   81
expense   82

"Everyone's chasing money these days!"

money and cash

Verb + money	Adjective + money	Verb + cash
lend or borrow money	extra money	pay cash
earn money	missing money	accept / take cash
inherit money	spending money	carry cash
run out of money	pocket money	have cash on (you)
save money		
raise money		
pay money		
refund money		

1. Verb + money

Complete the sentences with the correct form of the above verbs:

1. We're organising a concert to . . . . money for charity.
2. I . . . . a lot of money for that car. It cost me over £20,000.
3. If you're unhappy with the product, just bring it back and we'll . . . . your money.
4. Could you . . . . me £5? I'm flat broke.
   > You already owe me £10, so . . . . it from somebody else!
5. When her father dies, she's going to . . . . a lot of money!
6. Building has stopped because the construction company has . . . . out of money.
7. What's your salary? How much money do you . . . . ?
8. I try to . . . . some money each week. I usually manage about £20.

2. Adjective + money

Complete the sentences below with the above adjectives:

1. How much . . . . money are you taking with you on holiday?
2. I'm paid badly, so I work in a bar in the evening to make a bit of . . . . money.
3. How much . . . . money did your parents use to give you?
4. All bank employees are being questioned by police about the . . . . money.

3. Verb + cash

Complete the sentences with the correct form of the above verbs:

1. The shops only . . . . cash. You won't be able to use your credit card.
2. Do you . . . . any spare cash on you? I've left my wallet at home.
3. I never . . . . much cash with me, just enough to pay for lunch and my bus fare.
4. Customers are offered a 20% discount on all products if they . . . . cash.

Notes

1. Note the following ways of talking about a lot of money:
   He's making good / loads of / fantastic amounts of money.
2. Note the expression:
   The council spent £1,000,000 on the Queen's visit. What a waste of public money!
3. Note the following expressions with 'cash':
   I'm short of cash / strapped for cash just now. (don't have enough money)
   Do you wish to be paid in cash or by cheque?
   The plumber says he wants cash in advance.
   You can make a withdrawal from most cash machines / cash dispensers with this card.

savings, fortune and debt

Verb + savings	Verb + fortune	Verb + debt
build up your savings	make a fortune	get into debt
put your savings into (the bank)	spend a fortune	run up debts
fall back on your savings	come into a fortune	pay off your debts
spend your savings	lose a fortune	write off debt
cheat somebody out of	save a fortune	be faced with debts
their savings	cost a fortune	

1. Verb + savings

Complete the sentences with the correct form of the above verbs:

1. We .... all our savings on an expensive holiday.
2. When she lost her job she had to .... back on her savings to get by.
3. He was jailed for .... thousands of investors out of their life savings.
4. I've decided to .... up my savings by putting 20% of my salary in the bank.
5. He won't .... his savings into the bank. He says his money is safer at home!

2. Verb + fortune

Complete the sentences with the correct form of the above verbs:

1. Her dress must have .... an absolute fortune.
2. He .... into a considerable fortune when his uncle passed away.
3. My grandfather was a millionaire, but he .... his fortune when the stock market crashed in 1929.
4. If you install double glazing, you'll .... a fortune on heating bills.
5. The Rolling Stones have .... a fortune from sales of their music.
6. My sister .... a fortune on clothes. I don't know where she gets all the money from.

3. Verb + debt

Complete the sentences with the correct form of the above verbs:

1. He tried to borrow money from me to .... off his gambling debts.
2. It's very easy to .... into serious debt by using a credit card.
3. She's .... up debts of nearly £6,000 on her credit card.
4. .... with mounting debts, they were forced to sell their house.
5. I think that the World Bank should .... off the debts of poor countries.

Notes

1. Note these expressions with 'savings':
   I paid for the car out of my savings.
   With this account you have instant access to your savings.
   Repair bills can make a big hole in your savings. (use up a lot of your savings)
2. Note these expressions with 'fortune':
   I thought the painting would be worth a fortune, but they only offered me £100.
   A lot of young people come to the city in search of fame and fortune.
3. Note the following ways of describing a lot of debt:
   Many students are heavily / deeply in debt by the time they finish university.
   She's up to her ears / up to her neck in debt.

price

Verb + price	Adjective + price
agree on a price	competitive prices
afford the price	extortionate prices
haggle over the price	a fixed price
prices rise or fall	the full price
the price includes (postage and packing)	half price

1. Verb + price

Complete the sentences with the correct form of the above verbs:

1. The price of oil has . . . . steeply this year.
2. The price . . . . flights and two weeks' accommodation. Please note that the price excludes local taxes.
3. It's customary in many countries to negotiate how much you pay for things at the market, so it is important that you learn how to . . . . over prices.
4. We didn't buy the house. It was impossible to . . . . on a price with the owners.
5. Few people can . . . . the prices they're asking. £55 is far too much for a ticket.

2. Increase and decrease in price

Mark the sentences (I) if they mean increase in price and (D) for a decrease in price:

1. There's a shortage of housing in the area, so house prices are expected to rise.
2. The theatre is hoping to increase its audience by cutting the price of tickets.
   > Yes. They've slashed their prices by almost 50%.
3. It's amazing how much computers have come down in price over the past few years.
   > Yes. Prices have dropped quite a bit since I bought my first computer 15 years ago.
4. Prices shot up last year. They are nearly three times as expensive now.
5. Oil prices fell to $5 a barrel – the lowest for ten years.
6. The government has put up the price of cigarettes again. I'll have to stop smoking.

3. Adjective + price

Complete the sentences below with the above adjectives:

1. The table was slightly damaged, so he only charged me . . . . price for it.
2. I'm sorry – children over five must pay the . . . . entry price to the show.
3. Our prices are very . . . . They're as low as any other shop in the area.
4. Unlike the prices in the market, our prices are . . . . and not negotiable.
5. It's a good hotel, but their prices are . . . . It cost me £15 for a cup of coffee! How can they get away with charging such high prices?

Notes
1. Note the adverbs we use to describe a big increase or decrease in price:
   The price of materials has risen sharply, so we have been forced to increase our charges.
   The price of our shares on the stock market has fallen dramatically.
   Due to a shortage of flour, the price of bread has risen alarmingly.
   House prices in the city rose steeply last year.
2. Note the following expressions:
   They can do the work for you, at a price. (it will cost a lot of money)
   The people now want peace at any price. (willing to do anything to get it)
   You can't put a price on friendship. (impossible to say how valuable it is)

fee and charge

Verb + fee	Adjective + fee	Expressions with charge
charge a fee	an additional fee	add a service charge
increase / raise the fee	a flat fee	incur bank charges
pay a fee	a high fee	waive charges
waive the fee	a record fee	free of charge
	a nominal fee	
	the normal fee	
	a reasonable fee	

1. Verb + fee

Complete the sentences with the correct form of the above verbs:

1. If you have a television in Britain, you have to . . . . an annual licence fee.
2. The bank will . . . . you a small fee for setting up the account.
3. Tuition fees are . . . . for the unemployed, who get the course free.
4. They are thinking of . . . . the annual fee to £500 a year. I don't see how they can do that when the fees went up by over £100 last year.

2. Adjective + fee

Complete the sentences with the above adjectives:

1. For a . . . . fee of £2, hotel guests can use the facilities at the leisure centre.
2. We charge a . . . . fee of £25 per hour – the same for all our customers.
3. We only charge £500 per year. This is a considerable saving on the . . . . fee.
4. I think £20 for a check-up is a very . . . . fee! Pete paid over £50!
5. Tom Cruise commands one of the . . . . fees in Hollywood.
6. Zidane was transferred from Juventus for a . . . . fee of $76 million.
7. Once you've paid the annual £350 subscription, there are no . . . . fees.

3. Expressions with charge

'Charge' is not possible in Exercises 1 and 2. 'Fee' and 'charge' are both possible in this sentence:
> There is an admission charge / fee for adults, but children under 14 get in free.

However, only 'charge' is possible in the sentences below. Match the two halves:

1. The room's £30, and breakfast is provided at
2. In Britain, some restaurants add
3. Buy a dishwasher and you get a toaster
4. The bank will waive the charges

a. a 10 % service charge to the bill.
b. no extra charge.
c. as the mistake was partly ours.
d. free of charge.

"And the toaster came free of charge!"

Notes

1. Note this expression:
   The singer wanted half his fee paid up front.
2. Note how we describe a charge which covers administration costs:
   Your monthly payments include a handling charge of 50p per month.
   Please note that there's a £1 booking charge for each ticket.

expense

Verb + expense	Adjective + expense	Common expressions
be worth the expense	extra expense	at your own expense
spare no expense	living expenses	at great expense
go to the expense of	medical expenses	at no extra expense
justify the expense	operating expenses	
save the expense	travelling expenses	

1. Verb + expense

Complete the sentences with the correct form of the above verbs:

1. When I went to university, I decided to stay with my parents as it would . . . . me the expense of renting a flat.
2. Buying a bigger house. . . . . certainly worth the expense. Life is so much more comfortable now.
3. No expense was . . . . to make the film a success. Millions of pounds were spent on advertising alone.
4. Why . . . . to the expense of buying new clothes when you never go out!
5. We don't need another car. The one we've got is fine. I don't see how we can . . . . the expense of a second car.

2. Adjective + expense

Complete the sentences with the above adjectives:

1. Your insurance policy will cover all . . . . expenses incurred during your time in hospital.
2. I try to fly business class if it's a long flight. I think it's worth the . . . . expense.
3. They just manage to get by on his salary. It's just enough to meet the family's . . . . expenses.
4. The obvious way to reduce the company's high . . . . expenses is to cut staff.
5. Make sure you fill out a form to claim your . . . . expenses after you have finished the interview.

3. Common expressions

Match the halves:

1. We had to repair the damage to our house   a. at great expense to the college.
2. The old lifts were replaced   b. at no extra expense.
3. The price includes full use of the leisure facilities   c. at our own expense.

Notes

1. 'Expenses' are the extra costs involved in your job. For example, hotels, travelling, meals which you need while away from home. You 'incur' expenses. You 'claim them back'. They are then 'reimbursed' to you.
   Your salary will be £40,000 a year, plus expenses.
   Don't worry about the cost of dinner – it's on expenses.
2. Note these expressions.
   I'm on an expense account.
   I get all my out-of-pocket expenses reimbursed.
3. Some people 'cheat' or 'fiddle' their expenses when they claim money which they did not spend.

Section 11

Food

food   84

drink   85

meal and dish   86

diet and appetite   87

party   88

"Trying to keep to a balanced diet!"

food

Verb + food	Adjective + food	Noun + of + food
eat food	delicious food	the consumption of food
prepare food	disgusting food	a portion of food
waste food	fresh food	a shortage of food
pick up food	frozen food	a variety of food
be off your food	raw food	
serve food	hot / spicy food	

1. Verb + food

Complete these sentences with the correct form of the above verbs:

1. It's a shame to . . . . all this food when so many people go hungry in the world.
2. No wonder he's so fat. He . . . . vast amounts of junk food.
3. A food processor makes the job of . . . . food a lot easier.
4. Ever since the stomach upset I had last month, I've . . . . off my food.
5. We stopped at the supermarket on the way home to . . . . up some food.
6. Try the hotel restaurant. It . . . . good food at affordable prices.

2. Adjective + food

Complete the sentences with the above adjectives:

1. The sight of all that . . . . food on the table makes my mouth water.
2. Having a garden means that we get a lot of . . . . food to eat.
3. I bought some Japanese food, but I don't know if I eat it . . . . or cooked.
4. The food was absolutely . . . . I was almost sick.
5. You should defrost . . . . food completely before you cook it.
6. Indian food is too . . . . for me. I can only eat it if I drink lots of water.

3. Noun + of + food

Complete the sentences with the above nouns:

1. Avoid the Raj if you're very hungry. You only get tiny . . . . of food there.
2. There's a greater . . . . of food available today than there was fifty years ago.
3. The harvest has failed again, so there is a desperate . . . . of food in the area.
4. The increasing . . . . of junk food is worrying health officials everywhere.

Notes

1. Note this expression:
   She described her operation at the dinner table and it put me right off my food.
2. Note these types of food:
   'Junk food' is unhealthy food which contains a lot of fat, salt, and sugar.
   'Convenience food' is quick to prepare. It only needs to be heated as it is already cooked.
   'Fast food' is food that you can get quickly in a restaurant or which you take away.
   'Organic food' is food produced without the use of artificial chemicals.
3. Note that we talk about food in the following ways:
   a) who eats it – *pet food, baby food, plant food*
   b) the country of origin – *Italian / Chinese / Indian food*
   c) its purpose – *health food*
4. 'Food poisoning' is an illness you get from eating food that contains harmful bacteria:
   Poor hygiene is the most common cause of food poisoning.

drink

Verb + drink	Adjective + drink	Adjective + drink (non-alcoholic)
have a drink	a celebratory drink	a hot / cold drink
order a drink	a farewell drink	a long drink
sip your drink	a free drink	a refreshing drink
spill your drink	a quick drink	soft drinks
offer somebody a drink	a relaxing drink	
	a stiff drink	

1. Verb + drink

Complete these sentences with the correct form of the above verbs:

1. Tom went to the bar to . . . . another round of drinks for the group.
2. Try not to . . . . your drink. We don't want to ruin the carpet.
3. Can I . . . . you a drink? I've got beer, wine, or a soft drink if you prefer.
4. He'd . . . . a few drinks, and it was difficult to make out what he was saying.
5. He gulped down his drink, then ordered another one. I took my time and just . . . . my drink in order to make it last.

2. Adjective + drink

Complete the sentences with the above adjectives:

1. We're having a . . . . drink for Harry tomorrow night. He's moving to a new job next week.
2. How about a . . . . drink after work? We'll only be ten minutes or so.
3. When we heard that his wife had given birth to their first child, we all went for a . . . . drink.
4. There's . . . . drinks at the bar tonight. The company is paying!
5. After the accident he poured himself a . . . . drink to calm his nerves.
6. Before dinner we had a long, cool, ... drink on the balcony, watching the sun go down over the sea.

3. Adjective + drink (non-alcoholic)

Complete the sentences with the above adjectives:

1. I had a cold, so I made myself a . . . . drink and went straight to bed.
2. Water makes a . . . . drink when served with ice and a slice of lemon.
3. We're not licensed to serve alcoholic drinks. I have tea, coffee and . . . . drinks.
4. I needed a . . . . drink of water to quench my thirst. I had at least a litre.

Notes

1. Note how we describe our level of drinking:
   I'm a heavy / light drinker. (I drink / don't drink a lot of alcohol.)
   I'm a moderate drinker. (I drink a sensible amount.)
   I'm not much of a drinker. (I don't drink much alcohol.)
   I'm teetotal. (I never drink alcohol.)
2. Note the following ways of saying you want a drink:
   I'm desperate for a drink.
   I'm dying for a drink!
   I could do with a drink.

meal and dish

Verb + meal	Adjective + meal	Adjective + dish
make a meal	a delicious meal	an expensive dish
have a meal	a heavy or light meal	a local dish
go out for a meal	a hot meal	a rice dish
miss / skip a meal	a proper meal	a vegetarian dish
order a meal	a ready meal	the national dish
serve a meal	your main meal (of the day)	

1. Verb + meal

Complete these sentences with the correct form of the above verbs:

1. He's so thin. He looks as though he hasn't . . . . a square meal for weeks.
2. My local pub . . . . excellent bar meals. You should try them.
3. The meals my mother . . . . for us were good for us, but not that tasty.
4. We're . . . . out for a meal to celebrate my birthday tonight.
5. Every time she flies, my wife has to . . . . a vegetarian meal.
6. It's not a good idea to . . . . meals and replace them with snacks like biscuits.

2. Adjective + meal

Complete the sentences with the above adjectives:

1. You ought to eat . . . . meals instead of snacking all the time.
2. He threw together a . . . . meal out of a few leftovers. It was wonderful.
3. When do you have your . . . . meal of the day? We have ours in the evening.
4. Lots of students have little time to cook, so they live on . . . . meals.
5. We're only serving sandwiches. We stopped serving . . . . meals at 6pm.
6. I usually have a . . . . meal of bread and fruit at lunchtime. If I eat a . . . .
   meal, it makes me sleepy and I find it difficult to work.

3. Adjective + dish

Complete the sentences with the above adjectives:

1. If you don't eat meat, there are several . . . . dishes on the menu.
2. In the restaurant I ordered the most . . . . dish, a large sirloin steak.
3. I don't have a lot of money so I mainly cook pasta and . . . . dishes.
4. We sampled all the . . . . dishes while we were on holiday in the Algarve.
5. The . . . . dish of Scotland is 'haggis' – a kind of spicy meat sausage.

Notes
1. A 'dish' is an individual type of food *(lamb curry, steak and chips, mushroom soup)*.
2. Note this expression:
   The restaurant wasn't that expensive. The meal worked out at £20 a head / £20 per person.
3. In 1-1 a 'square meal' is a large meal that satisfies you.
   I haven't had a square meal in over a week. I've lived on nothing but sandwiches and biscuits.
   A 'buffet' is a meal where people serve themselves.
   Come and try our buffet – all you can eat for only £8.
   A 'side dish' is a small amount of food that you order with your main meal.
   We had curried chicken with a side dish of fried vegetables.
   The 'dish of the day' is a special meal in addition to the rest of the menu.
   I had the dish of the day – cod fillet in a cheese and mustard sauce.

Key Words for Fluency – Intermediate

diet and appetite

Adjective + diet	Verb + diet	Verb + appetite
a balanced diet	follow a diet	lose your appetite
a healthy diet	go on a diet	sharpen your appetite
a low-fat diet	stick to / keep to your diet	work up an appetite
a poor diet	watch your diet	give you an appetite
	cut out of your diet	spoil your appetite

1. Adjective + diet (what we usually eat)

Complete the sentences with the above adjectives:

1. Fruit is an essential part of a . . . . diet. Try to eat two or three pieces a day.
2. It's important that children eat a . . . . diet. They need a variety of foods.
3. His diet consists mainly of fried food. Such a . . . . diet will lead to illness.
4. If you eat a . . . . diet, you'll live longer. So, no more butter for me!

2. Verb + diet (losing weight)

Complete the sentences with the correct form of the above verbs:

1. I've decided to . . . . on a strict diet to see if I can lose a few kilos.
2. I've been advised to . . . . sugar out of my diet if I want to shed a few kilos.
3. If you . . . . this low calorie diet, you'll lose weight. But you must . . . .
   to it rigidly.
4. He's got an ulcer, so he has to . . . . his diet. He's got to keep off fatty foods.

3. Verb + appetite

Match these halves:

1. All this exercise has
2. I'm sorry I don't feel like eating just now.
3. I went for a long walk to see if I could
4. Don't eat snacks between meals.
5. All that fresh air has sharpened my appetite.

a. I've lost my appetite.
b. given me an appetite.
c. I could eat a horse.
d. work up an appetite.
e. You'll spoil your appetite.

"I've decided to go on a strict diet"'

Notes

1. Note these verb + 'on a diet of' expressions:
   When we were lost in the jungle we survived on a diet of insects and wild fruit.
   Children in the West seem to exist on a diet of burgers and chips.

2. Note these expressions:
   There is good evidence that a diet rich in fruit and vegetables can prevent disease.
   A diet deficient in vitamin C can lead to a number of skin diseases.
   The staple diet of the giant panda is bamboo.

3. Note the following adjectives that are used to describe a good appetite:
   The children have all got healthy appetites. They eat more than their parents do!
   Although she's over eighty she still has a hearty appetite.

4. 'Loss of appetite' is common among people who are ill.

party

Verb + party	Adjective + party	Types of party
arrive at a party	an all-night party	a dinner party
come away from a party	a fantastic party	a fancy-dress party
go to a party	a noisy party	a farewell / leaving party
invite (you) to a party	a surprise party	a house-warming party
plan a party		a street party
throw a party		

1. Verb + party

Complete these sentences with the correct form of the above verbs:

1. She . . . . a lot of people from her office to her birthday party.
2. I didn't really want to . . . . to my neighbours' party but I thought I'd better put in an appearance in case they felt offended.
3. We're . . . . a farewell party for Marion. She's retiring next week. Any ideas?
4. I try not to be the first to . . . . at parties. I'm not very good at small talk.
5. We . . . . away from the party early after a phone call from our babysitter.
6. After the final performance, the director . . . . a huge party for everyone involved in the production of the play. Champagne all round!

2. Adjective + party

Complete the sentences with the above adjectives:

1. We're organising a . . . . birthday party for my husband next week. Do you think you can manage to keep the party a secret until then?
2. Thanks for a . . . . party. I wouldn't have missed it for anything.
3. Dad, can I go to an . . . . party at Darren's at the weekend?
   > No way! You can go to the party, but make sure you're home by midnight.
4. There was a . . . . party going on next door which kept me awake most of the night. Unfortunately, it didn't break up until 5am.

3. Types of party

Match these halves:

1. Our new neighbours threw	a. a farewell party.
2. Andy's leaving so we're planning	b. the fancy-dress party dressed as a carrot.
3. I'm going to	c. were held to celebrate independence day.
4. Street parties	d. their dinner party?
5. Should I take some wine to	e. a house-warming party after moving in.

Notes

1. Note these expressions:
   When we arrived, the party was just starting to warm up. When we left, the party was in full swing.
   He's having a party to celebrate his 84th birthday.
2. A 'celebration' is a party for a special occasion:
   I didn't feel like joining in the celebrations.
   Peter got the job. I think that calls for a celebration!
   They planned a special celebration for her homecoming.
   As part of the celebrations, they staged a big, open-air concert in Hyde Park.

Section 12

Fun and entertainment

fun and entertainment   90
joke   91
television and programme   92
concert   93
fan and audience   94
film   95
music and song   96

"I'm a great fan of his."

fun and entertainment

Verb + fun	Expressions with fun	Adjective + entertainment
have fun	It sounds like fun.	popular entertainment
spoil (your) fun	Have fun!	free entertainment
join in the fun	full of fun	in-flight entertainment
miss out on the fun	It's great / no fun.	live entertainment
get fun out of	(She's) great fun to be with.	family entertainment
	(It's) just a bit of fun.	

1. Verb + fun

Complete the sentences with the correct form of the above verbs:

1. Why do grown-ups always . . . . your fun and tell you to be quiet?
2. I haven't . . . . so much fun for ages. We must do this again soon.
3. Don't be such a wet blanket! Come over to our place and . . . . in the fun!
4. Our children . . . . a lot of fun out of playing with water.
5. Of course I'm coming to the party. I don't want to . . . . out on all the fun!

2. Expressions with fun

Match the halves:

1. It's great fun watching	a. He's very entertaining.
2. The trip to the castle	b. full of fun.
3. Have fun!	c. It was just a bit of harmless fun.
4. Frank is always so cheerful and	d. But don't stay out too late.
5. I didn't mean to hurt her.	e. the dog chase the cat.
6. Harry's great fun to be with.	f. when everyone else is free.
7. It's no fun having to work on Sundays	g. sounds like fun.

3. Adjective + entertainment

Complete the sentences with the above adjectives:

1. There wasn't any . . . . entertainment on the plane so the children were bored.
2. Amusement parks offer good . . . . entertainment for both young and old.
3. We provide . . . . entertainment for children staying at the hotel.
4. There's no doubt that television is the most . . . . form of entertainment.
5. Local musicians provided . . . . entertainment while we ate and drank.

Notes

1. Note the following ways of saying something is not fun:
   Walking all day in the pouring rain and freezing cold is not my idea of fun.
   Being a film star isn't all fun and games.
   I enjoy golf as a hobby, but if I had to do it as a job, it would take all the fun out of it.

2. Note the expression 'just for fun':
   I write just for fun, not because I expect to make any money out of it.
   I decided to learn Japanese just for fun.

3. Note these expressions with 'entertainment':
   What do you do for entertainment around here?
   > I'm afraid there's not much in the way of entertainment. There's only a cinema and a pub.
   The zoo is good entertainment value. It keeps the kids amused for hours.

Key Words for Fluency – Intermediate

joke

Verb + joke	Adjective + joke	Verb + joke	Expressions
tell a joke	a corny joke	play a joke on (him)	meant as a joke
get the joke	a dirty joke	can't take a joke	your idea of a joke
hear a joke	a hilarious joke	a joke goes too far	the joke fell flat
laugh at a joke	a private joke		do something for / as a joke

1. Verb + joke (amusing story)

Complete these sentences with the correct form of the above verbs:

1. Have you . . . . any good jokes lately?
2. What's so funny? I don't . . . . the joke.
3. My mother always . . . . at my father's jokes. We just sit there and groan.
4. We all sat around the table drinking beer and . . . . jokes late into the night.

2. Adjective + joke

Complete the sentences with the above adjectives:

1. I think his jokes are . . . . They are extremely funny.
2. I'm tired of hearing these old jokes again and again. They're so . . . .
3. Please don't tell any . . . . jokes at the party. My mother's going to be there!
4. I don't know what those two girls in the corner over there are up to. They seem to be sharing a . . . . joke.

3. Verb + joke (a trick played on someone)

Choose the correct collocation:

1. They decided to make / play a joke on their father by hiding his jacket in his bed.
2. This stupid joke has come / gone far enough! Where are my shoes?
3. Relax! If you can't do / take a joke you won't find it easy working in this office!

4. Common expressions

Match the halves:

1. I tried to tell a joke to lighten the atmosphere
2. The children put flour in my hat
3. If putting salt in my tea is your idea of a joke,
4. Come on. Don't be so serious.

a. as a joke.
b. but it fell flat.
c. What I said was meant as a joke.
d. then I don't find it very funny.

"This is not my idea of a joke!"

Notes   1. Note the expression 'make a joke at the expense of somebody':
      It's unkind to make jokes at the expense of your friends.
     2. A 'sense of humour' is the ability to laugh at funny situations:
      Sally is a friendly person with a great sense of humour.
      He is not noted for his sense of humour.
      You need a sense of humour to work here!

television and programme

Verb + television	Verb + programme
switch the television on or off	interrupt a programme
turn the television up or down	record a programme
watch television	broadcast / show a programme
show on television	programmes attract viewers
Television + noun	**Adjective + programme**
television coverage	your favourite programme
a television licence	the following programme
a television presenter	a live programme
a television series	a violent programme

1. Verb + television

Complete these sentences with the correct form of the above verbs:

1. In Britain, the average viewer . . . . television for about three hours a day.
2. The television is quite loud. Could you . . . . it down please?
3. They edited out most of the sex scenes when the film was . . . . on television.
4. I can . . . . the television off if it's disturbing you.

2. Television + noun

Complete the sentences with the above noun phrases:

1. His book has been made into a successful television . . . .
2. Television . . . . of the match was lost because of a technical fault.
3. Why are television . . . . all so slim, healthy, and good-looking?
4. Our television . . . . expires next month. We'll need to remember to renew it.

3. Verb + programme

Choose the correct collocation:

1. We are disturbing / interrupting this programme to bring you a newsflash.
2. I'd like to copy / record a programme tonight at 9. Have you got a blank tape?
3. This kind of programme never fails to bring in / attract millions of viewers.
4. Don't worry, the programme will be delivered / shown again at the weekend.

4. Adjective + programme

Complete the sentences with the above adjectives:

1. The soap opera, *Eastenders,* is my . . . . programme. I never miss an episode.
2. Is *University Challenge* a . . . . programme, or is it pre-recorded?
3. We don't allow our children to watch . . . . programmes.
4. The . . . . programme contains scenes which you may find disturbing.

Notes

1. Note that 'the television' refers to the television set, while 'television' refers to programmes:
   There's an interesting programme on television tonight.
   They have the television on all the time.
2. We refer to the television informally as the 'TV', the 'telly', or the 'box'.
3. Note these expressions:
   I was glued to the television last night. (could not stop watching something special)

concert

Verb + concert	Adjective + concert	Noun + preposition + concert
attend a concert	a brilliant concert	a live broadcast of the concert
cancel a concert	a farewell concert	a ticket for the concert
give a concert	a live concert	a venue for the concert
put on a concert	an open-air concert	the proceeds from the concert
perform in a concert	the concert is well / badly organised	

1. Verb + concert

Complete these sentences with the correct form of the above verbs:

1. Ivan Patrovi's decision to . . . . the concert is bound to disappoint his fans.
2. A crowd of about 50,000 . . . . the concert in Central Park.
3. The opera star, Rory Watson, will . . . . a concert in Hyde Park in London.
4. Because of work, I wasn't able to see my son . . . . in the school concert.
5. The school is . . . . on a concert to raise money for cancer charities.

"An open-air concert with fireworks."

2. Adjective + concert

Complete the sentences with the above adjectives:

1. The concert was absolutely . . . . It lived up to all my expectations.
2. It's the band's . . . . concert – definitely their last. Tickets are like gold dust.
3. The Festival ends with an . . . . concert with a huge fireworks display.
4. I love the excitement of . . . . concerts. I saw David Bowie in London last month.
5. The concert was very . . . . The whole thing was a real fiasco.

3. Noun + preposition + concert

Complete the sentences with the above nouns:

1. I've got a spare . . . . for Friday's concert. Are you doing anything?
2. I watched a live . . . . of the concert on giant video screens outside the stadium.
3. The . . . . from the concert will go to help homeless people.
4. After the fire at the theatre, the organisers are now looking for an alternative . . . . for the concert.

Notes

1. Note the following ways of explaining the reason for a concert:
   Tonight's concert will be held in aid of famine relief.
   A concert will be held to mark the tenth anniversary of the country's independence.
2. Note this way of announcing a concert:
   The Berlin Philharmonic are in concert at the Festival Hall this evening.
3. Note these different kinds of concert:
   a pop concert   a rock concert   a classical concert

fan and audience

Verb + fan	Verb + audience	Adjective + audience
disappoint the fans	attract an audience	a captive audience
thank your fans	play to an audience	a family audience
fans pack (stadiums)	thrill an audience	a delighted audience
fans besiege (hotels)	an audience claps	an invited audience
		a live audience
Adjective + fan		the target audience
devoted fans		
rival fans		
a big fan of (the band)		

1. Verb + fan

Complete these sentences with the correct form of the above verbs:

1. I'd like to . . . . all my fans for their support throughout the years.
2. The singer's decision to cancel the concert is bound to . . . . her fans.
3. Hundreds of fans . . . . Sting's hotel, hoping to catch a glimpse of him.
4. Thousands of football fans . . . . the National Stadium for the cup final.

2. Adjective + fan

Choose the best collocation:

1. I'm a big / large fan of country and western music. It's all I ever listen to.
2. Fighting broke out between competitive / rival fans at the end of the match.
3. Madonna was mobbed by devoted / beloved fans as she left her hotel.

3. Verb + audience

Complete these sentences with the correct form of the above verbs:

1. The audience . . . . and cheered at the end of the performance.
2. He's a well-known figure in politics, so he should . . . . a large audience.
3. Charlie Chaplin's films . . . . audiences throughout the world for decades.
4. The rock group Oasis . . . . to an audience of over 100,000 at the festival.

4. Adjective + audience

Complete the sentences with the above adjectives:

1. She got a standing ovation from a . . . . audience.
2. He's the kind of singer who performs best before a . . . . audience.
3. The . . . . audience for this programme are people between 20 and 25.
4. The magician had a . . . . audience. We couldn't get our children to leave.
5. The film contains no sex or violence. It is obviously aimed at a . . . . audience.
6. A specially . . . . audience attended the opening night of the play. The selected guests included Prince Charles and his two sons.

Notes
1. Note this expression:
   The audience was composed largely of young people.
2. Note how we describe the feelings of the fans:
   Pavarotti cancelled his concert – to the great disappointment of his fans.
   The team won the game easily – to the delight of all their fans.

film

Verb + film	Adjective + film	Noun + preposition + film
see a film	an action-packed film	a part in a film
watch a film	an award-winning film	a review of a film
shoot a film	a good film	a screening of a film
show a film	a low-budget film	your enjoyment of a film
release a film		
ban a film		
appear in / star in a film		

1. Verb + film

Complete these sentences with the correct form of the above verbs:

1. Go and . . . . Woody Allen's latest film. I've never laughed so much in all my life.
2. The film was made for television. It was mostly . . . . on location in Egypt.
3. We stayed up to . . . . the late-night film.
4. For your in-flight entertainment today, we are . . . . the film *Men in Black*. It will start in approximately ten minutes.
5. The film was . . . . in my country for having too many explicit sex scenes.
6. It's ridiculous that Tom Cruise was paid $10 million for . . . . in that film.
7. The film was . . . . in the US two months ago, but only came out in the UK the week before last.

2. Adjective + film

Choose the correct collocation:

1. He has made a number of award-winning / prize films in his short career. He's already picked up Oscars for best director and best film.
2. *Indiana Jones and the Temple of Doom* is an action-packed / a thriller film full of adventure and exciting events.
3. Have you seen any fine / good films recently?
4. Spaghetti westerns were cheap / low-budget films made in the 1970s with very little money. They went on to become surprise box office hits.

3. Noun + preposition + film

Complete the sentences with the above nouns:

1. I'm an actor, but I've only had one or two minor . . . . in films so far.
2. I'd read the book and knew the ending, but it didn't spoil my . . . . of the film.
3. Film critics attended a special . . . . of the film in Los Angeles.
4. . . . . of the film are poor. They say it will flop and lose a lot of money.

Notes

1. Note these expressions:
   In India, the film was dubbed. (the language spoken by the actors was changed)
   In China, the film had subtitles. (a written translation was provided on screen)
2. Note how we describe the content of a film:
   The film is based on the real-life story of a woman who survived the sinking of the Titanic.
   The film Saving Private Ryan depicts the full horror of war.
   This film contains scenes of violence and bad language and has been rated 18.

music and song

Verb + music	Noun + preposition + music
compose / write music	a piece of music
listen to music	the beat of the music
perform music	your taste in music
music appeals to (you)	a gift for music
Adjective + music	**Expressions with song**
background music	a love song
folk music	a pop song
live music	a protest song
classical music	a theme song
the music is deafening	burst into song

1. Verb + music

Complete these sentences with the correct form of the above verbs:

1. . . . . to very loud music leads to hearing loss in young people.
2. The theme music was specially . . . . for the programme.
3. Annie Lennox is a popular singer whose music . . . . to a wide audience.
4. He's a well-known singer-songwriter. He writes and . . . . his own music.

2. Adjective + music

Complete the sentences with the above adjectives:

1. The music was . . . . We had to shout to make ourselves heard above it.
2. While I'm working in my study, I always have some kind of . . . . music on.
3. The club has . . . . music every night. There's always a band playing.
4. Every country has its own . . . . music.
5. Not everyone can appreciate . . . . music.

3. Noun + preposition + music

Complete the sentences with the above nouns:

1. The . . . . of the music was quite hypnotic and I began to feel quite sleepy.
2. Mendelssohn's Wedding March is a popular . . . . of music played at weddings.
3. Mandy has a . . . . for music. Her mother is also extremely talented.
4. What's your . . . . in music? What sort of music are you into?

4. Expressions with song

Match the halves:

1. He's very romantic and he	a. burst into song.
2. *Blowing in the Wind* by Bob Dylan is	b. I can listen to it again and again.
3. There's nothing but endless pop songs	c. a well-known protest song.
4. He was so happy he just	d. on the radio these days.
5. I love the theme song from *Neighbours*.	e. sings beautiful love songs.

Note   'Lyrics' are the words of a song:
> *He writes the lyrics for most of his own songs.*
> *I know the lyrics to every Beatles song.*

Section 13

People

life   98
death   99
age   100
character   101
clothes and fashion   102
appearance   103
habit and routine   104

"They're very close – despite the age difference."

life

Verb + life	Adjective + life	Noun + of + life
lose your life	an easy life	every aspect of your life
prolong your life	a new life	loss of life
risk your life	your private life	the pace of life
save your life	your social life	the quality of life
take your own life	everyday life	the rest of your life
		a new lease of life

1. Verb + life

Complete the sentences with the correct form of the above verbs:

1. Fasten your seatbelt. It could . . . . your life.
2. Doctors say that regular exercise and a good diet can . . . . your life.
3. My friend . . . . her own life. Nobody can understand why she killed herself.
4. Firemen . . . . their lives rescuing people from burning buildings.
5. The war claimed the lives of thousands of soldiers. Hundreds of civilians also
   . . . . their lives.

2. Adjective + life

Match the two halves:

1. She wants to make a clean break with her past and start	a. her private life.
2. Computers are now very much a part of	b. a new life.
3. It really irritates me when people say that teachers have	c. social life.
4. She's got a lot of friends here, so she has a good	d. everyday life.
5. She's not the sort of person who likes to talk about	e. an easy life.

3. Noun + of + life

Complete the sentences with the above nouns:

1. I love him, but I'm not sure I want to spend the . . . . of my life with him.
2. The two trains crashed into each other with serious . . . . of life.
3. Our . . . . of life has improved tremendously in the last 20 years. Most people
   now have a much higher standard of living.
4. I don't like the . . . . of modern life. It's too fast and stressful for me.
5. His illness is debilitating. It affects almost every . . . . of his life.
6. The operation has given my mother a new . . . . of life. It means she can now
   do the things she used to enjoy.

Notes

1. Note the expression 'to lead a . . . . life':
   Before going to university, I had little experience of the world. I had led a very sheltered life.
   My father has a minor heart problem, but he is able to lead a normal life despite his illness.
   *Most of us lead such dull and humdrum lives in the city, but some people seem to lead such exciting
   lives travelling from country to country.*
2. The expression 'a matter of life and death' is often used with a non-literal meaning:
   Keeping this factory open is a matter of life and death for this town.
3. Note this expression:
   She's so full of life – always running around and laughing.

death

Verb + death	Verb + to death	Adjective + death
cause death	be crushed to death	an early death
escape death	bleed to death	a horrible death
hear of a death	fall to your death	a violent death
get over a death	freeze to death	a sudden death
mourn a death	starve to death	certain death
	condemn to death	

	Noun + of + death	
the cause of death	on the point of death	in the event of (his) death

1. Verb + death

Complete the sentences with the correct form of the above verbs:

1. I was sorry to . . . . of your father's death.
2. He . . . . death by a millimetre. The bullet just missed his heart.
3. I don't think parents ever really . . . . over the death of a child.
4. It's a serious disease that . . . . thousands of deaths a year.
5. When Eva Peron died, the whole country . . . . her death.

2. Verb + to death

Match the halves:

1. The knife severed an artery in his leg and he   a. starved to death.
2. He lost his footing on the mountain and   b. froze to death.
3. When the crowd pushed forward, several people   c. was condemned to death.
4. He was lost in deep snow and he   d. fell to his death.
5. When the crops failed, thousands of people   e. were crushed to death.
6. He was caught spying in the 60s and   f. bled to death.

3. Adjective + death

Complete the sentences with the above adjectives:

1. Everyone was shocked by his . . . . death – it was completely unexpected.
2. It was his dependence on drugs that led to his . . . . death at the age of 24.
3. Many asylum seekers claim they face . . . . death if they are sent back home.
4. Unable to escape from the burning house, he died a . . . . death.
5. She died in her sleep, unlike her husband, who met a . . . . death during the war.

4. Noun + of + death

Complete the sentences with the above nouns:

1. The missing climber was on the . . . . of death when she was found.
2. The doctor said that the most likely . . . . of death was heart failure.
3. He left a letter for me to read in the . . . . of his death.

Note   Note these death + noun collocations:
Famous people often receive death threats.
The club was a death trap. The fire exits had been locked and nobody could escape from the fire.
The death penalty has been abolished in Britain, but some people want to re-introduce it.

age

Verb + age	Adjective + age	Preposition + age	Age + noun
feel your age	the average age	from the age of 4	age range
get to my age	an early age	at the age of 16	age gap
guess your age	an impressionable age	over the age of 18	age limit
lie about your age	a mental age	people of all ages	
look your age	your old age	mature for your age	

1. Verb + age

Complete the sentences with the correct form of the above verbs:

1. When you . . . . to my age, you have to start taking things easy.
2. He's always looked young, but recently he has started to . . . . his age.
3. I'm beginning to . . . . my age. I'm no longer as young as I like to think I am.
4. I think he's . . . . about his age. He doesn't look anywhere near 18.
5. Because of beauty treatments, it's difficult to . . . . the age of some movie stars.

2. Adjective + age

Complete the sentences with the above adjectives:

1. The three sisters have been singing together from an . . . . age.
2. My grandmother is getting a bit forgetful in her . . . . age.
3. He's at that . . . . age when he's easily influenced by other children at school.
4. The . . . . age of the soldiers who fought in the war was only 18.
5. My brother is mentally disabled. He's 16, but he only has a . . . . age of 8.

3. Preposition + age

Complete the sentences with the above prepositions:

1. He left home . . . . the age of 16 and went to work in London.
2. The competition is open to anyone . . . . the age of eighteen.
3. Your daughter is very mature . . . . her age.
4. He was a fast learner. He could read . . . . the age of three.
5. The programme is designed to appeal to people . . . . all ages.

4. Age + noun

Match the halves:

1. The drinks are being marketed at
2. There is a 15-year age gap
3. The age limit at the club is 18,

a. between me and my older brother.
b. so you'll need to show some form of ID.
c. people in the 20-30 age range.

Notes

1. Note these expressions:
   His age will count against him in the interview. (be a disadvantage)
   I'm not allowed to sell you alcohol. You're under age.

2. Note these types of age:
   The voting age was lowered from 21 to 18 to allow younger people to vote in elections.
   I can't wait until I reach retirement age and stop working.

3. We use 'generation' to refer to different age groups:
   The younger generation smoke less than their parents did, but they drink more.
   I was aware of the generation gap between my parents and myself.

character

Verb + character	Noun + prep + character	Adjective + character
reveal your character	defamation of character	a forceful character
transform your character	a flaw in your character	a likeable character
blacken your character	a stain on your character	a reformed character
	strength of character	a shady character
	a good / bad judge of character	

1. Verb + character (personality)

Complete the sentences with the correct form of the above verbs:

1. Therapy has . . . . his character. He's given up drinking and gambling.
2. Why are you trying to . . . . the Prime Minister's character? He's not a liar!
3. He's a very private person. He . . . . his true character to very few people.

2. Noun + preposition + character

Complete the sentences with the above nouns:

1. Anyone responsible for employing people has to be a good . . . . of character.
2. He's too easily persuaded. He hasn't got the . . . . of character to say no.
3. His inability to admit that he's wrong is the only . . . . in his character.
4. Being caught shoplifting was a terrible . . . . on his character.
5. The model, Zoe Foo, is suing the magazine *Goodbye* for . . . . of character.

3. Adjective + character (person)

Match the halves:

"He's a bit of a shady character."

1. Jim's such a likeable character.
2. David's a reformed character these days.
3. My neighbour's a bit of a shady character.
4. Jill's a very forceful character.

a. Yes, he's stopped drinking and he's got a job.
b. Yes, he's really nice, isn't he?
c. Yes, she's used to getting her own way.
d. I know. Nobody has a good word to say about him.

Notes

1. Note the expressions used to describe uncharacteristic behaviour:
   It's not in his character to hurt anybody. He would never deliberately try to do that.
   His behaviour was completely out of character. He has never acted like this before.
2. Note these character + noun collocations:
   I gave my teacher as a character reference on the application form.
   Some people argue that physical games like rugby are character building.
   The article on the Director of the BBC in today's paper was a perfect example of character assassination.
3. 'Character' is also a person in a book or film.
   George Clooney plays the central character in the movie 'Perfect Storm'.
4. Note that we use 'personality' and not 'character' in these expressions:
   He has a very outgoing personality and makes friends very easily.
   She has a very warm personality. You'll enjoy her company.
   All applicants for the job must undergo a personality test.

clothes and fashion

Verb + clothes	Adjective + clothes	Verb + fashion
put on your clothes	casual clothes	be in fashion
take off your clothes	clean clothes	keep up with fashion
wear clothes	loose clothes	go out of fashion
pack your clothes	warm clothes	come back into fashion
make your clothes		
clothes fit you		

1. Verb + clothes

Complete the sentences with the correct form of the above verbs:

1. My sister and I are the same size, so we can . . . . each other's clothes.
2. I need to . . . . my clothes. Does anyone know where the suitcases are?
3. My mother has a sewing machine and . . . . most of her own clothes.
4. Many of us feel embarrassed about . . . . our clothes off in front of the doctor.
5. Very tall people often have problems finding clothes to . . . . them.
6. You can . . . . your clothes back on now, Mr Smith. I've finished my examination.

2. Adjective + clothes

Complete the sentences below with the above adjectives:

1. If you're travelling in hot climates, wear . . . . clothes and light shoes.
2. If you don't put some . . . . clothes on, you'll catch your death of cold!
3. I went home, showered and shaved, then put on some . . . . clothes.
4. Most people who work for large computer companies wear . . . . clothes to work. It is unusual to see somebody in a suit and tie.

"She makes most of her own clothes!"

3. Verb + fashion

Complete the verb phrases in the sentences below with the above prepositions:

1. At my age I've stopped trying to keep . . . . with the latest fashions.
2. I hear green's . . . . fashion this summer. Last summer it was purple!
3. Flared trousers went . . . . of fashion twenty years ago. They came back . . . . fashion two years ago, but now they've gone out of fashion again!

Notes
1. We have names for clothes worn at certain times. We talk about school clothes, work clothes and maternity clothes (worn by a pregnant woman).
   I always change out of my school clothes as soon as I get home.
2. We usually prefer 'clothing' when we talk about clothes that protect against heat, water, machines or dangerous substances. We talk about outdoor / waterproof / protective clothing:
   Always wear protective clothing when handling these chemicals.
3. 'Fashion' is also used about other things:
   The modern fashion in education is to let the child decide everything!

appearance

Verb + appearance	Adjective + appearance	Common expressions
change your appearance	a deceptive appearance	a change in your appearance
improve your appearance	an outward appearance	pride in your appearance
neglect your appearance	your physical appearance	similar in appearance
judge people by appearances	an untidy appearance	self-conscious about your ...
worry about your ...	a youthful appearance	despite appearances

1. Verb + appearance

Complete the sentences with the correct form of the above verbs:

1. That hat cost £500, but it does nothing to . . . . her appearance.
2. Stop . . . . about your appearance. You look fine!
3. She has definitely started to . . . . her appearance. She looks terrible.
4. We all know that you shouldn't . . . . people by appearances. But we all do it!
5. I'd never dream of . . . . my appearance with plastic surgery.

2. Adjective + appearance

Complete the sentences below with the above adjectives:

1. He has such an . . . . appearance – I don't think he ever brushes his hair.
2. Cliff has a remarkably . . . . appearance. He certainly doesn't look his age.
3. Remember that appearances can be . . . . People aren't always what they seem.
4. He maintained an . . . . appearance of calm, but inside he was furious. You should have heard what he said after the meeting!
5. In my view, people today place too much emphasis on . . . . appearance.

3. Common expressions

Complete the sentences with the correct words:

1. Although . . . . in appearance, the twins are entirely different in character.
2. My friend is very . . . . about his appearance. He thinks his nose is too big.
3. The British monarchy has no power whatsoever – . . . . appearances to the contrary.
4. You need to smarten up! You should take more . . . . in your appearance.
5. We were amazed by the . . . . in his appearance. He looked so much better!

Notes
1. Note how we describe giving a false impression:
   He gives the appearance of being relaxed, but underneath he's really quite a nervous person.
2. Note these expressions:
   My sister spends an inordinate amount of time on her appearance. She's in the bathroom for hours!
   I think women tend to be more concerned about their personal appearance than men.
   I think what first attracted me to him was his physical appearance.
3. Note the expression 'to all appearances', which means 'on the surface':
   To all appearances, he was enjoying his birthday party, but I think he was just pretending in order to please me.
4. Appearance can also refer to an actor's part in a play, film or television programme:
   Last night's programme contained one of Bogart's rare television appearances.

habit and routine

Verb + habit	Adjective + habit	Verb + routine	Noun + prep + routine
form a habit	an anti-social habit	have a routine	a break from ...
break a habit	an annoying habit	stick to a routine	a change of routine
kick a habit	a good habit	change your routine	a matter of routine
pick up a habit	a disgusting habit	get back to a ...	
give up a habit		upset someone's ...	
get out of the habit			

1. Developing habits and ending habits

Mark the sentences (D) if they mean 'develop a habit' and (E) for 'end a habit':

1. I've tried to stop smoking many times, but I just can't kick the habit.
2. My brother taught me to drive and I know I've picked up some of his bad habits.
3. My daughter is finding it hard to give up the habit of reading aloud.
4. Try to break the habit of eating snacks between meals.
5. It's very important that children form good habits early in life.
6. I've got out of the habit of practising the piano since I stopped going to lessons.

2. Adjective + habit

Complete the sentences below with the above adjectives:

1. Taking regular exercise is a . . . . habit to develop.
2. Peter has the . . . . habit of talking to himself while he's working.
3. I think he's repulsive. He has some . . . . habits – like picking his nose.
4. In many countries today, smoking is now considered an . . . . habit.

3. Verb + routine

Complete the sentences with the correct form of the above verbs:

1. New babies . . . . no set routine. You never know when they want food or sleep!
2. My mother doesn't like anything or anyone to . . . . her daily routine.
3. Try . . . . your exercise routine to include more stretching movements.
4. After my holiday, it was actually nice to . . . . back to my old routine.
5. I . . . . to a rigid routine of studying for 4 hours at night. I never change this.

4. Noun + preposition + routine

Match the halves:

1. The bags of all visitors to the art gallery are searched as   a. the change of routine.
2. Some of the children were confused by   b. a break from routine.
3. Why don't you take some time off work? You need   c. a matter of routine.

Notes

1. Note these expressions:
   I'm not in the habit of lying to my friends / letting strangers into my apartment.
   It's all right to borrow money occasionally, but don't make a habit of it.
2. We talk about having a 'drug habit':
   He started breaking into houses to finance his heroin habit.
3. An 'exercise routine' or 'dance routine' describes a particular set of movements.
4. Note that a 'routine task / inspection / dental check-up' means a regular one.

Section 14

Relationships

friend   106
enemy   107
marriage   108
divorce   109
love   110
respect   111
family   112

"Friends – reunited!"

friend

Verb + friend	Verb + prep + friends	Adj + friend	Common expressions
make friends	approve of your ...	your best friend	your circle of friends
become friends	depend on your ...	a close friend	family and friends
remain friends	fall out with your ...	a mutual friend	a friend of a friend
meet a friend	lose touch with	an old friend	
visit a friend	your friends	a friend from work	
bring a friend		just good friends	

1. Verb + friends

Complete the sentences with the correct form of the above verbs:

1. I'm . . . . a friend of mine for lunch at the Carlton Hotel later today.
2. In spite of the bitter argument they had, they . . . . the best of friends.
3. Mike and I . . . . friends at university.
4. I'm afraid Ken's not here tonight. He's . . . . friends.
5. Can I . . . . a friend to the party?
6. Henry's the kind of person who doesn't find it easy to . . . . friends.

Now complete the multi-word verbs in the sentences with the correct preposition:

7. I've lost touch . . . . most of my school friends.
8. My parents don't approve . . . . my friends! They say they're a bad influence.
9. In times of crisis you know you can depend . . . . your best friends.
10. They used to be good friends, but they've fallen . . . . recently – over money!

2. Adjective + friend

Complete the sentences with the above adjectives:

1. She says that she and George aren't going out. They're just . . . . friends.
2. Heather was my . . . . friend at school. We did everything together.
3. Ivor and I are . . . . friends. We lived next door to each other as kids.
4. He knows a lot of people, but only one or two that he'd call . . . . friends.
5. On a Saturday I usually play football with some friends from . . . .
6. My wife and I were introduced to each other by a . . . . friend.

3. Common expressions

Match the halves:

1. Carol is a very sociable person. She has
2. I met Helen through
3. Roberta managed to recover

a. a friend of a friend.
b. with the help of her family and friends.
c. a wide circle of friends.

Note

Note these expressions:
Hilda's a friend of mine.
At our school reunion party we drank a toast to absent friends.
What a terrible way to treat a friend!
We usually have friends round on a Saturday night for a meal.
Since going to university, I've grown apart from many of my old school friends. (developed different interests)

enemy

Verb + enemy	Adjective + enemy	Enemy in war
make enemies	a bitter enemy	attack your enemy
have an enemy	a dangerous enemy	kill your enemy
face your enemy	a former enemy	defeat your enemy
	an old enemy	the enemy advances /
	your sworn enemy	retreats

1. Verb + enemy

Complete the sentences with the correct form of the above verbs:

1. He's such a likeable person. He doesn't seem to . . . . an enemy in the world.
2. The manager is arrogant. He's . . . . a lot of enemies since joining the company.
3. I think it's better to . . . . your enemies than to hide or run away from them.

2. Adjective + enemy

Match the halves:

1. The two leaders signed the peace agreement.
2. The sisters hate each other.
3. My father and his neighbour are old enemies.
4. I'll never forget the sight of the President
5. Make sure you get on with the manager's secretary.

"They used to be sworn enemies!"

a. They became bitter enemies after one of them stole the other's boyfriend.
b. They've been fighting for years over the hedge that separates their gardens.
c. shaking hands with his sworn enemy.
d. She's a dangerous enemy to have around here!
e. Then the former enemies shook hands for the cameras.

3. Enemy in war

Complete the sentences with the correct form of the above verbs:

1. The soldiers waited until nightfall so that they could . . . . the enemy under cover of darkness.
2. The battle didn't last long. We easily . . . . the enemy with our superior weapons.
3. We were under orders not to . . . . the enemy, but to take prisoners.
4. The enemy advanced 10 kms into our territory, but we eventually forced them to . . . .

Notes

1. Note these expressions:
   Male drivers are their own worst enemy. They drive too fast, and too close to the car in front. No wonder they have so many accidents!
   Being stuck in a lift with 20 people was an absolute nightmare. I wouldn't wish it on my worst enemy.
2. In war the opposite of 'enemy' is 'ally'.
   The Allies in the Second World War included Russia, the US, Canada, Australia, New Zealand and Britain.

marriage

Verb + marriage	Adj + marriage	Expressions with prepositions	Noun + of + marriage
believe in marriage	an arranged marriage	related by marriage	25 years of marriage
rush into marriage	a happy marriage	sex before marriage	offers of marriage
save a marriage	a previous marriage	at the marriage of	the basis of a ...
disapprove of a ...	the perfect marriage	a son by a previous	the break-up of a ...
marriages break down / up		marriage	the announcement of a marriage

1. Verb + marriage

Complete the sentences with the correct form of the above verbs:

1. The couple are trying to . . . . their marriage for the sake of the children.
2. She has been very depressed since her marriage . . . . down.
3. Your mum and I feel that you're far too young to . . . . into marriage.
4. My parents . . . . of my marriage. They think Pete's not good enough for me.
5. She said she didn't . . . . in marriage, but now she's on her third husband!

2. Adjective + marriage

Complete the sentences with the above adjectives:

1. Robert has three children – one with Lorna and two from a . . . . marriage.
2. I'm sure you'll join me in wishing Carol and Keith a long and . . . . marriage.
3. There are advantages to . . . . marriages, but I'd rather choose my own partner.
4. They seemed to have the . . . . marriage, so their divorce is a real surprise.

3. Expressions with prepositions

Choose the correct preposition:

1. We are related by / in marriage. He is my brother's father-in-law.
2. My mother doesn't believe in sex before / with marriage.
3. Bill has two daughters through / by a previous marriage.
4. We request the pleasure of your company at / for the marriage of our daughter Sonja.

4. Noun + of + marriage

Complete the sentences with the above nouns:

1. She moved to another town after the . . . . of her marriage.
2. In my opinion, trust in each other is the . . . . of a successful marriage.
3. The . . . . of her marriage appeared in *The Times*.
4. She separated from her husband after 25 . . . . of marriage.
5. She's received several . . . . of marriage, and rejected them all.

Notes

1. Note the following ways of saying that a marriage is not going well:
   I think their marriage is going through a bad patch.
   Their marriage is on the rocks. I can't see it lasting much longer.
   I think the children have put a tremendous strain on the marriage.

2. Note this expression:
   We've had a few problems in our marriage, but we're both determined to make a go of it.

divorce

Verb + divorce	Divorce + noun
want a divorce	divorce proceedings
get a divorce	the divorce rate
go through a divorce	a divorce settlement
grant a divorce	a divorce lawyer
end in divorce	
their divorce has come through	

1. Verb + divorce

Complete the sentences with the correct form of the above verbs:

1. I think it's far too easy to . . . . a divorce nowadays. I think it's the reason there are so many one-parent families in this country.
2. I watched my parents . . . . through a long, painful and messy divorce. It was a difficult time for my brother and me.
3. It's a sad fact that one in every three marriages today . . . . in divorce. And you wonder how many others are unhappy.
4. The Church is worried by the increasing number of failed marriages. Over 70,000 divorces were . . . . last year.
5. Jane . . . . a divorce from her husband, but he won't agree to one. It's a horrible situation to be in.
6. Bill was telling me that his divorce . . . . through last week. He says he's now a free man and has no intention of ever getting married again!

2. Divorce + noun

Match the halves:

1. As part of their divorce
2. There's been a dramatic rise in the divorce
3. My wife has threatened to start divorce
4. With a wife like Miranda, what you need is a good divorce

a. rate in the last twenty years.
b. proceedings if I continue working till midnight every day.
c. settlement, Paul agreed to let his wife keep the house.
d. lawyer! She'll try to get the kids, the house, the car, and at least £100,000 a year!

"What you need is a good divorce lawyer!"

Notes

1. Note the kind of things that happen after a divorce:
   They remained friends after their divorce.
   After divorce many women revert to their maiden name.
2. Note the expression:
   The fact that he admitted having an affair was sufficient grounds for divorce.

love

Verb + love	Love + noun	Common expressions
need love	a love affair	madly in love
fall in love	a love child	love at first sight
feel love	a love song	no love lost between them
declare your love	your love life	true love
your love grows	love letters	a mother's love
send your love		undying love

1. Verb + love

Complete the sentences with the correct form of the above verbs:

1. I . . . . in love with one of my students, and we were married within a month.
2. He married her to please his parents. I don't think he . . . . any love for her.
3. We all know that young children . . . . lots of love and affection.
4. At the wedding ceremony the bride and groom . . . . their love for each other.
5. Uncle Charlie . . . . his love and hopes you'll feel better soon.
6. We're still very much in love. In fact, our love has . . . . stronger over the years.

2. Love + noun

Complete the sentences with the above nouns:

1. He's having a love . . . . at work. I hope his wife finds out and leaves him.
2. *Wonderful Tonight* is a classic love . . . . , written by Eric Clapton.
3. I came across some old love . . . . at the back of a drawer in my bedroom.
4. The love . . . . of the young prince is never out of the papers!
5. It's no secret that he fathered a love . . . . with a young actress some years ago.

3. Common expressions

Match the halves:

1. They can't take their eyes off
2. When I saw her across
3. There's no love lost between them.
4. On their wedding day they pledged
5. Nothing can be stronger than
6. His latest partner's called Sue. Do you think it's

a. the room, it was love at first sight!
b. a mother's love for her child.
c. They can't stand each other.
d. true love this time?
e. each other. They're madly in love.
f. undying love for each other.

Notes
1. 'Unrequited love' is when you love someone, but they do not return your love.
2. A 'love-hate relationship' is when feelings frequently change from love to hate. We also call this a 'stormy relationship'.
3. We talk about 'having a great love of things' but not of people:
   My father had a great love of music.
4. To 'make love' is to have sex with someone.
5. 'Brotherly love' is the love between two brothers.
6. Note this common expression:
   Carol and Jim are obviously head over heels in love!

respect

Verb + respect	Adjective + respect
show respect	the greatest respect
gain respect	grudging respect
have respect	a healthy respect
lose respect	a mutual respect
treat with respect	

1. Verb + respect

Complete the sentences with the correct form of the above verbs:

1. As a manager he's a disaster because he doesn't . . . . the respect of his staff. If the company wants to succeed, they will need to replace him.
2. It's important that new teachers gain the respect of their students.
   > Yeah, the job becomes impossible if you . . . . the respect of the class.
3. The driver shouldn't have shouted at the old lady in that way. Everyone has a right to be . . . . with respect.
4. I think young people today need to . . . . more respect to the older generation. Offering your seat on a bus to an old person is just one example.
5. The Prime Minister has . . . . the respect of many leaders all round the world for his attempts to prevent war between India and Pakistan.

2. Adjective + respect

Match the halves:

1. The new player is not liked, but he's very talented
2. A successful marriage is based not only on love
3. Although I don't agree with his theories,
4. Don't worry, I know what my opponent is capable of and I won't underestimate him.

a. but also on a mutual respect for each other.
b. I have a healthy respect for his abilities.
c. I have the greatest respect for his ideas.
d. and so he's won the grudging respect of the team.

"Showing respect!"

Notes

1. Note the expressions we use to mean 'showing respect' towards somebody:
   No alcohol was served at the dinner, out of respect for Muslim customs.
   A minute's silence was observed as a mark of respect for the victims of the disaster.
2. Note how we describe disrespect:
   Many of these young men are out of control. They show a complete lack of respect for authority.
3. Note the following formal expression:
   Sir, with all due respect, I think that you are wrong.
4. Note this expression:
   I've got a lot of respect for my gran. She lost her husband when she was young and still managed to give her family a decent upbringing.

family

Verb + family	Adjective + family	Noun + prep + family
have a family	your immediate family	an addition to the family
support a family	your extended family	a friend of the family
bring up / raise a family	a respectable family	a member of the family
start a family	a single-parent family	the brains of the family
come from a (large) family	a close family	the baby of the family
	the whole family	the interests of the family
		opposition from your ...

1. Verb + family

   Complete the sentences with the correct form of the above verbs:

   1. Do you . . . . a family? I've got two boys and a girl.
   2. I . . . . from a large family. I have five brothers and three sisters.
   3. Many women today successfully combine a career with . . . . up a family.
   4. Are they planning to . . . . a family? I know Jenny loves children.
   5. People in low-income jobs often find it hard to . . . . their families.

2. Adjective + family

   Complete the sentences with the above adjectives:

   1. My family has always been very . . . . We ring each other and get together a lot.
   2. Only Diana's . . . . family and closest friends were invited to the wedding.
   3. He comes from a very . . . . family. His father is a judge.
   4. As a boy, I was surrounded by my . . . . family. Most of my aunts and uncles lived in the same village.
   5. The . . . . family had colds last week!
   6. Some people think that children brought up by both parents are less likely to get into trouble than children from . . . . families.

3. Noun + preposition + family

   Complete the sentences with the above nouns:

   1. No, he's not a relation. He's just a . . . . of the family – somebody we've known for years.
   2. She is the sole surviving . . . . of her family.
   3. Despite . . . . from her family, Sue married a man 40 years older than herself.
   4. I hear you're expecting a small . . . . to the family. When's the baby due?
   5. Good parents always put the . . . . of the family first.
   6. Jerry may be the . . . . of the family, but he's also the . . . . of the family. He's just finished his degree at Cambridge University.

Notes
   1. Note the following family + noun phrases:
      I know nothing about his family background.
      I have a family history of heart disease.
      If you would like advice on contraception, contact your local family planning clinic.
      With three young kids, I can't really join the club because of family commitments.
   2. Note this expression:
      Diabetes tends to run in the family. So, if your mother is diabetic, you might develop it later in life.

Section 15

The body and the senses

head 114
hand 115
heart 116
eye 117
sight 118
view 119
smell 120
taste 121
voice 122
breath 123
sleep and dream 124

"Arnold has a very acute sense of smell!"

head

Verb + head	Adjective + head	Common expressions
hit / bang your head	a bald head	a blow to the head
nod your head	a big head	a roof over your head
turn your head	a clear head	cover from head to toe
shake your head	a level head	pat someone on the head
hang your head		
your head aches		

1. Verb + head

Complete the sentences with the correct form of the above verbs:

1. The director . . . . her head in approval and told them to go ahead with the plan.
2. My mother . . . . her head in disagreement. She didn't like the idea at all.
3. I . . . . my head on the low ceiling when I stood up.
4. When I woke up, I had a fever and my head was . . . .
5. I thought he hadn't seen me, but then he . . . . his head and saw me.
6. The children . . . . their heads in shame when the teacher asked who had opened the letter on her desk.

2. Adjective + head

Complete the sentences with the above adjectives:

1. Just don't think about anything else. You'll need a . . . . head for your history exam today.
2. Tim's always boasting about how good he is. He has such a . . . . head.
3. You never see him without a baseball cap. He hates showing his . . . . head.
4. In this job it is important that you keep a . . . . head. If you lose your head, you'll lose the respect of the staff.

3. Common expressions

Match the halves:

1. The woman was killed by a heavy blow   a. on the head.
2. My grandfather patted his dog affectionately   b. to the head.
3. Some people don't even have a roof   c. from head to toe.
4. At the end of the game the players were covered in mud   d. over their head.

Notes

1. Note these 'head for' expressions:
   Let Henry work out the bill. He has a good head for figures. (good at counting)
   I couldn't be a mountaineer. I don't have a head for heights.
2. Note these verb + preposition + head expressions:
   You must be off your head if you think Dad'll let you take the car. (be crazy)
   I tried to understand the lecture, but most of it went over my head. (too difficult for me to understand)
   Don't let fame or success go to your head. (think you are more important than you are)
3. Note these idiomatic expressions:
   If we put our heads together, we might come up with a solution to the problem. (try together)
   I don't want to put any ideas into your head. (influence your thinking)
   I wish you'd use your head more often. (think more carefully before you do something)

hand

Verb + hand	Adjective + hand	Common expressions
raise / put up your hand	a free hand	do something by hand
wave your hand	an outstretched hand	be good with your hands
wash your hands	a steady hand	put your hands over your (ears)
hold hands	your bare hands	keep your hands off my (book)
join hands	capable / safe hands	get / lay your hands on (tickets)
shake hands	dirty / filthy hands	
tie (his) hands		

1. Verb + hand

Complete the sentences with the correct form of the above verbs:

1. The two leaders . . . . hands when they were introduced to each other.
2. . . . . your hand if you think you know the answer to the question.
3. There was nowhere to . . . . my hands, so I just wiped them clean on a cloth.
4. He . . . . my hand tightly, but he loosened his grip as he became less afraid.
5. The robbers . . . . the shopkeeper's hands behind his back before escaping.
6. I . . . . my hand madly to attract his attention, but he never looked my way.
7. At the end of the party we all . . . . hands and formed a large circle.

2. Adjective + hand

Match the two halves:

1. There are marks on her dress where she wiped her
2. He claims that he can kill a man with only his
3. When I go to work, I leave my child in my parents'
4. Hold the baby for a moment, so I'll have
5. I put a few coins into the beggar's
6. If you want to be a brain surgeon, you need a

a. bare hands.
b. safe and capable hands.
c. dirty hands.
d. outstretched hand.
e. steady hand.
f. a free hand to open the door.

3. Common expressions

Complete the sentences with the correct preposition:

1. Rory made all the furniture himself. He's very good . . . . his hands.
2. Woollen garments are best washed . . . . hand and not in a washing machine.
3. We can't get our hands . . . . tickets for the Stones concert.
4. I warned her to keep her hands . . . . my new bike.
5. She put her hands . . . . her ears to shut out the noise of the traffic.

Notes   1. Note these expressions:
I got down on my hands and knees and looked under the sofa.
When I realised I had made a fool of myself, I buried my head in my hands.
I know this part of town like the back of my hand. (I know it very well).
This tiny television is so small that it fits into the palm of your hand.
Give the singers a big hand, ladies and gentlemen! (clap to show you enjoyed the show)

2. 'Hand' also means 'help':
Do you need a hand to pack your shopping?
Can you give me a hand to move the bed?
Olga is always willing to lend a hand.

heart

Verb + heart	Adjective + heart	Common expressions
your heart beats	a broken heart	speak from the heart
your heart leaps	a cold heart	love with all your heart
your heart sinks	a kind heart	learn by heart
transplant a heart	a heavy heart	have a change of heart
break (his) heart		affairs of the heart
		from the bottom of your ...

1. Verb + heart

Complete the sentences with the correct form of the above verbs:

1. The fallen climber had a faint pulse. His heart was still . . . .
2. She . . . . Robert's heart when she left him for another man.
3. My heart . . . . when I heard my uncle was coming to stay. He's such a bore.
4. My heart . . . . when he asked, 'Will you marry me?' It certainly missed a beat!
5. Doctors have successfully . . . . the heart of a 30-year-old man into the body of a fifteen-year-old boy.

2. Adjective + heart

Complete the sentences with the above adjectives:

1. My music teacher has a . . . . heart – a real heart of gold.
2. I watched him go with a . . . . heart. I knew it was the last time I'd see him.
3. People say that she died of a . . . . heart.
4. He rarely thinks of other people. He has a . . . . heart – a real heart of stone.

3. Common expressions

Complete the sentences with the correct preposition:

1. You could tell from his voice that his speech at the funeral came . . . . . . the heart.
2. I love you . . . . . . all my heart. Will you marry me?
3. For homework we had to learn a poem . . . . . . heart.
4. I love you and I mean it . . . . . . the bottom . . . . . . my heart.
5. You'll be pleased to hear I've had a change . . . . . . heart. I'm giving you a second chance.
6. Barbara Cartland's novels are mostly about affairs . . . . . . the heart.

Notes

1. Note these expressions:
   My heart was in my mouth as the lorry came towards us. (was very afraid)
   I could feel my heart pounding with excitement as I went up to the stage to collect my prize.
   He can seem a bit aggressive at times, but his heart is in the right place (he means well).
   I tried to look interested in the game we were playing, but my heart wasn't in it. (I didn't really want to do it.)
   Have a heart! I need a rest. Please don't make me do it again! (be sympathetic)

2. 'Heart' also describes being determined to do something:
   She has set her heart on becoming a doctor.
   You're doing really well. Keep going, you're almost there – don't lose heart now.

3. 'Heart' can also mean 'centre':
   We live right in the very heart of the city.
   They have a cottage right in the heart of the countryside.

eye

Verb + eye	Adjective + eye	Common expressions
protect your eyes	a black eye	gaze into (her) eyes
strain your eyes	a close / watchful eye	bring tears to your eyes
make eyes at (her)	the naked eye	poke someone in the eye
have your eye on (it)	sore eyes	see (it) with my own eyes
keep your eye on (it)		have bags under your eyes
can't take your eyes off (him)		
your eyes water		

1. Verb + eye

Complete the sentences with the correct form of the above verbs:

1. Don't try to read in this poor light – you'll . . . . your eyes!
2. Always wear goggles to . . . . your eyes when using these machines.
3. How do you stop your eyes from . . . . when you're cutting up onions?
4. Could you . . . . an eye on my bags while I go to the toilet?
5. She was so beautiful that I couldn't . . . . my eyes off her.
6. I . . . . my eye on a new car, but my wife says we can't afford one.
7. I think she fancies me. She's been . . . . eyes at me all day.

2. Adjective + eye

Match the two halves:

1. How did she get that black eye?
2. Make sure you keep a close eye on the children
3. I bathed my sore eyes
4. The comet will be visible to the naked eye.

a. when they go swimming.
b. with some warm water.
c. You shouldn't need a telescope to see it.
d. Did someone punch her?

"I have my eye on a new car!"

3. Common expressions

Complete the sentences with the above prepositions:

1. If I hadn't seen it . . . . my own eyes, I would never have believed it possible.
2. The pain of the injection brought tears . . . . my eyes.
3. The two lovers were holding hands and gazing . . . . each other's eyes.
4. If you don't get enough sleep, you'll get bags . . . . . . your eyes.
5. You'll poke someone . . . . the eye with that umbrella if you're not careful.

Note

Note these expressions:
I knew he was lying because he wouldn't look me in the eye.
I couldn't believe my eyes when I opened the letter and found a cheque for £10,000.
I'm afraid I can't come. I'm up to my eyes in reports this week. (very busy)
Could you try to catch the waiter's eye and get the bill.
I don't see eye to eye with my father on lots of things. (not have the same opinions)
Her paintings are very realistic. She has a good eye for detail.

sight

Verb + sight	Adjective + sight	Expressions with
come into sight	a terrifying sight	**prepositions**
disappear from sight	a beautiful sight	at first sight
be hidden from sight	a common sight	by sight
keep out of sight	a pretty sight	in sight
let out of your sight	a pathetic sight	on sight
	a rare sight	out of sight
	a welcome sight	within sight

1. Verb + sight

Complete the sentences with the correct form of the above verbs:

1. He didn't leave the pier till the boat had . . . . from sight over the horizon.
2. The castle . . . . into sight as the bus climbed over the top of the hill.
3. Don't . . . . him out of your sight. It's so easy to lose a child in a busy street.
4. We didn't see the sign because it was . . . . from sight behind some bushes.
5. He's . . . . out of sight until his mother has cooled down. She's really angry with him.

2. Adjective + sight

Complete the sentences with the above adjectives:

1. After we'd been walking for 30 kilometres, the hotel was a . . . . sight.
2. There can be no more . . . . sight than a tiger coming towards you.
3. The huge display of flowers at the flower show was a . . . . sight.
4. The children were a . . . . sight – starving, frightened and very cold.
5. She's not a . . . . sight when she gets out of bed in the morning!
6. Butterflies used to be a . . . . sight on farms but the modern use of pesticides has meant that they are now a . . . . sight.

3. Expressions with prepositions

Choose the correct prepositional phrase:

1. I know him on sight / by sight, but I've never talked to him.
2. I went looking for the children, but they were nowhere in sight / out of sight.
3. Don't tempt thieves. Keep any valuables in your car out of sight / within sight.
4. Soldiers have been ordered to shoot rioters at first sight / on sight.
5. The question looked easy at first sight / on sight, but I found I couldn't answer it.
6. My house is situated by sight / within sight of the school. You can actually see my classroom from my bedroom.

Notes

1. Note these verb + 'sight of' expressions:
   As she stood up, she caught sight of her reflection in the mirror.
   They used to be good friends, but now they can't stand the sight of each other. (hate each other)
2. Note that 'sight' also means the ability to see:
   He lost his sight in an accident but the doctors managed to restore the sight of his left eye.
   As you get older, it is important that you have your sight checked regularly.
3. The 'sights' of a city are the places worth seeing:
   Let's spend the day seeing the sights.

view

Verb + view	Adjective + view
admire the view	a bird's eye view
get a view	a clear view
block your view	in full view
come into view	a panoramic view
spoil your view	a poor view
be hidden from view	a sea view

1. Verb + view

Choose the correct collocation:

1. Don't stand in front of me – you're blocking / stealing my view. I can't see the stage.
2. I stood near the front to get / take a better view.
3. After a while the fog lifted, and the mountains suddenly came into / arrived in view.
4. We stopped at the top of the mountain pass and admired / watched the marvellous views across the hills and valleys.
5. The countryside is magnificent, but the electricity pylons damage / spoil the view. Why can't they put electric cables underground?
6. You can't see the house from the road because it's hidden from / lost from view behind a high hedge.

2. Adjective + view

Complete the sentences with the above adjectives:

1. We had a . . . . view of the stage from where we were sitting. A pillar restricted our view.
2. The revolving restaurant at the top of the hotel has . . . . views across the city.
3. We had a . . . . view of the castle from our room. There was nothing blocking our view.
4. The President was shot in . . . . view of the public. Hundreds saw the assassin pull out his gun.
5. We'd like to reserve a double room with a . . . . view, please.
6. From the top of the roof the police had a . . . . view of what was going on in the street below.

"I can't see!
You're blocking my view!"

Notes

1. Note the adjectives we use to describe a marvellous view:
   It's a long climb up the mountain, but once you get there the view is breathtaking.
   From our hotel room we had a spectacular view of the New York skyline.
   We got a magnificent view of the coastline from the plane.
   The view of the mountains from our room was fantastic.

2. Note the following prepositional phrase:
   There are a number of paintings by Picasso on view at the Tate Gallery at the moment.

3. 'View' also means 'opinion'. You can find information on the collocations for this meaning in Key Words for Fluency – Upper Intermediate.

smell

Verb + smell	Adjective + smell
detect a smell	a disgusting / revolting smell
have a smell	a funny / strange smell
get rid of a smell	an off-putting smell
love the smell of	a delicious smell
smells get worse	an overpowering smell
smells fill the (air / room / building)	a stale smell of
	the unmistakable smell of
	a distinct smell of

1. Verb + smell

Complete the sentences with the correct form of the above verbs:

1. I hate grilled sardines. They . . . . such an unpleasant smell.
2. I wish we could . . . . rid of that awful smell in the kitchen. I don't know where it's coming from.
3. I hate it when my mother boils cabbage. The smell . . . . the house for days.
4. I . . . . the smell of new sheets, fresh coffee, and newly cut grass.
5. I think the smell from the toilets is . . . . worse. Let's get the plumber in.
6. I could . . . . the faint smell of gas when I walked into the house, so I called the gas board immediately.

2. Adjective + smell

Match the halves:

1. There's a funny smell
2. I couldn't finish my soup. It tasted OK,
3. You've been drinking again, haven't you?
4. There was a delicious smell of
5. The next day the stale smell of
6. I couldn't stand the overpowering
7. Did you put your cigarette out properly?
8. There's a revolting smell outside.

a. freshly-baked bread in the small shop.
b. cigarette smoke still clung to my clothes.
c. There's a distinct smell of burning.
d. coming from the engine.
e. but the smell was a bit off-putting.
f. It's disgusting! It must be the drains.
g. smell of garlic on his breath.
h. There's the unmistakable smell of alcohol on your breath.

Notes

1. Note these smell + verb collocations:
   The smell of curry lingered in the kitchen for days after we'd cooked it.
   The acrid smell of burning rubber hung in the air for days after the fire at the tyre factory.
2. Note these effects of smells:
   The smell of my mother's cooking always makes my mouth water.
   I got very drunk on whisky when I was 16, and now the mere smell of it makes me feel sick.
3. Note that 'smell' also describes the ability to notice or recognise smells:
   Dogs are used to search for drugs because they have an acute sense of smell.
   Have a smell of this milk. Do you think it's all right?
4. In English you don't 'feel' a smell. You smell it! The following is correct:
   What's that? I can smell a strange smell!
   But it is more likely that you would say:
   There's a strange smell in here.

taste

Verb + taste	Adjective + taste	Common expressions
improve the taste	an authentic taste	share a taste in
leave a taste	a fresh taste	acquire a taste for
spoil the taste	a metallic taste	suit your taste
take away the taste	a strange / peculiar taste	a matter of personal taste
lose its taste	a sour / bitter taste	
	a strong taste	

1. Verb + taste

Complete the sentences with the correct form of the above verbs:

1. I don't like black coffee. It . . . . a bitter taste in your mouth.
2. Don't smoke just before eating – you'll . . . . the taste of the food.
3. Adding some freshly-chopped herbs will . . . . the taste of the sauce.
4. Vegetables . . . . some of their taste when frozen. Buy fresh ones if you can.
5. I sucked a mint to . . . . away the nasty taste in my mouth.

2. Adjective + taste

Choose the correct collocation:

1. The medicine had a biting / bitter taste.
2. I prefer bottled beer. Beer from a can usually has a slight iron / metallic taste.
3. Toothpaste leaves a clear / fresh taste in your mouth.
4. Add some soya sauce to give the dish the actual / authentic taste of Chinese food.
5. I've never eaten Thai food before. It has a foreign / strange taste that I don't recognise.
6. Some Italian cheeses have a very severe / strong taste and smell. My mother won't have them in the house!

3. Common expressions

'Taste' also means what we like. Match the halves:

1. He acquired a taste for whisky
2. Although we share a taste in books,
3. Our organisation has a range of hotels
4. No one colour or style is best.

a. It's a matter of personal taste.
b. while he was studying in Scotland.
c. our taste in music differs.
d. to suit all tastes and budgets.

Notes
1. Note these adjective collocations:
   The sauce had a slightly sweet / bitter / salty taste.
   Olives are an acquired taste – I hated them the first time I tried them.
2. Note the preposition that follows the different meanings of taste:
   I don't like the taste of olives.
   She's got very expensive tastes – particularly in clothes!
3. Note 'flavour' means the same as 'taste', but only 'flavour' is possible in the following sentences:
   Add flavour to your meal by using more herbs and garlic.
   This product is organic. It contains no artificial colours, flavours, or preservatives.
   We sell 21 different flavours of ice cream.
4. Note this usage:
   The colour of their sitting room isn't to my taste. I prefer something lighter.

voice

Verb + voice	Adjective + voice	Noun + prep + voice
hear a voice	muffled voices	your tone of voice
lose your voice	a loud voice	the clarity of your voice
lower your voice	a deep voice	at the top of your voice
raise your voice	a soft voice	the sound of your voice
recognise a voice	a whining voice	
your voice shakes		

1. Verb + voice

Complete the sentences with the correct form of the above verbs:

1. I had to . . . . my voice to make myself heard above the noise in the classroom.
2. I didn't . . . . your voice, Helen! You sound so different on the phone.
3. The woman's voice . . . . as she described the man who had attacked her.
4. We can . . . . the voices of the people in the next apartment.
5. It is not unusual to . . . . your voice when you're suffering from a sore throat.
6. Please . . . . your voices. Keep them down or you'll frighten the animals.

2. Adjective + voice

Complete the sentences with the above adjectives:

1. Margaret has a rather . . . . voice for a woman.
2. Henry speaks quietly in a . . . . , gentle voice – unlike his brother who has the
   . . . . voice of anybody I know.
3. Aunt Hilda is always complaining, but it's her . . . . voice that I can't stand.
4. They said the house was empty, but I could hear . . . . voices coming from inside.

3. Noun + preposition + voice

Match the halves:

1. I've never seen him so upset and angry.
2. Although he was phoning all the way from Australia,
3. His problem is that he talks far too much in meetings.
4. It's his patronising tone of voice that I can't stand.

a. He's too fond of the sound of his own voice.
b. He talks to me as if I were an idiot.
c. I was amazed at the clarity of his voice.
d. He was screaming at the top of his voice.

"Helen! I didn't recognise your voice! You sounded just like your mother!"

Notes

1. Note these expressions:
   There was a hint / note / touch of sarcasm in her voice.
   I could tell he was nervous by the slight tremor in his voice.
   Our son, Peter, was almost 14 before his voice broke.
3. Note this expression:
   He just won't listen to the voice of reason / experience. (good advice)
4. 'Voice' is often used to talk about opinions:
   Protests are one of the most effective ways of making your voice heard.
   The committee represents the voice of the students.

breath

Verb + breath	Preposition + breath	Common expressions
catch your breath	on your breath	pause for breath
hold your breath	out of breath	take your breath away
take a breath	in one breath	get your breath back
struggle for breath	under your breath	a breath of fresh air
(his) breath smells		with bated breath

1. Verb + breath

Complete the sentences with the correct form of the above verbs:

1. How long can you . . . . your breath? I can stop breathing for two minutes.
2. I was so short of breath I had to stop halfway up the stairs to . . . . my breath.
3. The doctor told me to . . . . a deep breath so that he could listen to my chest.
4. His breath . . . . strongly of garlic. I had to cover my nose with my hand.
5. When he got to A & E, his chest pains were worse and he was . . . . for breath.

2. Preposition + breath

Complete the sentences with the above prepositions:

1. It was obvious he'd been drinking. You could smell the alcohol . . . . his breath.
2. During the meeting he muttered rude remarks about the chairman . . . . his breath.
3. He recited the short poem . . . . one breath.
4. I was completely . . . . of breath after running upstairs. I had to sit down for a few minutes to recover.

3. Common expressions

Match the halves:

1. It's pretty stuffy in this room.
2. He was so excited,
3. We waited with bated breath
4. The beauty of the countryside
5. I needed about five minutes to

a. he talked for 5 minutes, hardly pausing for breath.
b. took my breath away.
c. get my breath back after the run.
d. Shall we go outside for a breath of fresh air?
e. to see who the overall winner was.

"I was completely out of breath!"

Notes
1. People can have bad breath:
   He can't find a girlfriend because of his bad breath.
2. We use 'breathing' to talk about the act of breathing:
   Deep breathing is good for relaxing your mind and your body.
   When I picked up the phone, all I could hear was the sound of heavy breathing.
   Rapid, shallow breathing is a classic symptom of an anxiety attack.
   You can learn to control your breathing.
3. Note this expression about the weather: *There hasn't been a breath of wind all day.*

sleep and dream

Verb + sleep	Adjective + sleep	Verb + dream	Adjective + dream
go to sleep	broken sleep	appear in a dream	a bad dream
get to sleep	a deep sleep	have a dream	a recurring dream
get some sleep	a light sleep	wake from a dream	a vivid dream
get back to sleep	a good night's sleep		sweet dreams
catch up on sleep			
disturb your sleep			
send you to sleep			

1. Verb + sleep

Complete the sentences with the correct form of the above verbs:

1. If I don't . . . . at least seven hours sleep at night, I feel tired all day.
2. I've been out late a lot. I'll need to use the weekend to . . . . up on my sleep.
3. My sleep was . . . . by the noise of the traffic passing the hotel.
4. The rhythmic sound of trains always . . . . me to sleep.
5. I couldn't . . . . to sleep last night for worrying about my exams.
6. My younger brother always says his prayers before he . . . . to sleep.
7. The storm woke me up and I couldn't . . . . back to sleep.

2. Adjective + sleep

Choose the correct collocation:

1. I must've fallen into a deep / heavy sleep and didn't hear the phone when you rang.
2. Don't worry. You'll feel better after a long night's / a good night's sleep.
3. After lunch, I often lie on the sofa and allow myself to drift into a light / soft sleep.
4. We've had nothing but nights of broken / damaged sleep since the baby was born.

3. Verb + dream

Complete the sentences with the correct form of the above verbs:

1. Have you ever . . . . a dream in which somebody is trying to kill you?
2. For some strange reason, you often . . . . in my dreams.
3. I . . . . from a dream with a start, and wondered where I was.

4. Adjective + dream

Complete the sentences with the above adjectives:

1. Our five-year-old comes to sleep in our bed when she has a . . . . dream.
2. I had a . . . . dream about my first day at school. Everything was so clear.
3. Good night and . . . . dreams. Sleep well.
4. I have this . . . . dream in which I'm flying. I have it about three times a week.

Notes

1. Note these expressions with 'sleep':
   Her irritability is probably due to a lack of sleep.
   I didn't get a wink of sleep with all the noise going on outside the hotel.
   I cried myself to sleep at night for weeks after my boyfriend left me.
   It's not that important. Don't lose any sleep over it. (don't worry about it)

2. Note this expression:
   Every night, he relives the horror of the crash in his dreams.

Section 16

Feeling and mood

feeling   126
mood   127
happiness and pleasure   128
anger   129
fear and anxiety   130
worry   131
confidence   132
disappointment and relief   133
surprise and shock   134

"Now, there's nothing to be afraid of!"

feeling

Verb + feelings	Adjective + feeling	Feeling + of + noun
show your feelings	a bad feeling	a feeling of apprehension
suppress your feelings	a sinking feeling	a feeling of dissatisfaction
control your feelings	true feelings	a feeling of loneliness
hide your feelings	mixed feelings	a feeling of guilt
hurt your feelings	the feeling is mutual	a feeling of well-being

1. Verb + feelings

Complete the sentences with the correct form of the above verbs:

1. I'm sorry if I upset you. I didn't really mean to . . . . your feelings.
2. She's not afraid to . . . . her feelings.
3. You can't . . . . your feelings from me. I've known you far too long.
4. It's unhealthy to . . . . your feelings. So don't be afraid to cry!
5. Young children find it difficult to . . . . their feelings. This is something they learn to do later in life.

2. Adjective + feeling

Choose the correct collocation:

1. It was better to lie rather than let everybody know my correct / true feelings.
2. He has mixed / opposite feelings about going back to his home town. He's looking forward to seeing his friends again, but he doesn't want to stay with his parents.
3. I had that falling / sinking feeling in the pit of my stomach. I knew that something terrible had happened.
4. Her careless remarks have caused a lot of bad / poor feeling in the community.
5. Jo can't stand Dave, and the feeling is equal / mutual. They totally avoid each other.

3. Feeling + of + noun

Complete the sentences with the above nouns:

1. Parents can experience deep feelings of . . . . if their children fail in life.
2. People who do yoga benefit from increased feelings of . . . .
3. I remember the horrible feeling of . . . . as I waited for my examination results.
4. There is a strong feeling of . . . . with the way the government is running the country.
5. When my parents left me at boarding school for the first time, I remember being overwhelmed by a deep feeling of . . . .

Notes

1. Note how we describe showing your feelings:
   English people are reserved and don't usually talk openly about their feelings.
   She's a woman of few words. She expresses her feelings through her paintings.
   At times, I have difficulty putting my feelings into words.

2. Note these noun + preposition + feeling(s) expressions:
   She shows a total disregard for other people's feelings.
   > Yes, she seems totally insensitive to the feelings of others.
   I was taken aback by the strength of feeling of the meeting. He didn't think it was that important.
   He spoke with great depth of feeling about how kind and helpful they had been to him.

mood

Verb + mood	Adjective + mood	Mood + of + noun
your mood changes	a bad mood	a mood of despair
depend on your mood	a good mood	a mood of optimism
affect your mood	in confident mood	the mood of the crowd
lighten / lift your mood	a defiant mood	the mood of the occasion
	a festive mood	the mood of the time
	a lazy mood	

1. Verb + mood

Complete the sentences with the correct form of the above verbs:

1. Why has her mood . . . . so dramatically? Was it something I said or did?
2. A phone call from a friend did nothing to . . . . my mood. I still felt down.
3. I really do believe that a full moon can . . . . your mood.
4. I've no favourite type of music. What I listen to . . . . very much on my mood.

2. Adjective + mood

Complete the sentences with the above adjectives:

1. The players are in . . . . mood and expect to win today's game quite easily.
2. Why are you in such a . . . . mood? You've been rude to people all day!
3. The workers are in a . . . . mood, and are refusing to accept the new pay deal.
4. I don't feel like doing anything today. I'm in a bit of a . . . . mood.
5. At Christmas, everybody was in a . . . . mood, buying presents and cards.
6. My dad is usually very grumpy, but this morning he woke up in a . . . . mood!

3. Mood + of + noun

Match the halves:

1. Nelson Mandela's election as President created
2. The film accurately reflects
3. There was a mood of despair
4. At the funeral, the music reflected
5. The mood of the crowd turned nasty and

"He looks as if he's in one of his moods again!"

a. the sombre mood of the occasion.
b. people started throwing stones at the police.
c. the mood of the time.
d. a mood of optimism in South Africa.
e. after the team's tenth defeat in a row.

Notes

1. Note these ways of saying you feel / don't feel like doing something:
   I'm in the mood for dancing. Let's go to the club.
   You go alone. I'm just not in a party / the holiday mood, so I wouldn't be very good company.
   I wouldn't try to discuss the matter with him just now. He's in no mood for talking.

2. Note these ways of saying someone is in a bad mood:
   Watch out! She's been in a real mood all day.
   He's in one of his moods again.

happiness and pleasure

Verb + happiness	Noun + prep + happiness	Verb + pleasure	Adj + pleasure
bring happiness	a guarantee of ...	be a pleasure	endless pleasure
find happiness	the key to ...	give pleasure	great pleasure
wish you happiness	the pursuit of ...	get pleasure	few pleasures
		read for pleasure	a simple pleasure
		combine business with pleasure	an unexpected ...

1. Verb + happiness

Complete the sentences with the correct form of the above verbs:

1. After two failed marriages, he seems to have . . . . happiness with his third wife.
2. I'd like to take this opportunity to . . . . you every happiness for the future.
3. People think that money . . . . happiness. That's why they buy lottery tickets.

2. Noun + preposition + happiness

Complete the sentences with the above nouns:

1. I've spent my life trying to find the . . . . to true happiness and peace of mind.
2. Basic human rights are the right to life, liberty, and the . . . . of happiness.
3. I think living together before you get married is no . . . . of future happiness.

3. Verb + pleasure

Complete the sentences with the correct form of the above verbs:

1. Lots of people . . . . great pleasure from painting in water colours.
2. Few things in this world . . . . me more pleasure than a long, hot bath.
3. The trip to New York will enable me to . . . . business with pleasure.
4. It certainly . . . . a real pleasure to hear from you after all these years.
5. Some people . . . . Shakespeare's plays for pleasure, while most schoolchildren read them because they have to!

4. Adjective + pleasure

Choose the correct collocation:

1. After the operation she was able to enjoy easy / simple pleasures like walking again.
2. I can't give up smoking – it's one of the few / small pleasures I have left in life.
3. Well, fancy meeting you here! This is an unusual / unexpected pleasure!
4. Children find constant / endless pleasure in playing with simple things like water.
5. His music has given big / great pleasure to many people over the years.

Notes

1. Note these expressions:
   It's a pleasure to meet you.
   The car is beautifully made and a real pleasure to drive.
2. Note how we describe taking a lot of pleasure in something:
   His music has given tremendous pleasure to many people over the years.
   For me, shopping for clothes is one of life's greatest pleasures!
   I rolled about in the snow just for the sheer pleasure of it.
3. 'Taking great pleasure in something' can mean enjoying doing something bad to other people:
   Tom seems to take great pleasure in annoying his younger brother.

anger

Verb + anger	Noun + of + anger	Common expressions
arouse anger	a moment of anger	shake your fist in anger
express your anger	an outburst of anger	raise your voice in anger
control your anger	a surge of anger	stamp your foot in anger
feel anger towards (him)		your eyes blaze with anger
your anger subsides		

1. Verb + anger

Complete the sentences with the correct form of the above verbs:

1. Drivers are blockading the motorway to . . . . their anger over high fuel costs.
2. The player couldn't . . . . his anger and shouted at the referee.
3. The destruction of the mosque has . . . . anger throughout the Muslim world.
4. She waited for his anger to . . . . before asking him if he wanted anything.
5. I still . . . . a lot of anger towards my father, who left home when I was 3.

2. Noun + of + anger

Complete the sentences with the above nouns:

1. I'm sorry for what I said last night. It was said in a . . . . of anger.
2. I felt a sudden . . . . of anger welling up inside me. I had to fight to control it.
3. Her comments provoked an uncharacteristic . . . . of anger from the Minister of Education.

3. Common expressions

Match the halves:

1. The cyclist shouted at the driver and shook
2. From behind the door I could hear voices
3. He looked straight at me and his dark eyes
4. When my son doesn't get his way, he stamps

a. his feet in anger.
b. his fist in anger.
c. raised in anger.
d. blazed with anger.

"I was seething with anger!"

Notes

1. Note the verbs we use to describe showing anger:
   Psychologists say that it is better to express your anger rather than let it fester inside you.
   The rioters vented their anger on the police by throwing stones and bottles at them.
   All the passengers exploded in anger when they learned that their flight was cancelled.
   He's seething with anger at the way he was treated during his interview.
2. Note the verbs we use to describe controlling anger:
   She had stored up all her anger against him for years and eventually she snapped.
   I held back my anger and kept quiet. I didn't want to say something I would later regret.
   It was an unfair question but the Prime Minister managed to suppress his anger.
3. Note this expression:
   Don't take your anger out on me, I had nothing to do with it!

fear and anxiety

Verb + fear	Adjective + fear	Verb + anxiety	Noun + of + anxiety
have a fear	a constant fear	cause anxiety	an effect of anxiety
confront your fear	a deep fear	hide your anxiety	a level of anxiety
overcome your fear	an irrational fear	reduce your anxiety	a sign of anxiety
show fear	a sudden fear	increase your anxiety	
live in fear	your worst fear		

1. Verb + fear

Complete the sentences with the correct form of the above verbs:

1. You have to . . . . your fear in order to conquer it. Now try holding the spider!
2. . . . . fear is generally seen as a sign of weakness.
3. I . . . . a terrible fear of heights. I avoid tall buildings whenever I can.
4. Many old people . . . . in fear of being attacked and never go out at night.
5. Our daughter has . . . . her fear of the dark and she can now sleep with the light off.

2. Adjective + fear

Complete the sentences with the above adjectives:

1. My wife has an . . . . fear of all dogs – which she can't explain.
2. Since the publication of his controversial book, the author has lived in . . . . fear of assassination.
3. A . . . . fear gripped me as I entered the meeting.
4. The news that the factory was to close confirmed everyone's . . . . fears.
5. Many old people have a . . . . fear of being abandoned by their families.

3. Verb + anxiety

Complete the sentences with the correct form of the above verbs:

1. She tried to . . . . her anxiety from me, but I could tell from her voice.
2. I regret any anxiety I may have . . . . you. Please, forgive me.
3. The smile on the air steward's face did nothing to . . . . my anxiety.
4. Thanks, but you've only . . . . my anxiety by reminding me about the speech I have to give next week!

4. Noun + of + anxiety

Match the halves:

1. At the dentist's, it is not uncommon to experience high   a. signs of anxiety.
2. People with stressful jobs often experience the destructive   b. levels of anxiety.
3. During the examination period, many children show   c. effects of anxiety.

Notes

1. Note how we describe the effects of fear:
   The child stood there, crying and shaking / trembling / quaking with fear.
   When she saw the snake, she couldn't move. She was paralysed with fear.
2. Note how we describe a lot of anxiety:
   Your husband is suffering from acute / intense anxiety.
   My son has caused us considerable anxiety over the years.

worry

Verb + worry	Adjective + worry	Common expressions
cause / give worry	a nagging worry	sick with worry
discuss your worries	the main worry	a constant source of worry
forget your worries	unnecessary worry	the least of my worries
add to your worries	a constant worry	my only worry

1. Verb + worry

Choose the correct collocation:

1. I'd love to be able to lie back and just forget / lose all my worries for a little while.
2. His father's strange behaviour is causing / making him considerable worry.
3. I've got money problems, but when I lost my job, it only added to / worsened my worries.
4. It's important that children can discuss / examine their worries with their parents.

2. Adjective + worry

Complete the sentences with the above adjectives:

1. There will always be a . . . . worry at the back of my mind that if I'd acted sooner, the problem would not have arisen.
2. Why didn't you ring and say you'd be late? You've caused us a lot of . . . . worry.
3. My . . . . worry is that in his present state of mind, he'll do something stupid.
4. I think it was the . . . . worry of the business that drove him to resign.

3. Common expressions

Match the halves:

1. Where on earth have you been?
2. Money is a constant source of worry.
3. My only worry is that
4. What they think of me is the least of my worries.

a. I have more important things to worry about.
b. We've been sick with worry!
c. I worry about my credit card debt all the time.
d. I won't find a job when I get there.

"Where on earth have you been?"
We've been sick with worry?"

Notes

1. Note this useful way of expressing your worries about something:
   We have no worries about his ability to do the course.
   It's his poor attendance that's a problem.
2. Note these expressions:
   She said that her worries were a thing of the past. (She no longer has them.)
   My financial worries have cost me many sleepless nights. I now wish I hadn't borrowed so much.
   Despite our worries everything turned out well. There were no major problems.
   We're going through a worrying time at the moment. My wife's been ill and I've just been made redundant.
3. You can describe someone as 'a worry':
   Our youngest daughter is a bit of a worry at the moment. She's not eating.

confidence

1. Verb + confidence

Complete the sentences with the correct form of the above verbs:

1. If you have an accident, it is important that you get back in a car as soon as possible, so that you don't . . . . confidence in your ability to drive.
2. He used to be shy but he's . . . . a lot of confidence since going to school.
   > Yes, he seems to be growing in confidence all the time.
3. Our teacher tried to . . . . our confidence by telling us we'd all pass the exam.
4. He . . . . confidence. I've never known anyone so unsure of himself.
5. The accident seems to have completely . . . . his confidence.
   > Yes. Something like that really shatters your confidence in yourself.
6. I like Jane, but I don't . . . . the confidence to go up to her and ask her out!

2. Noun + preposition + confidence

Complete the sentences with the above nouns:

1. I suffer from a . . . . of confidence. I blame it on my sheltered upbringing.
2. Failing the exam was a severe . . . . to my confidence. I thought I'd pass easily.
3. My manager's encouraging comments were a . . . . to my self-confidence.
4. There is an . . . . of confidence about Tiger Woods at the moment. He is so full of confidence that I can't see anybody beating him.

3. Losing confidence

Match the halves:

1. After 3 defeats in a row, the team's confidence	a. Try to believe in yourself.
2. His confidence has taken a knock	b. has been badly shaken.
3. Self-doubt can only undermine your confidence.	c. my confidence deserted me!
4. When I saw the questions in the exam paper,	d. with that bad review of his book.

Notes

1. Note these ways of saying you have great confidence in somebody or something:
   She has a lot of experience and I have every confidence in her ability to do the job.
   Our bank manager advises us on our investments. We have complete confidence in his financial judgement.
   For peace of mind, a sick person needs to have absolute confidence in their doctor.
2. Note how we use 'confidence' to express certainty:
   No one can predict with total confidence what will happen in the future.
3. 'In confidence' means in secret:
   Can I speak to you in confidence?
   This is between you and me and nobody else – in strict confidence. I've just won the Lottery!

disappointment and relief

Verb + disappointment	Noun + of + disappointment	Verb + relief
avoid disappointment		feel relief
be a disappointment	a sense of disappointment	sigh with relief
end in disappointment	a look of disappointment	come as a relief
express disappointment	a string of disappointments	
hide your disappointment		
get over a disappointment		

1. Verb + disappointment

Complete the sentences with the correct form of the above verbs:

1. The Prime Minister . . . . disappointment at the lack of progress in the talks.
2. It's a very popular restaurant, so book early to . . . . disappointment.
3. I found it difficult to . . . . my disappointment at not being picked for the team.
4. He didn't get the job, but I'm sure he'll soon . . . . over the disappointment.
5. Failing the exam . . . . a bitter disappointment to me.
6. The match . . . . in disappointment when we lost two goals late in the closing minutes of the game.

2. Noun + of + disappointment

Complete the sentences with the above nouns:

1. I'll never forget the . . . . of disappointment on his face when I told him I couldn't marry him.
2. There was a real . . . . of disappointment when we failed to reach the final.
3. We've suffered a whole . . . . of disappointments this week. Nothing seems to be going right for us at the moment.

3. Verb + relief

Complete the sentences with the correct form of the above verbs:

1. When our neighbours left at one in the morning, I . . . . an incredible sense of relief. I was beginning to think they were going to stay all night!
2. News of the child's safety . . . . as a great relief to all involved in the search.
3. We had to fly through some pretty scary weather over the Alps, and when the plane eventually touched down, many of us . . . . with relief.

Notes

1. Note these expressions with disappointment:
   Cher had to cancel the concert – to the great disappointment of her fans.
   Hingis described the defeat as the biggest disappointment of her tennis career.
2. Note that you can be a disappointment to someone:
   I'm afraid I was a disappointment to my parents. They wanted me to be a doctor.
3. Note these expressions with 'relief':
   I breathed / let out / heaved / gave a sigh of relief when the exam finished.
   I don't have to make a speech when I receive the prize tonight. What a relief!
   It was such a relief to hear that he was safe and well.

surprise and shock

Verb + surprise	Adjective + surprise	Verb + shock	Expressions with shock
get a surprise	a complete surprise	die of shock	in a state of shock
express surprise	a pleasant surprise	get a shock	be in for a shock
have a surprise	the best possible ...	get over a shock	get the shock of
spring a surprise		come as a shock	(my) life
take (me) by surprise		a shock wears off	

1. Verb + surprise

Complete the sentences with the correct form of the above verbs:

1. Close your eyes. I . . . . a surprise for you!
2. I . . . . a pleasant surprise when I received my wages. I had a bonus of £100.
3. He . . . . surprise at the result. He'd expected the workers to reject the deal.
4. His announcement about becoming a priest . . . . us all by surprise.
5. She's always organising birthday parties. She loves . . . . surprises on people.

2. Adjective + surprise

Complete the sentences with the above adjectives:

1. Your letter was a . . . . surprise. We must meet up soon.
2. I wanted the party to be a . . . . surprise, but a friend let the cat out of the bag.
3. Seeing my sister again was the best . . . . surprise anyone could have given me.

3. Verb + shock

Complete the sentences with the correct form of the above verbs:

1. I . . . . a terrible shock when I saw him. He looked so ill.
2. I nearly . . . . of shock when he came into the bathroom without warning.
3. Once the initial shock . . . . off, I began to get used to my son's blue hair.
4. I don't think she'll ever . . . . over the shock of losing her husband.
5. The news of the leader's death . . . . as a great shock to the people.

4. Expressions with shock

Match the halves:

1. When I found out who my real mother was,
2. When the young star died, the whole country was in
3. If you think it's easy looking after a young baby,

a. then you are in for a shock!
b. I got the shock of my life.
c. a state of shock.

Notes

1. Note the expression 'come as a complete / no surprise':
   I had no idea about the holiday. It came as a complete surprise to me.
   It came as no surprise to learn that she had failed her exams. She hardly did any work for them.
2. Note these expressions:
   To everyone's surprise, his prediction of a long hot summer came true.
   Much to my surprise, I passed the exam.
   Imagine our surprise when the brother we hadn't seen for 20 years walked into the room!
3. Note the expression 'full of surprises':
   Life's full of surprises. (unexpected but nice things happen to us all)
   My brother is full of surprises. (always doing unexpected things)

Section 17

Society

government and election   136
vote   137
society   138
justice   139
law   140

"What's Society coming to!"

government and election

Verb + government	Verb + election	Expressions with election
bring down the government	boycott the election	a candidate in the election
criticise the government	hold the election	gains in the election
elect the government	stand for election	an issue in the election
form the government	win / lose the ...	win / lose a seat in the ...
lead the government	rig the election	the turnout in the election
resign from the government		

1. Verb + government

Complete the sentences with the correct form of the above verbs:

1. The government was . . . . last year. They've now been in office for 5 months.
2. This crisis could . . . . down the government. We could be facing an election.
3. The government is . . . . by a man who couldn't succeed in business.
4. The government has been . . . . for not doing enough for the elderly.
5. After the scandal, the minister was forced to . . . . from the government.
6. Who do you think will . . . . the next government?

2. Verb + election

Complete the sentences with the correct form of the above verbs:

1. The military government promises to . . . . democratic elections within a year.
2. The Labour Party . . . . the election by a huge majority.
3. A number of parties are threatening to . . . . the forthcoming election because they don't believe that it will be a free and fair one.
4. In 1967 Lyndon Johnson decided not to . . . . for election as President.
5. United Nations observers reported that the elections in the country were . . . . by the ruling party to ensure that they would be returned to power.

3. Expressions with election

Complete the sentences with the above nouns:

1. Unemployment will be one of the big . . . . in the next election.
2. A number of well-known politicians lost their . . . . in the general election.
3. The Green Party continues to make big . . . . in local elections.
4. There was a low . . . . in the local elections. Only 15% of people voted.
5. He's been selected by the local branch of the Liberal Party as their . . . . in the next election.

Notes

1. Note the different kinds of government in the sentences below:
   The people have been promised a democratically-elected government, but the country's military rulers have yet to set an election date.
   In Britain there is a trend towards taking power away from central government and giving more to local government.
2. Note the following election + noun phrases:
   The government has failed to fulfil its election promises.
   There's no doubt in my mind that the media played an important part in the election campaign.

Key Words for Fluency – Intermediate

vote

Verb + vote	Adjective + vote	Noun + of + vote	Common expressions
have the vote	the casting vote	thousands of votes	take a vote on (it)
cast your vote	the popular vote	a share of the vote	put it to the vote
count the votes	a single vote	the result of the ...	a vote can go
win votes	a vote is unanimous	the majority of the votes	(against you)

1. Verb + vote

Complete the sentences with the correct form of the above verbs:

1. The Prime Minister conceded defeat before all the votes had been . . . .
2. There are some countries in the world where women still don't . . . . the vote.
3. Lowering the rate of tax before an election is a sure way of . . . . votes.
4. The front page of this morning's paper shows a picture of the new President
   . . . . his vote in the country's first free elections for 30 years.

2. Adjective + vote

Complete the sentences below with the above adjectives:

1. There were ten votes in favour of the plan, ten against, with three abstentions.
   The chairperson, with the . . . . vote, voted for the proposal.
2. The vote was . . . . Nobody voted against the proposal.
3. The socialists can no longer be sure of the . . . . vote. Most ordinary people
   feel that the party has failed to fulfil its election promises.
4. The result couldn't have been closer. The bill was passed by a . . . . vote.

3. Noun + of + vote

Complete the sentences with the above nouns:

1. The ruling democratic party received the . . . . of the votes and were re-elected.
2. This will not be a popular policy. It will cost the government . . . . of votes.
3. The . . . . of the vote will be announced in parliament tomorrow.
4. The Labour Party hope to take a larger . . . . of the vote than they did last time.

4. Common expressions

Match the halves:

1. Unless anyone has anything to add,
2. Let's put it to the vote.
3. The vote went against him,

a. All those in favour, raise your hands.
b. and he had to step down as leader.
c. I think we should take a vote.

"The President casting his vote."

Note   Note these expressions:
The motion to go on strike was carried / passed by 400 votes to 67.
The proposal to change the rules was narrowly defeated by 120 votes to 118.
Parliament approved the use of military force by a margin of 450 votes to 340.
Democracy rests on the principle of one person, one vote.

society

Verb + society	Adjective + society	Noun + prep + society
create a society	an affluent society	a cross-section of society
destroy a society	a civilised society	a member of society
live in a society	an open society	a danger to society
drop out of society	an industrial society	a role in society
integrate into society	a multicultural society	

1. Verb + society

Complete the sentences with the correct form of the above verbs:

1. I think we now . . . . in a society that values money more than people.
2. He gave up his job and . . . . out of society. He's now living on the streets.
3. We need to take stronger action against drug use. It's . . . . our society.
4. We all need to work together to . . . . a fair and just society.
5. The government has set up a number of resettlement programmes to help new immigrants . . . . into society.

2. Adjective + society

Complete the sentences with the above adjectives:

1. Many people believe that the death penalty has no place in a . . . . society.
2. Large numbers of immigrants have come to Britain, making it a . . . . society.
3. In today's . . . . society people are becoming less content with their lives. This is yet another indication that money does not always bring happiness.
4. I like to think that I live in an . . . . society where I can express my opinions.
5. In order to protect the environment, modern . . . . societies need to reduce the amount of energy they use.

3. Noun + preposition + society

Complete the sentences with the above nouns:

1. We must remember to consider the needs of the older . . . . of society.
2. Today women are playing an increasingly important . . . . in society.
3. The judge described the murderer as a . . . . to society and sentenced him to twenty years in jail.
4. The demonstrators came from a complete . . . . of society – male and female, black and white, old and young, rich and poor.

Notes

1. Note these expressions:
   Couples who cannot have children often feel excluded from the rest of society.
   People tend to look upon drug addicts as the dregs of society. (worthless)
2. Note how we use 'society' to refer to people:
   Society is deeply divided on the issue of abortion.
3. 'High society' refers to the group of people who are rich and powerful in a country.
   A 'consumer society' is one in which people are frequently encouraged to buy new things.
4. A 'society' can also be a club or an association:
   The local Folk Song Society meets on Tuesdays.
   I support the work of the National Society for the Prevention of Cruelty to Children.

justice

Verb + justice	Noun + preposition + justice
demand justice	a fight for justice
escape justice	a miscarriage of justice
fight for justice	a sense of justice
uphold justice	a travesty of justice
bring someone to justice	
deny someone justice	

1. Verb + justice

Complete the sentences with the correct form of the above verbs:

1. Although unhappy with the court ruling, Mrs Sheldon will continue to . . . . for justice. She said that she would not rest until she had cleared her son's name.
2. Some criminals use their political connections to . . . . justice. We need to get rid of this kind of corruption.
3. We will not rest until we . . . . those responsible for this crime to justice.
4. Soldiers exposed to radiation during nuclear bomb tests have been . . . . justice far too long. Compensation to the victims should have been paid years ago.
5. It's up to the courts to . . . . justice. People shouldn't take the law into their own hands.
6. Crowds of angry protestors gathered in the streets, ... justice for the innocent victims of the bombing.

2. Noun + preposition + justice

Complete the sentences with the above nouns:

1. We appealed to his . . . . of justice and fairness.
2. They claim that they are victims of a . . . . of justice, and they are demanding a retrial.
3. The rest of the workforce came together to support their colleague in his . . . . for justice.
4. The press described the verdict as a . . . . of justice. Many feel that killing somebody as a result of drink driving deserves a prison sentence and not a fine.

"Is there no justice?"

Notes

1. Note these expressions:
   He got ten years in prison for conspiring to pervert the course of justice by withholding evidence from the court.
   Many people no longer have confidence in the criminal justice system.
   Justice must not just be done – it must be seen to be done!
   Where is the justice in this world!
2. In 2-2 the expression 'miscarriage of justice' means that a decision has been made which is unfair.

law

Verb + law	Law + verb	Preposition + law	Noun + prep + law
break the law	the law applies	above the law	a change in the law
change the law	the law prohibits	against the law	respect for the law
introduce a law	the law requires	under the law	an infringement of
enforce the law	the law states	within the law	the law
obey the law		by law	an interpretation of
			the law

1. Verb + law

Complete the sentences with the correct form of the above verbs:

1. The main role of the police force is to uphold and . . . . the law.
2. Should you do what you think is right even if it means . . . . the law?
3. I think speed cameras are effective in getting drivers to . . . . the law.
4. The government is . . . . a law to reduce the hours worked by junior doctors.
5. The government is coming under increasing pressure to . . . . the law on the use of soft drugs like cannabis. Many people believe the present law is out of date.

2. Law + verb

Complete the sentences with the correct form of the above verbs:

1. The law . . . . the sale of alcohol to people under the age of 18.
2. The new law will . . . . equally to men and women.
3. The law . . . . that everyone has the right to practise their own religion.
4. In the UK the law . . . . all motorcyclists to wear crash helmets.

3. Preposition + law

Choose the correct preposition:

1. You're obliged by / in law to notify us of any change in your circumstances.
2. The star was fined for speeding just like you or me. Nobody is above / over the law.
3. It is against / below the law to leave young children alone in the house.
4. We all have basic human rights that are recognised from / under international law.
5. The MD claims his company is operating entirely inside / within the law.

4. Noun + preposition + law

Match the halves:

1. Many people have voiced concern over	a. often go unpunished.
2. Minor infringements of the law	b. the proposed change in the law.
3. Some young people today show	c. differing interpretations of the law.
4. The dispute is based on	d. a total disregard for the law.

Note   Note the verbs used in these expressions to mean 'breaking the law':
It is a well-known fact that motorists regularly flout the law.
Restaurants that violate hygiene laws will be heavily fined.
The penalties for contravening the employment laws are very serious.
He took the law into his own hands and attacked the driver who had killed his son.

Section 18

Crime and punishment

crime and criminal 142
offence, offender and victim 143
arrest and charge (criminal) 144
evidence 145
trial and verdict 146
sentence and fine 147
punishment and prison 148

"Now officer, I know what you're thinking, but I have a perfectly good explanation."

crime and criminal

Verb + crime	Adj + crime	Noun + prep + crime	Adj + criminal
fight crime	(a) petty crime	**crime**	a common criminal
cut crime	(a) serious crime	a life of crime	a convicted criminal
solve a crime	a terrible crime	the war on crime	a hardened criminal
commit a crime	a violent crime	the scene of the ...	a known criminal
be charged with a ...		the victim of a ...	
be convicted of a ...			

1. Verb + crime

Complete the sentences with the correct form of the above verbs:

1. The prisoner has . . . . several crimes, including murder.
2. The government hopes to . . . . serious crime in the inner cities by 30%.
3. To . . . . crime effectively, we need more police officers on the streets.
4. He was . . . . of five separate crimes and sentenced to 10 years in jail.
5. He was taken to the police station, but he hasn't been . . . . with any crime yet.
6. The police hope to . . . . this crime with the help of the general public.

2. Adjective + crime

Choose the correct adjective:

1. Aggressive / Violent crime is a growing problem in the city's parks.
2. A lot of police time is spent on small / petty crime instead of severe / serious crime.
3. Terrorists are believed to have been responsible for this extreme / terrible crime.

3. Noun + preposition + crime

Complete the sentences with the above nouns:

1. In a recent report the police claim to be winning the . . . . on crime.
2. In some cities, poverty condemns some young children to a . . . . of crime.
3. Two people saw the murderer running away from the . . . . of the crime.
4. The chances of being the . . . . of a crime are much higher if you live in a city.

4. Adjective + criminal

Complete the sentences with the above adjectives:

1. He's a . . . . criminal – he's been in and out of prison all his life.
2. I had done nothing wrong, but I was treated like a . . . . criminal.
3. . . . . criminals – as soon as they are found guilty – should not sell their stories.
4. The police have evidence that he's been associating with . . . . criminals.

Notes
1. Note these expressions:
   Many addicts turn to crime to support their drug habit.
   Everyone wants the government to get tough on crime.
2. Note the following types of crime:
   juvenile or under-age crime – crime committed by young people
   organised crime – organisations like the Mafia that commit crimes.
3. Note these crime + noun collocations:
   The crime rate in the city has risen alarmingly over the past year.
   A crime wave is sweeping the country. The latest crime figures show a rise in violent crime.

offence, offender and victim

Verb + offence	Adj + offence	Adj + offender	Adj + victim
commit an offence	your first offence	a first-time offender	an easy victim
make it an offence	a capital offence	a persistent offender	an innocent victim
charge with an ...	a minor offence	a sex offender	a murder victim
be convicted of an ...	a serious offence	the worst offenders	
be fined for an ...			

1. Verb + offence

Complete the sentences with the correct form of the above verbs:

1. Javid Khan has .... no offence under British law and should be freed.
2. Drivers will be .... on the spot for motoring offences such as speeding.
3. The two tourists were .... of drug offences and immediately deported.
4. The law .... it an offence to take a sharp object onto an aeroplane.
5. The fans arrested yesterday have been .... with public order offences.

2. Adjective + offence

Choose the correct collocation:

1. I thought the punishment was extremely harsh for such a minor / small offence.
2. Giving false information to the police is a major / serious offence.
3. As it was her first / initial offence, she was let off with only a caution.
4. Selling drugs is a capital / death offence in some countries. It carries the death penalty.

3. Adjective + offender

Complete the sentences with the above adjectives:

1. He's a .... offender. He's been arrested ten times this year for shoplifting.
2. As she was a .... offender, the judge did not send her to prison.
3. When it comes to speeding, most of the .... offenders are young men.
4. As a .... offender, he was separated from other prisoners for his own safety.

4. Adjective + victim

Match the halves:

1. Police say that the murder victim
2. Tourists on the underground are
3. Who will compensate

a. easy victims for pickpockets.
b. the innocent victims of violent crime?
c. had been shot at close range.

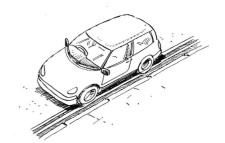

"Parking on double yellows is a serious offence."

Notes

1. Note these expressions:
   It's an offence to park on double yellow lines.
   He has a long record of previous convictions for drug offences.
   In most sexual offences, the attacker is known to the victim.
   The judge gave him the maximum possible sentence in order to discourage similar offences.

2. A 'young offender' is someone who has committed a crime, but is not old enough to be treated as an adult by the courts.

arrest and charge (criminal)

Verb + arrest	Adjective + arrest	Verb + charge	Expressions with charge
escape arrest	close arrest	deny a charge	be arrested on a charge
make an arrest	house arrest	face a charge	plead guilty to a charge
resist arrest	wrongful arrest	prove a charge	be cleared of a charge
lead to an arrest		press charges	appear in court on a ...

1. Verb + arrest

Complete the sentences with the correct form of the above verbs:

1. The police . . . . several arrests, following the discovery of a large haul of drugs.
2. A reward has been offered for information . . . . to the arrest of the kidnappers.
3. The businessman, Yore Idal, has left the country to . . . . arrest for tax evasion.
4. Ten hooligans have been charged with violent behaviour and . . . . arrest.

2. Adjective + arrest

Complete the sentences below with the above adjectives:

1. The President has been placed under . . . . arrest. He can't leave his palace.
2. He is under . . . . arrest. Two policemen are always at his side.
3. A tourist is suing the police for . . . . arrest during a riot in central London.

3. Verb + charge

Complete the sentences with the correct form of the above verbs:

1. Aitken goes on trial next week to . . . . two charges of armed robbery.
2. With all this new evidence against him, I can't see how it's possible for him to . . . . the charges against him. It's obvious he's guilty!
3. According to his lawyer, these fraud charges will be difficult to . . . . in court.
4. The police announced they would not be . . . . charges, and Adnan was released.

4. Expressions with charge

Complete the sentences with the correct form of the verbs:

1. The youth . . . . guilty to two charges of theft and three motoring offences. He asked for several more charges to be taken into account.
2. In court, the three protesters were . . . . of all charges and released.
3. He was . . . . on a charge of assault and taken to the local police station.
4. The businessman, Lesley Muller, is due to . . . . in court on charges of fraud.

Notes

1. Note these expressions with 'arrest':
   The court has issued a warrant for his arrest.
   The husband of the dead woman is under arrest on suspicion of murder.
2. A 'citizen's arrest' is when a member of the public, not a police officer, arrests somebody.
3. Note these expressions with 'charge':
   He says he's been arrested on a trumped-up charge. He claims the police planted the drugs on him.
   A number of arrests were made, but all detainees were later released without charge.

evidence

Verb + evidence	Adj + evidence	Noun + of + evidence
have evidence	false evidence	a shred of evidence
destroy evidence	circumstantial evidence	the lack of evidence
gather evidence	overwhelming evidence	in the light of the evidence
give evidence		
withhold evidence		

Common expressions

the evidence points to   there is no evidence that

the evidence proves   used in evidence

1. Verb + evidence

Complete the sentences with the correct form of the above verbs:

1. Prosecutors believe they . . . . enough evidence to convict Jones of the crime.
2. I was one of many witnesses called to . . . . evidence at the trial.
3. The journalist was sent to prison for . . . . evidence and obstructing the course of justice. He had refused to give vital information to the police.
4. Detectives spent months . . . . evidence against his illegal gambling activities.
5. The drug dealer tried to . . . . the evidence by flushing it down the toilet.

2. Adjective + evidence

Complete the sentences below with the above adjectives:

1. She was charged with perjury – giving . . . . evidence in court.
2. There was no way he could maintain his innocence. The evidence against him was
. . . .
3. The . . . . evidence is strong. He was the only person in the building when the money was taken.

3. Noun + of + evidence

Match the two halves:

1. Lack of evidence meant
2. In the light of the new evidence,
3. There isn't a shred of evidence

a. to support his alibi. Nobody will believe him.
b. that the police had to release him.
c. he couldn't deny the charges against him.

4. Common expressions

Match the halves:

1. All the evidence points to suicide.
2. The documents may be used in evidence
3. The evidence proves beyond any doubt
4. There was no evidence that

a. either driver had been drinking.
b. It looks like she took her own life.
c. at the trial.
d. that the defendant is guilty.

Note   Note that we use evidence to talk about other topics such as health:
Scientists have shown that there is clear evidence of a link between exercise and a healthy heart.
We have compelling evidence of the health risks posed by the use of pesticides on fruit.
There is convincing evidence that eating a little can help you to live longer.
There's evidence that people who drink a glass of red wine a day are less likely to develop heart disease.
When the doctors examined him they found no evidence of infection.

trial and verdict

Verb + trial	Noun + prep + trial	Expressions with trial	Verb + verdict
await trial		reach a verdict
receive a fair trial	the right to a trial	throughout the trial	return a verdict of
guarantee a fair trial	the costs of the ...	without trial	appeal against the ...
stand trial	the conduct of the ...	the trial collapsed	
bring to trial		the trial ended in ...	
go on trial			

1. Verb + trial

Complete the sentences with the correct form of the above verbs:

1. The prisoner claims that he did not . . . . a fair trial.
2. The terrorists were finally . . . . to trial three years after the hijacking.
3. Doctors declared that the prisoner was perfectly fit to . . . . trial.
4. He's in prison, ... trial for murder.
5. Because of all the publicity, he claims that he will not be . . . . a fair trial.
6. A 25-year-old man has . . . . on trial. He's accused of murdering his girlfriend.

2. Noun + preposition + trial

Complete the sentences with the above nouns:

1. Under British law, everyone has the . . . . to a fair trial.
2. The newspapers attacked the judges and their . . . . of the trial.
3. If he loses the court case, he will have to pay the full . . . . of the trial.

3. Expressions with trial

Match the halves:

1. The trial ended in
2. The trial collapsed
3. The protesters were thrown into jail
4. She maintained her innocence

a. without a trial.
b. throughout the trial.
c. the acquittal of the defendant.
d. after a witness admitted lying.

"In prison awaiting trial."

4. Verb + verdict

Complete the sentences with the correct form of the above verbs:

1. After three days the jury had still not . . . . a verdict.
2. He maintains his innocence and he'll certainly . . . . against the guilty verdict.
3. The jury in the Rodham murder trial . . . . a verdict of not guilty.

Note   A court is where trials take place:

Three people will appear in court today, charged with possessing explosives.
The minister threatened to take the newspaper to court if they didn't publish an immediate apology.
The police admitted that they didn't have enough evidence to bring the case to court.

sentence and fine

Verb + sentence	Adjective + sentence	Verb + fine
defer sentence	a life sentence	carry a fine
pass sentence	a light sentence	face a fine
receive a sentence	a lenient sentence	get a fine
reduce the sentence	a stiff sentence	get away with a fine
serve a sentence	a suspended sentence	impose a fine
		pay a fine

1. Verb + sentence

Complete the sentences with the correct form of the above verbs:

1. His father is in Wandsworth Prison, ... a five-year sentence for burglary.
2. In court today he . . . . a long prison sentence for armed robbery.
3. We will be appealing to the court to . . . . his prison sentence to a fine.
4. The judge has. . . . . sentence until he receives medical reports on the defendant.
5. The accused has been found guilty. The judge will . . . . sentence later today.

2. Adjective + sentence

Complete the sentences below with the above adjectives:

1. The woman was given a one-year . . . . sentence for assaulting her neighbour.
2. He will serve a . . . . sentence for the murder of his wife. In the past that meant what it said, but today it usually means something between 10 and 20 years.
3. He got off with a fairly . . . . sentence because it was his first conviction.
4. Rapists should be given . . . . prison sentences. The ones they get now are far too . . . .

3. Verb + fine

Complete the sentences with the correct form of the above verbs:

1. Someone who mugs an old lady . . . . away with only a fine. Is that justice?
2. The offence . . . . a maximum fine of £500. However, the usual fine is £50.
3. I had to . . . . a £30 fine when I got a parking ticket yesterday.
4. Tougher fines are to be . . . . on companies who ignore safety regulations.
5. I . . . . a fine for parking on double yellow lines.
6. Taxpayers who fail to send in tax forms will . . . . an automatic fine of £150.

Notes

1. In 2–1 a 'suspended sentence' is when the person is guilty, but allowed to go free. If they commit another crime in the next year, they automatically go to prison.
2. Note the adjectives we use to describe fines:
   If found guilty, he faces six months in jail and a heavy / hefty / stiff / substantial fine.
   The council has introduced on-the-spot fines of £50 for people caught dropping litter. (to be paid immediately)
3. Note the verb phrases we use to describe being punished lightly:
   Instead of a prison sentence, he got off with / got away with / was let off with / escaped with a small fine.
4. Note the expression:
   Offenders will be liable to fines of up to £500.

punishment and prison

Verb + punishment	Adj + punishment	Verb + prison	Prison + noun
deserve punishment	capital punishment	go to prison	a prison cell
escape punishment	barbaric punishment	send to prison	a prison sentence
receive punishment	harsh punishment	escape from ...	prison conditions
	lenient punishment	release from ...	the prison service
			the ... population

1. Verb + punishment

Complete the sentences with the correct form of the above verbs:

1. I have no doubt that he's guilty and I hope he gets the punishment he . . . .
2. What sort of punishments did you . . . . for misbehaving at school?
3. You were lucky to . . . . punishment. I had to scrub the graffiti off the wall.

2. Adjective + punishment

Complete the sentences below with the above adjectives:

1. Most European countries have abolished . . . . punishment.
2. The electric chair is considered a . . . . form of punishment for a civilised country to be still using in this day and age.
3. He claims that there is little evidence that . . . . punishments actually deter criminals any better than more . . . . ones.

3. Verb + prison

Complete the sentences with the correct form of the above verbs:

1. He was . . . . to prison for armed robbery.
2. She has such strong beliefs that she's even prepared to . . . . to prison for them.
3. He was . . . . from prison after serving only two years of a six-year sentence.
4. Three dangerous criminals . . . . from a high security prison last night.

4. Prison + noun

Complete the sentences with the above nouns:

1. He received a 10-year prison . . . . for attempting to hijack a plane.
2. Prison . . . . are appalling. Up to six prisoners are being held in prison . . . . , designed for one.
3. Britain's prison . . . . continues to rise. As a result, the prison . . . . is now being stretched to its limits.

Notes

1. Note these expressions with 'punishment':
   He was sent to his room as a punishment for not eating his dinner.
   The judge said the punishment would serve as a warning to others.
   I believe that the punishment should fit the crime.
2. Note these expressions with 'prison':
   Matthews faces up to 24 years in prison if convicted.
   The judge ordered the politician to serve at least 3 years in prison.
   Some people think that people who abuse children should be sent to prison for the rest of their lives.

Section 19

Conflict

war   150

peace   151

attack   152

defence   153

bomb and explosion   154

casualty   155

weapon and gun   156

dispute and strike   157

campaign and demonstration   158

"I always think that attack is the best form of defence!"

war

Verb + war	Adjective + war	Noun + of + war
be at war	a civil war	the horror of war
declare war	a conventional war	an outbreak of war
prepare for war	a full-scale war	a prisoner of war
prevent war	a futile war	the threat / risk of war
win / lose a war	a nuclear war	
war breaks out		

1. Verb + war

Complete the sentences with the correct form of the above verbs:

1. The government has . . . . war on drug dealers as from today.
2. The UN is doing everything it can to . . . . war between the two countries.
3. They . . . . the war, but it cost millions of lives and ruined the economy.
4. Billions are being spent on weapons and arms as the country . . . . for war.
5. While the men . . . . away at war, many women went to work in the factories.
6. Peace lasted in Europe for over 20 years before war . . . . out again in 1939.

2. Adjective + war

Complete the sentences with the above adjectives:

1. There are fears that this minor border dispute could escalate into a . . . . war.
2. Some people say that the scars left by . . . . war never heal.
3. It will be a long and . . . . war. Neither side will achieve anything by it.
4. There is always the frightening possibility that what begins as a . . . . war could easily become a . . . . one.

3. Noun + of + war

Match the two halves:

1. British nationals were advised to leave the country,
2. Thousands of prisoners of war were kept in camps and
3. Countries justify having nuclear weapons by
4. Today, television can carry the full

a. horror of war directly into our homes.
b. subjected to inhuman treatment.
c. claiming that they reduce the threat of war.
d. following the outbreak of civil war.

Notes

1. We use the verb 'rage' to describe fierce fighting:
   The war, which has been raging in the mountains, has already claimed thousands of lives.
2. In 1-1 'war' is used to describe an attempt to deal with crime. It can be used in these situations:
   The government has declared war on corruption.
   The police will continue to wage war on organised crime.
   Customs officials believe that they are winning the war against drug smuggling.
   The World Health Organisation is constantly waging war on malaria.
3. A 'price war' is where businesses compete to attract customers by lowering prices:
   When petrol companies engage in a price war, it's good news for the motorist!
4. In the late 1960s 'Make love not war' was a popular anti-war slogan.

peace

Verb + peace	Peace + noun	Noun + prep + peace
bring peace	a peace campaign	a commitment to peace
make peace	a peace treaty	hopes of peace
live in peace	the peace process	a period of peace
work for peace	peace talks	a plea for peace
keep / preserve the peace		a symbol of peace
threaten world peace		a threat to peace

1. Verb + peace

Complete the sentences with the correct form of the above verbs:

1. A UN force is in the area to . . . . the peace between the two ethnic groups.
2. He . . . . tirelessly for world peace and received the Nobel Prize in 1978.
3. We hope the signing of the treaty will . . . . peace and stability to the region.
4. Let's hope that the two communities can learn to . . . . together in peace.
5. Spain and France . . . . peace in 1659 after a war lasting 25 years.
6. This small war creates a dangerous situation which could . . . . world peace.

2. Peace + noun

Complete the sentences with the above nouns:

1. Peace . . . . between the two sides ended in deadlock last month.
2. After years of war, the peace . . . . was signed last month.
3. These latest killings are the work of people trying to de-rail the peace . . . .
4. The peace . . . . starts in earnest this weekend with a big meeting in Paris.

3. Noun + preposition + peace

Complete the sentences with the above nouns:

1. The war was followed by a long . . . . of peace and prosperity.
2. Terrorism constitutes a very real . . . . to world peace.
3. The dove is often used as the . . . . of peace.
4. At Easter, the Pope made a passionate . . . . for world peace.
5. In his speech, the President stressed his . . . . to world peace.
6. These suicide bombings seem to have ended any . . . . of peace.

"Whenever I watch the setting sun, I always feel at peace with myself and the world."

Notes

1. Note how we describe how long we think the peace will last:
   This agreement offers the possibility of a lasting peace in the Balkans.
   A fragile peace exists between the two sides, but further fighting could break out at any time.
2. 'Peace-loving' describes people who do not want war:
   They are a peace-loving nation and will avoid war at all costs.
3. We also use 'peace' to describe feelings:
   As I watched the setting sun, I felt at peace with myself and the world.

attack

Verb + attack	Adj + attack	Noun + of + attack	Types of attack
carry out an attack	a devastating attack	attack	a knife attack
come under attack	a savage attack	the ferocity of an ...	a bomb attack
launch an attack	a surprise attack	the target of an ...	an arson attack
repel an attack	an unprovoked ...	the possibility of ...	a racial attack
protect against ...			a nuclear attack
claim responsibility for an ...			

1. Verb + attack

Complete the sentences with the correct form of the above verbs:

1. The city has . . . . under attack from both land and air.
2. Police believe that a lone gunman . . . . out the attack on the President.
3. Police are at the factory gates to . . . . workers against attacks from pickets.
4. The defenders managed to . . . . the first attack without losing any men.
   However, they expect the rebel army to . . . . further attacks in the days ahead.
5. An unknown rebel group has . . . . responsibility for yesterday's bomb attack.

2. Adjective + attack

Complete the sentences with the above adjectives:

1. A . . . . attack caught the guards sleeping and they were quickly overcome.
2. Rioters with machetes brutally hacked to death 30 villagers in a . . . . attack.
3. In court, he claimed he was a victim of an . . . . attack by the police. He says he was minding his own business at the time and doing nothing wrong.
4. The enemy surrendered after a . . . . attack by B-52 bombers.

3. Noun + of + attack

Complete the sentences with the above nouns:

1. The police are on red alert against the . . . . of further terrorist attacks.
2. The . . . . of the attack was the police headquarters in the centre of the city.
3. The police were shocked by the . . . . of the attack on the old woman.

4. Types of attack

Match the halves:

1. Ten classrooms were destroyed in	a. left one Leeds supporter dead.
2. Refugees are often the victims of	b. a car bomb attack.
3. Fifty civilians were killed in	c. the arson attack on the school.
4. Today, the threat of	d. racial attacks.
5. Tensions are high after a knife attack	e. nuclear attack has almost disappeared.

Notes

1. We also use 'attack' to refer to health problems:
   He suffered an acute attack of food-poisoning after eating some left-over chicken.
   One of the passengers had a heart attack and had to be rushed to hospital.
2. We also use 'attack' to mean 'criticism':
   The opposition mounted a scathing attack on the government's handling of education.
   The newspaper launched a personal attack on the President, claiming he was unfit for office.

defence

Verb + defence	Adjective + defence	Common expressions
break through a defence	an effective defence	do something as a defence
strengthen your defences	a strong defence	spend money on defence
come to the defence of	a vigorous defence	leap to your defence
defences are overwhelmed		speak out in your defence
		a form of defence

1. Verb + defence

Complete the sentences with the correct form of the above verbs:

1. We have been . . . . our border defences in case of attack.
2. Heavy seas . . . . through the coastal defences during last week's storms.
3. The patient dies when the body's natural defences are . . . . by the virus.
4. When I was attacked, a passer-by . . . . to my defence and the mugger ran away.

2. Adjective + defence

Complete the sentences with the above adjectives:

1. The team's got a . . . . defence but no attack. We badly need a goal scorer!
2. The PM launched into a . . . . defence of his decision to go to war.
3. Some people say that humour is a more . . . . defence than violence. So don't hit your enemy, tell him a joke!

3. Common expressions

Match the halves:

1. When I was wrongly accused of causing the disaster nobody spoke out
2. The villagers' only form of defence against the soldiers' guns
3. Huge amounts of government money are spent
4. When the boss criticised my work, a friend leapt
5. The town walls were built as a defence

a. against enemy attacks.
b. on defence.
c. was sticks and stones.
d. in my defence.
e. to my defence.

"Would you fight in your country's defence?"

Notes

1. Note the kind of things we defend:
   Would you be prepared to fight in defence of your country?
   Thousands of young men gave their lives in defence of freedom.
2. Note the expression 'self-defence':
   She claims that she killed him in self-defence.
3. Note how we talk about health matters using 'defence':
   The immune system is the body's defence against infection.
   Taking cod liver oil supplements is a good defence against colds.

bomb and explosion

Verb + bomb	Bomb + noun	Verb + explosion	Noun + of + explosion
make a bomb	a bomb attack	cause an explosion	a series of explosions
detonate a bomb	a bomb hoax	hear an explosion	the force of the ...
plant a bomb	a ... disposal expert	explosions shake	reports of an ...
drop a bomb		explosions shatter	the time of the ...
throw a bomb			
bombs explode / go off			

1. Verb + bomb

Complete the sentences with the correct form of the above verbs:

1. The newspaper received an anonymous tip-off about where the bomb had been
. . . . and police raced to the location.
2. If the car bomb had . . . . during the rush hour, it would have killed hundreds.
3. US planes . . . . thousands of bombs on the city during the war.
4. The army believe a remote control device was used to . . . . the car bomb.
5. Rioters . . . . petrol bombs in clashes with police last night.
6. Experts believe the country has enough uranium to . . . . a nuclear bomb.

2. Bomb + noun

Match the halves:

1. A bomb hoax forced
2. Bomb disposal experts have defused
3. The police suspect him of carrying out

a. the bomb attack on the embassy.
b. the police to evacuate the building.
c. a massive bomb at the railway station.

3. Verb + explosion

Complete the sentences with the correct form of the above verbs:

1. A huge explosion . . . . buildings and . . . . windows.
2. A court of inquiry has been set up to investigate what . . . . the explosion.
3. I . . . . a deafening explosion, then I saw a plume of black smoke in the distance.

4. Noun + of + explosion

Complete the sentences with the above nouns:

1. Fortunately, there was no one in the building at the . . . . of the explosion.
2. There was a . . . . of explosions, then the ship broke up and sank.
3. We were thrown backwards by the . . . . of the explosion.
4. In the last few minutes, we've received . . . . of an explosion aboard a ferry.

Notes
1. Note how we describe the effects of a bomb:
The bomb reduced the building to a heap of rubble.
The aircraft was blown apart by a terrorist bomb.
2. Note these expressions:
The police evacuated the shopping centre shortly before the explosion.
A number of innocent bystanders were injured in the explosion.
Ambulances, fire engines and police cars raced to the scene after the explosion.

casualty

Verb + casualties	Adjective + casualty	Common expressions
result in casualties	a civilian casualty	be among the casualties
suffer casualties	heavy casualties	there were no casualties
inflict casualties	road casualties	without suffering a single
reduce the number of		casualty
casualties		

1. Verb + casualties

Complete the sentences with the correct form of the verbs above:

1. Both sides . . . . appalling casualties at the Battle of the Somme.
2. A bomb exploded in the main railway station, ... in hundreds of casualties.
3. The use of body armour helped to . . . . the number of casualties in the war.
4. A small group of terrorists . . . . heavy casualties on government forces. More than five hundred troops were killed.

2. Adjective + casualty

Choose the correct collocation:

1. The general admitted that there were citizen / civilian casualties when the bomb missed its target.
2. The introduction of seat belts has helped to reduce the number of car / road casualties by a third.
3. British and US troops sustained heavy / large casualties when they landed on the open beaches.

"Seat belts have cut down the number of road casualties."

3. Common expressions

Match the halves:

1. The army managed to capture the building
2. The bomb caused serious damage to the building, but there
3. There are reports of an explosion in Spain. Women and children are feared to

a. be among the casualties.
b. without suffering a single casualty.
c. were no casualties.

Notes

1. Note that 'Casualty' also refers to the department of a hospital where people who need urgent treatment are taken:
   The seriously injured were rushed to Casualty by ambulance.
   I had to wait in Casualty for over an hour before a doctor saw me.
2. 'Casualty' can also be used in a non-literal sense:
   I'm afraid our department is going to be one of the first casualties in the government's next round of spending cuts.
3. Note that we use 'victim', not 'casualty', in these sentences:
   Unfortunately, children are always the innocent victims of war.
   The jury awarded damages of over £5 million to the victims of the air disaster.
   Police are trying to identify the murder victim.
   The train company have taken full responsibility for the accident and have agreed to compensate the victims.

weapon and gun

Verb + weapon	Adj + weapon	Verb + gun	Phrasal verbs
ban a weapon	a hidden weapon	carry a gun	**with gun**
develop a weapon	a lethal weapon	fire a gun	pull out a gun
supply weapons	the murder weapon	load a gun	point a gun at (him)
lay down your ...	an offensive weapon	a gun goes off	put a gun to
	a superior weapon		throw down your ...
			threaten with a gun

1. Verb + weapon

Complete the sentences with the correct form of the above verbs:

1. Who is . . . . weapons to the terrorists?
2. I hope that one day nuclear weapons will be . . . . internationally.
3. . . . . down your weapons or we'll open fire! We have you surrounded!
4. We have evidence that they are trying to . . . . chemical weapons in secret.

2. Adjective + weapon

Choose the correct collocation:

1. Police divers are still searching for the death / murder weapon.
2. Government troops with their greater / superior weapons defeated the rebel army.
3. It's against the law to carry knives – they're classified as criminal / offensive weapons.
4. Metal detectors are used to catch people carrying hidden / disguised weapons.
5. The machine gun is one of the most fatal / lethal weapons ever developed by man.

3. Verb + gun

Complete the sentences with the correct form of the above verbs:

1. The rebels . . . . their machine guns into the air to celebrate their victory.
2. Unlike many other police forces, British police do not . . . . guns.
3. The gun . . . . off as he was cleaning it. The bullet just missed his head!
4. He . . . . the gun with his last six bullets. He was now out of ammunition.

4. Phrasal verbs with gun

Complete the verb phrases with the correct preposition:

1. During the hold-up at the bank a masked man threatened staff . . . . a gun.
2. Suddenly the customer pulled . . . . a gun and demanded money.
3. He put a gun . . . . her head and told the manager to hand over the money.
4. She pointed a gun directly . . . . me and said 'Hand over your wallet.'
5. The police told the robber to throw . . . . his gun and put his hands in the air.

Notes

1. Note this expression:
   During the fight he used his steel comb as a weapon.
2. 'Weapons of mass destruction' are weapons which are capable of causing massive casualties. They include nuclear, chemical and biological weapons.
3. Note these expressions:
   It's dangerous to leave a loaded gun lying around. (with bullets in it)
   The robber was armed with a toy / replica gun.

dispute and strike

Verb + dispute	Expressions with dispute	Verb + strike
be involved in a dispute	settled beyond dispute	hold a strike
handle a dispute	in dispute with (them)	avert a strike
intervene in a dispute	a matter of dispute	break a strike
settle a dispute	the settlement of a dispute	lead to a strike
		disrupted by a strike

1. Verb + dispute

Complete the sentences with the correct form of the above verbs:

1. After lengthy negotiations the dispute over pay has been . . . .
2. I didn't like the way my boss . . . . the dispute, so I complained to my union.
3. If you are . . . . in a dispute with your landlord, you should seek legal advice.
4. The Secretary-General of the UN was asked to . . . . in the border dispute between the two countries.

2. Expressions with dispute

Match the halves:

1. The unions are in dispute
2. The matter was settled
3. Who fired the first shot is
4. The union leader was praised for his
5. We are optimistic that we can reach

a. handling of the dispute.
b. with management over pay.
c. beyond dispute in a court of law.
d. a peaceful settlement of the dispute.
e. a matter of dispute at the moment.

3. Verb + strike

Complete the sentences with the correct form of the above verbs:

1. Talks are taking place between management and unions in an attempt to . . . . next week's planned strike.
2. Workers have voted by a large majority to . . . . a one-day strike in support of their sacked colleagues.
3. Management have rejected the latest pay claim by the workers. This will almost certainly . . . . to further strikes.
4. The company brought in outside workers in an attempt to . . . . the strike.
5. Flights will be severely . . . . by the air traffic controllers' strike.

Notes

1. Note the following types of strike:
   The workforce staged a lightning strike / a series of wildcat strikes. (sudden and short)
   The student union has called for a rent strike. (protest by not paying).
2. Note these expressions:
   The car industry has been hit by a wave of strikes in recent months.
   The rail strike is now entering its fifth week and shows no signs of ending.
   Firefighters have voted to take strike action.
3. Note some of the ways we describe the effects of a strike:
   The rail network is still paralysed by the strike. No trains are running.
   A strike by dockers has crippled the port. No ferries can get in or out.
   The strike has left thousands of British holidaymakers stranded at Greek airports.

campaign and demonstration

Verb + campaign	Adjective + campaign	Verb + demonstration
launch a campaign	an advertising campaign	hold a demonstration
conduct a campaign	an anti-(obesity) campaign	take part in a demonstration
lead a campaign	an election campaign	lead to a demonstration
support a campaign	a publicity campaign	break up a demonstration

1. Verb + campaign

Complete the sentences with the correct form of the above verbs:

1. Most people .... the campaign to ban fox hunting. Only a tiny minority approve of killing animals for sport.
2. For over five years the prisoner's family have .... a tireless campaign for his release, without success.
3. The police have .... a new campaign against drink-driving.
4. The headmaster .... a successful campaign against the closure of the village school. He was certainly the driving force behind the whole campaign.

2. Adjective + campaign

Complete the sentences with the above adjectives:

1. Sales of the car increased, following a successful .... campaign.
2. The Health Service was the main issue in the recent .... campaign.
3. Despite a major .... campaign, few people recognised the star in the street.
4. The government's .... campaign seems to have made little impact. People simply refuse to change their eating habits.

3. Verb + demonstration

Complete the sentences with the correct form of the above verbs:

1. An anti-war demonstration will be .... in front of the embassy building this weekend. Thousands are expected to join the protest.
2. Yesterday in London, more than 2,000 students .... part in a demonstration against the government's planned increase in university fees.
3. The huge rise in the price of basic foodstuffs has .... to mass demonstrations throughout the country.
4. The police used tear gas and water cannon to .... up the demonstration and disperse the protesters.

Notes
1. Note these expressions:
   Local residents have mounted a campaign against the building of a new supermarket.
   Bertrand Russell was a leading figure in the Campaign for Nuclear Disarmament (CND).
   The campaign has succeeded in raising public awareness of the disease.
   Environmentalists are organising a campaign to draw people's attention to the dangers of genetically modified crops.
   If this policy doesn't change, there's going to be a campaign of civil disobedience.
2. Note that a demonstration can be peaceful or violent:
   Unfortunately, what was planned as a peaceful demonstration turned violent / degenerated into violence.
   Apart from one or two minor disturbances / incidents, the demonstration passed off peacefully. (there was no trouble)

Section 20

Communication

language   160
conversation   161
discussion   162
speech   163
secret, rumour and lie   164

"Your secret's safe with me!"

language

Verb + language	Adjective + language	Expressions with language
acquire a language	bad language	a flair for languages
master a language	a foreign language	a good command of a ...
speak a language	your first / native language	fluent in a language
translate into a language	ordinary / plain language	proficient in a language
	body language	

1. Verb + language

Complete the sentences with the correct form of the above verbs:

1. So, how many languages do you . . . . ?
2. I wish I was able to . . . . a language in the effortless way that children do.
3. His books have been . . . . into over 50 different languages.
4. Although I lived for many years in Greece, I never quite . . . . the language.

2. Adjective + language

Match the halves:

1. The film has been edited for bad or offensive language.
2. She didn't say anything, but I knew by her body language that
3. French, German and Spanish are
4. Make sure your explanation doesn't contain too much technical language.
5. German is her first language, but she speaks English with an impeccable accent.

a. she was angry about something.
b. The secret of a good talk is to express your ideas in plain language.
c. It no longer contains any swearing.
d. You'd think that it was her first language.
e. the most popular foreign languages taught in British schools.

3. Expressions with language

These expressions mean to 'speak a language well'. Choose the correct preposition:

1. I'm fluent at / in French, and I have a working knowledge of German.
2. He has a flair for / with languages. I think he can speak about ten.
3. After a year in Spain, I now have a good command in / of the language.
4. She's proficient at / in several languages, including Arabic.

Notes
1. Note these expressions:
   At the meeting the only common language was English.
   Watch your language! (Don't use language which will offend / upset people)
   This programme contains language which some viewers may find offensive.
2. Note these types of language:
   The official language of Singapore is English.
   Latin is a dead language.
3. Note these language + noun expressions:
   Listening is extremely important in language learning and teaching.
   This course will help to develop your mathematical and language skills.
   The country needs more modern language teachers.
4. Note that you talk about your 'native language', and your 'mother tongue'.

conversation

Verb + conversation	Adj + conversation	Noun + preposition + conversation
carry on a conversation	polite conversation	the art of conversation
interrupt a conversation	a civilised conversation	snatches of a conversation
monopolise a conversation	a private conversation	a topic of conversation
overhear a conversation	a sensible conversation	the tone of a conversation
get into conversation		in the middle of a ...
		a lull / break in the ...

1. Verb + conversation

Complete the sentences with the correct form of the above verbs:

1. A knock on the front door . . . . our conversation.
2. It's impossible to . . . . on a conversation with all this noise going on.
3. My sister completely . . . . the conversation. I could hardly get a word in.
4. At the bus stop, Henry . . . . into conversation with the girl standing next to him.
5. I . . . . their conversation. I think they're planning to close the business.

2. Adjective + conversation

Complete these sentences with the above adjectives:

1. Whenever we try to have a . . . . conversation, she tries to listen in on us.
2. He's losing his memory. It's almost impossible to hold a . . . . conversation with him.
3. I hate it when you're left alone at a party with a complete stranger and you've got to make . . . . conversation about things like the weather.
4. We can't have a . . . . conversation any more. We just argue all the time.

3. Noun + preposition + conversation

Complete the sentences with the above nouns:

1. We've exhausted this . . . . of conversation. Let's talk about something else.
2. People watch too much television. They're losing the . . . . of conversation.
3. I was cut off in the . . . . of the conversation. I wish they'd fix the phones.
4. Trust you to lower the . . . . of the conversation with your rude jokes.
5. I waited for a . . . . in the conversation so that I could ask a question.
6. Because of the noise in the room I only caught . . . . of the conversation.

Notes

1. Note these expressions:
   We had little in common and ran out of conversation after two minutes.
   The two lovers were locked in conversation in a quiet corner of the restaurant. They were so deep in conversation that they were oblivious to everyone around them.

2. Note that we use 'chat' to describe an informal conversation:
   I was just passing, so I thought I'd drop in for a chat.
   I had an interesting chat with your sister. I didn't know she worked for the BBC.
   If you're not sure what you want to do, go along to the careers office and have a chat with someone.
   I've got to get on with my work. I've got no time for idle chat.

3. A 'chat room' is a place on the internet where you use e-mail to discuss a topic with other people. A chat show is a TV programme where famous people are interviewed.

discussion

Verb + discussion	Adj + discussion	Noun + prep + discussion	Expressions
have a discussion	a fruitful discussion		be deep in discussion
generate discussion	a heated discussion	a great deal of ...	be under discussion
take part in a ...	lengthy discussion	the level of ...	a ... can be pointless
widen the ...	a detailed ...	an item for ...	a ... can go round in
	a full and frank ...		circles

1. Verb + discussion

Complete the sentences with the correct form of the above verbs:

1. The two governments are to . . . . discussions on a trade agreement.
2. We hope everyone will . . . . part in the discussion.
3. The report on poverty has . . . . a lot of discussion of the issues involved.
4. I think we should . . . . the discussion to include other points of view.

2. Adjective + discussion

Complete these sentences with the above adjectives:

1. The speech on euthanasia was extremely controversial. It provoked a very . . . . discussion afterwards. Some people got very angry at the views expressed.
2. After . . . . discussion, we reached a decision on the proposal about midnight!
3. We had a . . . . and . . . . discussion on who was responsible for the disaster. People were very honest with each other.
4. The report is far too long to allow . . . . discussion of all the 150 points it lists.
5. The meeting was extremely positive with some very . . . . discussion. We achieved much more than we could possibly have hoped for.

3. Noun + preposition + discussion

Complete the sentences with the above nouns:

1. If we are in agreement, can we move on to the next . . . . for discussion?
2. I thought the . . . . of discussion was rather poor at the meeting.
3. There's been a great . . . . of discussion about the new plans to reduce traffic.

4. Expressions

Match the halves:

1. Any further discussion seems pointless.
2. I wouldn't disturb them just now.
3. The discussion kept going round in circles.
4. I'm sorry I can't give you any details.

a. We achieved nothing in over two hours.
b. The matter is still under discussion.
c. We'll just have to agree to differ.
d. They're deep in discussion.

Notes

1. Note these expressions:
   Discussions have taken place between the two leaders on the crisis in the Middle East.
   Discussions with management over pay and conditions have broken down.
   I'd like to bring our discussion back to the original topic.

2. A discussion group is a group of people who meet to share ideas on a particular topic. Today this type of communication is often done on the internet.

speech

1. Verb + speech

Complete the sentences with the correct form of the above verbs:

1. The bridegroom . . . . a short speech, thanking all the guests for their gifts.
2. I hadn't . . . . a speech, so I had to make it up as I went along.
3. Over half of the speech was . . . . to the issue of unemployment.
4. A group of hecklers rudely . . . . the Queen's speech with shouts and jeers.
5. The Prime Minister was extremely careful and diplomatic in what he said. His speech managed to . . . . the controversial issue that divides the two countries.

2. Adjective + speech

Match the halves:

1. At the wedding reception the best man gave a very witty speech.
2. The poet, Tim Arden, delivered a passionate speech against the war.
3. He made a very moving speech at the funeral.
4. I knew my speech was controversial, but
5. A few jokes provided some light relief
6. In a democratic country all citizens are guaranteed
7. As part of your assessment you will have to give

"*I've never made a speech before*"

a. the right to free speech.
b. a short speech to the class.
c. He had everyone laughing.
d. I didn't expect it to upset so many people!
e. He obviously has strong feelings about it.
f. in an otherwise dull speech.
g. Many of the mourners were in tears by the time he had finished.

Notes

1. Note the following adverb + adjective collocations:
   It was a deadly boring speech. Most of the audience were asleep by the end of it!
   In a carefully worded speech, he criticised the way the royal family treated his sister.
2. Note these expressions for describing responses to a speech:
   The President's speech was received with cheers and a standing ovation.
   His speech was greeted with boos and jeers.
   The speech didn't go down well. It wasn't what the audience wanted to hear.
3. Speech also means the ability to speak:
   After he'd had a few drinks, his speech became slurred. I couldn't make out what he was saying.
   My grandfather lost his power of speech after he had a stroke.
   Our son has a slight speech impediment and has to have lessons with a speech therapist.

secret, rumour and lie

Verb + secret	Adj + secret	Verb + rumour	Verb + lie
have a secret	a dark secret	confirm a rumour	tell a lie
keep a secret	an open secret	deny a rumour	believe a lie
tell (her) a ...	a closely-guarded ...	hear a rumour	spread a lie
	one of the best-kept	start a rumour	
	secrets	rumours go round	

1. Verb + secret

Complete the sentences with the correct form of the above verbs:

1. Why did you have to tell John that I fancy him? You can't . . . . a secret, can you?
2. I only . . . . my secrets to my best friend.
3. My wife and I are very open with each other. We don't . . . . any secrets.

2. Adjective + secret

Complete these sentences with the above adjectives:

1. One problem with tracing your family tree is that you might discover some . . . .
   secret from the past – for example, that your great-grandfather was a murderer.
2. The location of the church where the pop star will get married is a . . . . secret.
3. Their affair is an . . . . secret. Everybody knows about it, but nobody mentions it.
4. It's a quiet restaurant with the most superb food. It must be one of the . . . .
   secrets in Paris. I just hope the guidebooks don't find out about it.

3. Verb + rumour

Complete the sentences with the correct form of the above verbs:

1. We've . . . . rumours that the factory is closing. Is there anything in them?
2. In an interview the actress . . . . rumours that she will be quitting the show.
   She said she would be leaving at the end of the current series.
3. There's a rumour . . . . around that Jim is leaving. Any idea if it's true?
4. Nobody seems to know who . . . . the rumour.
5. A Palace press officer has . . . . rumours that the royal couple are about to
   divorce.

4. Verb + lie

Complete the sentences with the correct form of the above verbs:

1. I always know when he's . . . . lies. He never looks me in the eye.
2. How could she . . . . such a pack of lies? It was obvious that he was lying.
3. I'd like to know who is . . . . lies about me around the neighbourhood.

Notes

1. Note these expressions:
   If you promise not to tell, I'll let you in on a little secret. (tell you a secret)
   Your secret is safe with me. (I won't tell anyone.)
2. Note the adjectives that describe a deliberate and obvious lie:
   How could he think that we would believe such a(n) blatant / barefaced / outright lie?
3. A 'white lie' is a harmless or small lie, especially one that you tell to avoid hurting somebody:
   All children tell their parents little white lies when they are young.

Section 21

Information

news   166
message   167
document   168
article   169
letter   170
mail   171
advertisement, publicity   172
and reputation

"I'm just checking my messages."

news

Verb + news	Adjective + news	Common expressions
hear news	good news	once the news gets out
tell (your) news	bad news	news travels fast
make news	great news	take news well or badly
wait for news	the latest news	news can come as a shock /
celebrate news		a surprise / a relief
catch up on news		
break bad news to (him)		

1. Verb + news

Complete the sentences with the correct form of the above verbs:

1. Write or phone and . . . . us all your news.
2. The world held its breath as it . . . . for news of the troubled spacecraft.
3. You've got the job! That's the best piece of news I've . . . . for a long time!
4. He phoned to say he's getting married! Let's have a party to . . . . the news.
5. We hadn't seen each other for ages, so we spent the evening . . . . up on each other's news. We had a lot to talk about.
6. Sebastian Coe . . . . news when he set a world record for the 1500 metres.
7. I didn't know how to . . . . the terrible news to my wife.

2. Adjective + news

Complete these sentences with the above adjectives:

1. Which do you want first, Mr Smith – the . . . . news or the . . . . news?
   > The good news, doctor.
   The good news is you have 24 hours to live. The bad news is I forgot to tell you yesterday!
2. The hospital haven't contacted us yet, but I suppose no news is . . . . news.
3. Have you heard the . . . . news? There's been another earthquake in Turkey.
4. You're expecting a twins! That's . . . . news!

3. Common expressions

Match the halves:

1. The news of his death came as	a. the rest of the staff will want one.
2. With satellite communication	b. a pleasant surprise. We all like him.
3. Harry's taken the news	c. news certainly travels fast these days.
4. News of the child's safety came as	d. a great relief to the worried family.
5. The news of his appointment came as	e. a shock to us all.
6. Once the news gets out about her pay rise,	f. of his father's death very well.

Notes

1. Note these expressions:
   News of the arrest of the President's son for murder caused a sensation.
   News of the assassination of President Kennedy shocked the entire world.
   Williams has been in the news a lot recently because of his health problems.
   Was there anything interesting on the news this evening?

2. The expression 'That's news to me' means that you didn't know about something.

message

Verb + message	Adjective + message	Message + of + noun
get a message	a garbled message	a message of support
leave a message	a good-luck message	a message of sympathy
pass on a message	a new message	a message of thanks
send a message	an urgent message	a ... of congratulation
take a message		
give (her) a message		

1. Verb + message

Complete the sentences with the correct form of the above verbs:

1. Dr Brown's line is busy at the moment. Can I . . . . a message?
2. Have you checked your e-mail today? I . . . . you a message last night.
3. His secretary said she'd see that the manager . . . . the message.
4. It's entirely my fault he missed the meeting – I forgot to . . . . him the message.
5. He's not in the office at the moment, but I'll . . . . your message on.
6. I'm sorry we can't take your call just now. Please . . . . a message after the tone.

2. Adjective + message

Complete these sentences with the above adjectives:

1. The newlyweds have received hundreds of . . . . messages from friends and family.
2. When I checked my e-mail this morning, I had 40 . . . . messages waiting for me.
3. He left a . . . . message on my answerphone which I couldn't make out.
4. Apologies for interrupting, but we've had an . . . . message that your mother's ill.

3. Message + of + noun

Match the halves:

1. The Prime Minister has sent a message of sympathy
2. We've had thousands of messages of support
3. He received many messages of congratulation
4. The committee sent a special message of thanks

a. following his success at the Olympic Games.
b. to the families of the soldiers killed in the attack.
c. for our campaign to ban land mines.
d. to everyone who helped with the Queen's visit.

"I think the message is pretty clear!"

Notes

1. A 'text message' is a way of communicating text by mobile phone:
   The cheapest way to communicate by mobile phone is through text messages.
2. An 'error message' appears on a computer screen when something is not working correctly.
   A 'warning message' appears on the screen when the computer's batteries are running low.
3. Note how we use 'message' to mean getting people to understand something:
   The advertisement sends a clear message about the dangers of smoking.
   Through national advertising, the government hopes to bring home the message / get across the message that regular exercise is essential for health.
4. Note this common expression:
   This afternoon's meeting has been cancelled. Can you spread the message?

document

Verb + document	Adjective + document
deliver a document	a confidential document
e-mail a document	a forged document
produce a document	an important document
check a document	an original document
shred a document	the enclosed document
sign a document	

Expressions relating to computers

create a document	save a document
edit a document	print out a document
send / receive a document	scroll through a document

1. Verb + document

Complete the sentences with the correct form of the above verbs:

1. It's a legally-binding document. It must be . . . . in the presence of two witnesses.
2. For security reasons, we use a courier service to . . . . all official documents.
3. I'll . . . . the documents to you. Check your inbox in about five minutes.
4. In our office, we have to . . . . all documents before putting them in the bin.
5. Have you . . . . the document for mistakes?
6. With basic word-processing skills, you can . . . . professional-looking documents.

2. Adjective + document

Complete these sentences with the above adjectives:

1. Only . . . . documents will be accepted as proof. We don't accept photocopies.
2. Please sign both copies of the . . . . document and return one of them to us.
3. Your birth certificate is an . . . . document and should be kept in a safe place.
4. Three men have been charged with using . . . . documents to enter the country.
5. A private letter from the Prime Minister to the Queen was published by a newspaper yesterday. It is a mystery who leaked the . . . . document to the press.

3. Expressions relating to computers

Note that 'document' is used to refer to information on a computer. Complete the sentences with the correct form of the above verbs:

1. Get into a routine of . . . . the document you're working on every 20 minutes.
2. To . . . . a new document, select 'New' from the 'File Menu'.
3. I'll . . . . out a copy of the document for you so that you'll have a hard copy.
4. E-mail allows you to . . . . or . . . . documents at the click of a button.
5. The great advantage of a computer is that you can . . . . a document as much as you like before finalising it.
6. The search function helps you to find the information you need, without having to . . . . through the entire document on the screen.

Note   'Travel documents' are the important papers, such as your passport or visa, which you need when travelling between countries:

Always keep your travel documents in a safe place.

article

Verb + article	Adjective + article	Noun + of + article
read an article	a critical article	a series of articles
write an article	a fascinating article	the end of an article
publish an article	an informative article	a copy of an article
articles contain (facts)	the whole article	a summary of an article
articles appear		
articles criticise		
an article covers (a topic)		

1. Verb + article

Complete the sentences with the correct form of the above verbs:

1. Two articles on sun spots . . . . in the November issue of *The Astronomer.*
2. The article . . . . lots of handy hints for making long journeys comfortable.
3. It's a very long article which . . . . a wide range of issues.
4. . . . . the whole article quickly and make notes on the main points.
5. I've . . . . a few articles for the local newspaper.
6. He got his article . . . . in *The New Scientist.*
7. The article . . . . the police for the methods they used to control the crowd.

2. Adjective + article

Complete these sentences with the above adjectives:

1. I came across a . . . . article on John Travolta. Did you know that he has a pilot's licence?
2. There's an . . . . article on digital photography in today's paper. It tells you all you need to know about the subject.
3. I didn't have time to read the . . . . article – just the title and the first couple of paragraphs.
4. One of the country's most respected daily newspapers published a highly . . . . article about the government's spending on defence.

3. Noun + of + article

Complete the sentences with the above nouns:

1. Our sources can be found in the bibliography at the . . . . of the article.
2. The making of unauthorised . . . . of this article is prohibited.
3. The newspaper ran a . . . . of articles on corruption in the police force.
4. This is only a brief . . . . of the article. The full text is available on the internet.

Notes
1. Note these expressions:
   I'm in the process of collecting material for an article that I'm writing on culture shock.
   If you have any comments on this article, please e-mail us.
   I cut this article out of last night's newspaper – I thought it might interest you.
   We ran a short article about her in the last issue of our magazine.
2. Note these expressions with 'full of':
   The article is full of technical terms which I don't understand.
   The article is full of inaccuracies. Writers should check their facts before publishing them.
   The article is full of spelling mistakes.

letter

Verb + letter	Adjective + letter	Letter + of + noun
address a letter	a begging letter	a letter of application
reply to / answer a letter	a love letter	a letter of apology
get / receive a letter	an open letter	a letter of complaint
post a letter	a thank-you letter	a ... of recommendation
sign a letter		a letter of resignation
write a letter		letters of support
		letters of sympathy

1. Verb + letter

Complete the sentences with the correct form of the above verbs:

1. I . . . . a letter from my bank manager telling me my account is overdrawn.
2. The letter was . . . . correctly, but it was delivered to the wrong house.
3. Over a hundred MPs . . . . a letter demanding that the Prime Minister resign.
4. I've had this letter in my bag for over a week. I keep forgetting to . . . . it.
5. My mother . . . . an angry letter to the council complaining about the dirty streets. She was even more indignant when the council didn't . . . . to it.

2. Adjective + letter

Match the halves:

1. I came across some old love letters
2. 30 MPs sent an open letter to *The Times,*
3. I wrote my aunt a thank-you letter
4. After her lottery win, she received

a. for the birthday present she sent me.
b. hundreds of begging letters.
c. I sent my wife before we were married.
d. expressing their concerns about the war.

3. Letter + of + noun

Complete the sentences with the above nouns:

1. She said that she was deeply moved by all the letters of . . . . she had received after the death of her husband.
2. We've received countless letters of . . . . from the public in our fight to stop the council closing the local primary school.
3. I wrote a letter of . . . . about the problems we had on our holiday. Two weeks later I received a letter of . . . . from the company and a cheque for £100.

The following letters are all associated with jobs.

4. I could stand the job no longer, so I sat down and composed my letter of . . . .
5. Please enclose a CV with your letter of . . . .
6. His former employer speaks very highly of him in her letter of . . . .

Notes
1. Note these noun + of + letter phrases:
   For some unknown reason, she refuses to reveal the contents of the letter.
   The BBC have received a flood of letters complaining about the programme on child abuse.
   Please acknowledge receipt of this letter by phoning the following number.
2. A 'covering letter' is one you send with a document or package which describes the contents:
   Please enclose a covering letter with your CV.

mail

Verb + mail	Adjective + mail
answer your mail	first-class mail
check your mail	fan mail
open your mail	hate mail
deliver the mail	junk mail
sort the mail	snail mail
forward / redirect mail	unopened mail

I. Verb + mail

Complete the sentences with the correct form of the above verbs:

1. Mail is . . . . to our office twice a day.
2. The postcode on the letter allows the mail to be . . . . by machine.
3. I . . . . my mail before leaving the hotel, but there was nothing for me.
4. When you move house, arrange to get your mail . . . . to your new address.
5. Could you . . . . my mail for me and check if there's anything urgent.
6. I haven't had a chance to . . . . my mail. I've been too busy to write.

2. Adjective + mail

Complete these sentences with the above adjectives:

1. I throw . . . . mail straight into the bin without opening it.
2. After the match the referee received . . . . mail from angry supporters.
3. Send the letter by . . . . mail if you want to be sure it will get there tomorrow.
4. There's a stack of . . . . mail waiting for me at home. I've been away for 2 months.
5. I nearly always use e-mail now – I've almost given up . . . . mail.
6. The pop star Robbie Williams receives a lot of . . . . mail.

3. Mail or letter?

Put a line through the word which is not possible:

1. The letters are / mail is delivered twice a day.
2. The letter / mail had the wrong address on it.
3. All our products can be ordered by mail / letter.
4. Would you like it sent by air or surface letter / mail?
5. I will try to answer your letter / mail soon.
6. I wrote a long letter / mail to my parents explaining why I left home.

"Why didn't they get their mail redirected?"

Notes

1. Note that we use 'post' and not 'mail' or 'letter' in these sentences:
   I never received it. It must have got lost in the post.
   I'll put a copy of the document in the post tonight.

2. 'E-mail' is a system that allows you to communicate by computer. Note these expressions:
   Send me an e-mail when you arrive.
   I haven't had time to check my e-mail this morning.
   E-mail has revolutionised the way we communicate.
   I was getting so much spam mail that I had to change my e-mail address.

3. 'Internal mail' is a system of sending messages to people inside the same organisation:
   We send all our reports via internal mail.

advert, publicity and reputation

Verb + advert	Expressions with publicity	Verb + reputation
place an advert	generate publicity	gain a reputation
scan the adverts	receive publicity	have a reputation
respond to an advert	avoid / shun publicity	ruin your reputation
aim adverts at	in a blaze of publicity	save your reputation
adverts appear	publicity surrounds ...	live up to your reputation
adverts influence		lose a reputation

1. Verb + advert

Complete the sentences with the correct form of the above verbs:

1. I . . . . the job adverts in the hope of finding work as a gardener.
2. He . . . . an advert in the local paper to sell his car.
3. More than 50 people . . . . to the advert for the post of school caretaker.
4. Adverts for soft drinks are usually . . . . at young people.
5. There can be no doubt that adverts . . . . our choices.
6. A full page advert . . . . in *The Guardian* outlining the Liberal Party's manifesto.

2. Expressions with publicity

Match the halves:

1. The two film stars were married
2. They've received a lot of bad publicity
3. The broadcast of the programme was timed to
4. There has been a great deal of publicity
5. He's an actor who shuns publicity and

a. for the quality of their products.
b. rarely gives interviews.
c. in a blaze of publicity.
d. generate maximum publicity.
e. surrounding his disappearance.

3. Verb + reputation

Complete the sentences with the correct form of the above verbs:

1. After the scandal, the minister is making great efforts to . . . . his reputation.
2. Stevenson College . . . . an international reputation as a centre of learning.
3. During his time at university, he . . . . a reputation as a brilliant speaker.
4. The weather in Britain is . . . . up to its reputation. Rain every day!
5. The report in today's paper of his relationship with a married woman 10 years ago is enough for the Minister to . . . . his reputation for being a man of absolute integrity.
6. The school's good reputation has been . . . . by your appalling behaviour on the trip.

Notes

1. Note that you can use either 'advert' or 'advertisement'.
2. Note the following:
   The British have a reputation for being reserved.
   Over the years, the company has gradually built up a world-wide reputation for quality and reliability.
3. Note these expressions:
   After the story of the affair appeared in the newspapers, his reputation was in ruins / in tatters.
   The Prime Minister has emerged from the scandal with his reputation intact. (undamaged)

Section 22

Technology

machine   174

equipment   175

computer and internet   176

fault   177

repair   178

"Sorry, no time to talk – too busy chatting!"

machine

Verb + machine	Machine + verb	Types of machine
invent a machine	machines break down	an answering machine
install a machine	machines perform (tasks)	a cash machine
switch a machine on / off	machines run on (petrol)	a ticket machine
operate a machine	machines work	a vending machine
dismantle a machine		a washing machine
repair / fix a machine		

1. Verb + machine

Complete these sentences with the correct form of the above verbs:

1. Buy your dishwasher from us and we'll deliver and . . . . your machine free of charge.
2. The machine is fairly simple to . . . . Let me show you how it works.
3. The personal computer is without doubt the most useful machine to be . . . . in my lifetime.
4. The green button starts the machine. The red one is for . . . . the machine off.
5. I paid a lot of money to get this sewing machine . . . . and it still doesn't work!
6. Never . . . . a faulty machine without disconnecting it from the electricity supply. Always make sure it's unplugged before you attempt to take it to pieces.

2. Machine + verb

Complete these sentences with the correct form of the above verbs:

1. Modern machines are capable of . . . . many of the routine tasks that people used to do. For example, robots have almost replaced workers in the car industry.
2. Our washing machine . . . . down yesterday and flooded the kitchen.
3. Can you help me? I can't seem to get this machine to . . . .
4. The machine . . . . on solar power, but it can be powered by batteries in cloudy weather.

3. Types of machine

Match the halves:

1. Is it OK to put this woollen jersey into
2. There's a couple of messages on
3. I tried to get a cup of coffee out of
4. You can withdraw money from
5. I need some coins for

a. the answering machine for you.
b. the washing machine?
c. most cash machines with this card.
d. the ticket machine in the car park.
e. the vending machine, but it's not working.

Notes

1. Note the verbs we use to describe what a machine does:
   We use a special machine to monitor the patient's breathing.
   This machine measures your heart rate and this one calculates the amount of energy you are using.
   The machine is designed to detect very small movements of the earth's surface.
2. 'Out of order' means not working:
   The coffee machine in the staff canteen is out of order again, but the one in the student refectory is working.

equipment

Verb + equipment	Adjective + equipment
invest in equipment	faulty equipment
install equipment	fragile equipment
test equipment	proper equipment
use equipment	the latest equipment
handle equipment	sensitive equipment
hire out equipment	special equipment

1. Verb + equipment

Complete the sentences with the correct form of the verbs above:

1. A qualified instructor will show you how to . . . . the equipment in the gym.
2. All our equipment is . . . . regularly to make sure it's in good working order.
3. This high-tech equipment needs to be . . . . very carefully. Don't drop it!
4. I run a company that . . . . out office equipment to new businesses.
5. The company has . . . . millions of pounds in new computer equipment.
6. We've . . . . some new security equipment in our factory in an attempt to reduce theft.

2. Adjective + equipment

Complete the sentences with the above adjectives:

1. They didn't even have a rope with them! It's absolutely crazy to go mountain climbing without the . . . . equipment.
2. . . . . navigation equipment caused the ship to sail 100 miles off course.
3. Firefighters had to use . . . . equipment to cut the driver free from the car.
4. Be careful with this equipment. It's . . . . , and easily damaged if mishandled.
5. He spends an absolute fortune on golf. He always has the . . . . equipment.
6. The patient's brain waves are recorded on this . . . . piece of equipment which gives extremely accurate readings of brain activity.

3. Other words for equipment

In these sentences 'equipment' is not possible. Complete them with:

apparatus   appliances   devices   stuff   instruments   tools

1. I always keep a set of . . . . in the back of my car in case I break down.
2. The shop sells musical . . . . , sheet music, tapes and CDs.
3. Don't forget to bring your football . . . . There's a game after the meeting.
4. It's a good idea to switch off all electrical . . . . when you are not using them.
5. I hate using the climbing . . . . in the school gym. I keep falling off!
6. Labour-saving . . . . like dishwashers and microwaves have made life easier for people today.

Note   Note these types of equipment:

The store has a good range of sports equipment. There are some cheap tennis rackets on offer.
The rebel army was quickly defeated by the modern military equipment that government troops had available to them.
With this system you don't have to spend money on expensive new computer equipment every year.

computer and internet

Verb + computer	Computer + noun	Verb + internet
be on a computer	computer dating	connect to the internet
shut down a computer	computer games	surf the internet
hack into a computer	computer program	shop on the internet
a computer performs tasks	computer screen	spread over the internet
a computer crashes	computer software	download from the ...
	computer virus	

1. Verb + computer

Complete the sentences with the correct form of the above verbs:

1. Make sure you . . . . down your computer before you leave the office.
2. A bug in the program caused the computer to . . . . , so I had to restart it.
3. Banks have tight security systems to stop people from . . . . into their computers.
4. How long are you going to . . . . on the computer? I need to send something.
5. The difference between you and a computer is that a computer can multi-task. That is, it can . . . . many different tasks at the same time.

2. Computer + noun

Complete the sentences with the above nouns:

1. Computer . . . . spread from one machine to another through e-mail attachments.
2. Many children today would rather play computer . . . . than play outside.
3. The computer . . . . is installed on your machine. It comes with Windows XP.
4. Computer . . . . is an interesting way of meeting somebody of the opposite sex.
5. An error message flashed up on my computer . . . .
6. I've done a number of courses and I can now write simple computer . . . .

3. Verb + internet

Complete the sentences with the correct form of the above verbs:

1. It's very easy to . . . . on the internet if you have a credit card.
2. Most viruses are . . . . over the internet, so make sure you install anti-virus software on your PC to check the files that you . . . .
3. Parents should place limits on the time their children spend . . . . the net.
4. Just click on the Explorer icon and you'll be . . . . to the internet.

Notes

1. Note these expressions:
   The information is stored on computer.
   Documents are scanned into a computer and then sent by e-mail.
   My job is to key written texts into the computer.

2. Note the following verb collocations:
   Students should be encouraged to use the internet as a resource.
   It's impossible to police the internet.

3. Note these expressions:
   Our children have restricted / limited access to the internet at home.
   With broadband we have unlimited access to the internet. We are connected 24 hrs a day.
   The information is freely available on the internet.

Key Words for Fluency – Intermediate

fault

Verb + fault	Adjective + fault
develop a fault	a common fault
discover a fault	an electrical fault
repair a fault	a design fault
report a fault	a minor fault
check for faults	a serious fault
	a technical fault

1. Verb + fault

Complete the sentences with the correct form of the above verbs:

1. We had to call out an engineer to . . . . a fault in our alarm system.
2. The fault in the plane's landing gear was . . . . during a routine check.
3. If any of your appliances fail to work, you should . . . . the fault directly to the hire company.
4. If this product . . . . a fault, please return it to the shop where you bought it.
5. We have quality control staff who . . . . for any faults in our products before they are sent out to shops.

2. Adjective + fault

Complete the sentences below with the above adjectives:

1. The plane's been grounded due to a . . . . fault.
2. Overheating is a . . . . fault with this make of car. The fault was rectified in later models.
3. The fire was caused by an . . . . fault. It was traced to a short circuit in the dishwasher.
4. It was only a . . . . fault. A mechanic took 5 minutes to fix it and we were on our way again.
5. I had to take my new car back to the garage because it had a . . . . fault in its braking system, making it dangerous to drive in wet conditions. The problem appears to be a . . . . fault.

Notes

1. Note these expressions:
   A mechanic tested the engine and could find no fault with it.
   It sounds as if there's a fault in the ignition system.

2. Note that 'fault' and 'defect' are both possible in this sentence:
   All aircraft have been grounded, after a fault / defect was discovered in the fuel system.
   Only 'defect' is possible in the following sentences:
   I got these shoes quite cheaply because there are slight defects in them.
   The drug is known to cause birth defects.
   She's suffered from a speech defect all her life.

3. Note that we use 'faults' to describe weaknesses of character:
   I love him dearly in spite of all his faults.
   I know I've got many faults, but telling lies isn't one of them.

4. Note that fault also means being responsible for something:
   It's all / partly my fault – I forgot to tell him about the meeting.
   It's not my fault that we're late. I was ready on time.
   If you failed the exam, it's your own fault. You should have studied harder.

repair

Verb + repair	Adj + repair	Noun + of + repair	Common expressions
need repairs	essential repairs	the cost of repairs	be under repair
carry out repairs	major repairs	in need of repair	be in for repairs
undergo repairs	minor repairs	£400 worth of ...	keep in good repair
complete repairs	simple repairs	a programme of ...	damaged beyond ...
repairs cost money			

1. Verb + repair

Complete the sentences with the correct form of the above verbs:

1. The ferry will be out of service for several weeks while it . . . . repairs.
2. We were horrified to discover how much the repairs to our roof would . . . .
3. Our church urgently . . . . repairs, but we've no funds to carry out the work.
4. Repairs are being . . . . out on the motorway so expect delays in both directions. These repairs are expected to be . . . . by the end of the month.

2. Adjective + repair

Complete the sentences with the above adjectives:

1. The old house needs . . . . repairs. It needs a lot of work done to it – a new roof, new central heating, re-wiring – everything!
2. The car was OK. It only needed . . . . repairs, which cost very little.
3. The swimming pool is closed for 3 days for . . . . repairs and maintenance.
4. We should all be able to carry out . . . . repairs around the house. I find it hard to believe that some people don't even know how to change a light bulb!

3. Noun + of + repair

Complete the sentences below with the above nouns:

1. About £200 . . . . of repairs need to be done to get my car back on the road.
2. Parts of the building are dangerous and are in urgent . . . . of repair.
3. The council is carrying out an extensive . . . . of repairs on all its schools.
4. The other driver agreed to pay the full . . . . of repairs to my car.

4. Common expressions

Match the halves:

1. We're in temporary accommodation because our offices are
2. I'm using the bus because my car is in the garage
3. It is the responsibility of the landlord to keep the house
4. The car will need to be scrapped. It is damaged

a. in good repair.
b. beyond repair.
c. under repair.
d. for repairs.

Note   Note that 'maintenance' means to keep something in good condition:
This course is designed to give drivers a grounding (basic ability) in car maintenance and repairs.
The landlord, and not the tenant, is responsible for the maintenance and upkeep of the property.
I like old houses, but they need a lot of maintenance and I don't have the time to do it.
In order to save money, the council has had to cut back on road maintenance.

Answer Key

answer key

Section 1: A place to live

world 10

Ex 1:   1. see 2. change 3. destroying 4. taken
Ex 2:   1. whole 2. safer 3. changing 4. ideal 5. outside
Ex 3:   1. authority 2. record 3. affairs 4. peace

country 11

Ex 1:   1. fled 2. paralysed 3. enter 4. running 5. represent
Ex 2:   1. wealthy 2. foreign 3. free 4. neighbouring 5. underdeveloped
Ex 3:   1-e 2-d 3-a 4-c 5-b

home 12

Ex 1:   1. left 2. head 3. get 4. own 5. call 6. return
Ex 2:   1. cooking 2. address 3. delivery 4. town
Ex 3:   1. sent 2. saw 3. take 4. welcome
Ex 4:   1-d 2-c 3-a 4-b

building 13

Ex 1:   1. construct 2. restored 3. evacuated 4. convert 5. demolished
Ex 2:   1. empty 2. high-rise 3. public 4. derelict 5. main 6. fine
Ex 3:   1. Damage 2. floor 3. entry 4. tenants 5. appearance

accommodation and rent 14

Ex 1:   1. find 2. guaranteed 3. provide 4. lives
Ex 2:   1. temporary 2. self-catering 3. furnished 4. free
Ex 3:   1. pay 2. put 3. withholding 4. afford 5. owe

Section 2: The environment

environment 16

Ex 1:   1. pollute 2. harm 3. respect 4. protect
Ex 2:   1. pleasant 2. stress-free 3. hostile 4. male 5. safe
Ex 3:   1. effect 2. threat 3. harmony 4. destruction 5. damage

pollution, fumes, waste and rubbish 17

Ex 1:   1. reduce 2. risen 3. destroying 4. threatening
Ex 2:   1. pouring 2. inhaling 3. overcome
Ex 3:   1. recycle 2. dumping 3. creates 4. dispose
Ex 4:   1. collected 2. clearing 3. pick 4. recycle

earthquake and flood 18

Ex 1:   1. withstand 2. hit 3. predicting 4. devastated 5. shook 6. survived 7. set
Ex 2:   1. cut 2. hit 3. swept 4. caused

storm 19

Ex 1:   1. struck 2. broke 3. raged, died 4. destroyed 5. in 6. through
Ex 2:   1-d 2-a 3-e 4-c 5-b

answer key

damage 20
Ex 1:   1. prevent 2. caused 3. suffered 4. insured 5. repair
Ex 2:   1-LOT 2-LOT 3-LIT 4-LIT 5-LOT 6-LIT 7-LOT
Ex 3:   1. worth 2. extent 3. cost 4. signs 5. risk

Section 3: The natural world

weather. 22
Ex 1:   1. dressed 2. holds 3. turned 4. changing 5. sets
Ex 2:   1. hot 2. cold 3. wet 4. dry 5. glorious 6. unpredictable
Ex 3:   1-b 2-d 3-a 4-c

temperature and heat 23
Ex 1:   1. drop / fall 2. rise / increase 3. took 4. reach 5. control
Ex 2:   1. Freezing 2. constant / even 3. high 4. average
Ex 3:   1. feel 2. generate 3. lose 4. escape 5. withstand

air 24
Ex 1:   1. need 2. gasping 3. breathe 4. put 5. pollute
Ex 2:   1. fresh 2. polluted 3. thin 4. stale 5. still 6. cold
Ex 3:   1-d 2-a 3-b 4-c

light 25
Ex 1:   1. block 2. get 3. needs 4. let 5. fading
Ex 2:   1. bright 2. artificial 3. softer 4. poor 5. fading
Ex 3:   1. source 2. glimmer 3. flash
Ex 4:   1-b 2-c 3-a

fire 26
Ex 1:   1. caught 2. caused 3. fought, put 4. light 5. started
Ex 2:   1. destroyed 2. broke 3. spread 4. burning 5. go
Ex 3:   1. risk 2. alarm 3. escape 4. extinguisher 5. drills

water 27
Ex 1:   1. drink 2. boil 3. spilled or spilt 4. poured 5. dripping 6. flows
Ex 2:   1. drinking 2. boiling 3. fresh 4. mineral
Ex 3:   1. on 2. through 3. with 4. with 5. into 6. with
Ex 4:   1-c 2-a 3-b

noise and silence. 28
Ex 1:   1. making 2. shut 3. stand 4. sleep
Ex 2:   1. funny 2. deafening 3. background 4. squeaking 5. awful 6. piercing
Ex 3:   1. long 2. awkward 3. stunned 4. complete

Section 4: Work

job 30
Ex 1:   1. lose 2. looking 3. applied 4. hold 5. got
Ex 2:   1. responsible 2. stressful 3. rewarding 4. boring 5. challenging
Ex 3:   1. perks 2. qualifications 3. pressures

answer key

career 31
Ex 1: 1. wrecked 2. began 3. further 4. choosing 5. pursue
Ex 2: 1. worthwhile 2. brilliant 3. promising
Ex 3: 1-e 2-b 3-d 4-a 5-c

staff and duty 32
Ex 1: 1. lay off 2. trained 3. employs 4. recruiting
Ex 2: 1. vacancies 2. dedication 3. turnover 4. member
Ex 3: 1. report 2. carries 3. suspended 4. include 5. failing

qualification and interview 33
Ex 1: 1. leads 2. getting / obtaining 3. have 4. Studying
Ex 2: 1. academic 2. recognised 3. further
Ex 3: 1. had 2. invited 3. prepare 4. held 5. dreading
Ex 4: 1-c 2-a 3-b

skill 34
Ex 1: 1. test 2. learn 3. update 4. handed down 5. equip
Ex 2: 1. basic 2. practical 3. communication 4. computer 5. social
Ex 3: 1. test 2. degree 3. use

training 35
Ex 1: 1. provide 2. requires 3. receive 4. completed
Ex 2: 1. basic 2. proper 3. formal 4. regular 5. intensive

wages, salary and pay 36
Ex 1: 1. earns 2. go 3. live / survive 4. deducted 5. demanding
Ex 2: 1. wage 2. salary 3. wage 4. salary 5. salary 6. wage
Ex 3: 1-c 2-d 3-b 4-e 5-f 6-a

Section 5: Travel

trip 38
Ex 1: 1. go 2. afford 3. cancelled 4. made 5. ruined 6. planning
Ex 2: 1. long 2. free 3. good 4. round 5. abroad / overseas
Ex 3: 1. highlight 2. cost 3. souvenir 4. length

holiday 39
Ex 1: 1. spend 2. ruined 3. takes 4. enjoy 5. book 6. cancel
Ex 2: 1. paid 2. relaxing 3. dream 4. public 5 package
Ex 3: 1-d 2-b 3-a 4-c

flight 40
Ex 1: 1. catch 2. called 3. gets 4. delayed 5. miss 6. cancelled, diverted
Ex 2: 1. long-haul 2. direct, connecting 3. short 4. scheduled 5. bumpy, smooth
Ex 3: 1. call 2. duration 3. arrival 4. standby 5. cancellation

delay and destination 41
Ex 1: 1. expected 2. face 3. apologise 4. caused 5. avoid
Ex 2: 1. reason 2. apologies 3. series 4. liability
Ex 3: 1. popular 2. intended 3. top 4. new 5. exotic

Key Words for Fluency – Intermediate

answer key

passenger 42

Ex 1: 1. proceed 2. board 3. travelling 4. killed 5. stranded
Ex 2: 1. angry 2. nervous 3. Terrified 4. business class 5. drunken
Ex 3: 1-c 2-d 3-b 4-a

passport and visa 43

Ex 1: 1. expires, renew 2. show 3. stolen 4. surrender 5. stamped
Ex 2: 1. valid 2. new 3. forged
Ex 3: 1-e 2-c 3-a 4-f 5-b 6-d

luggage and fare 44

Ex 1: 1. weigh 2. lost 3. screen 4. insure 5. pack 6. searched
Ex 2: 1. full 2. return 3. flat 4. half-fare 5. exact
Ex 3: 1-b 2-c 3-e 4-a 5-d

Section 6: Traffic

traffic 46

Ex 1: 1. diverted 2. held 3. directing 4. reducing 5. builds, thin
Ex 2: 1. build-up 2. break 3. volume 4. queue 5. noise
Ex 3: 1-c 2-d 3-a 4-b

street 47

Ex 1: 1. wander 2. patrol 3. cross 4. paraded 5. Go 6. clean
Ex 2: 1. one-way 2. deserted 3. High 4. crowded 5. side
Ex 3: 1-b 2-c 3-a 4-e 5-d

route and map 48

Ex 1: 1. plan 2. marked 3. take 4. lined
Ex 2: 1. scenic 2. roundabout 3. alternative 4. escape 5. popular 6. direct
Ex 3: 1. read 2. showing 3. drew 4. bring 5. studied

accident 49

Ex 1: 1. avoided 2. reduced 3. witnessed 4. had 5. happened 6. caused
Ex 2: 1-c 2-b 3-e 4-a 5-d
Ex 3: 1. cause 2. event 3. series 4. scene

injury 50

Ex 1: 1. suffered 2. prevent 3. treated 4. escape 5. caused 6. recovered
Ex 2: 1. series 2. reports 3. risk 4. pain 5. extent
Ex 3: 1-d 2-a 3-b 4-e 5-c
serious injury = appalling, horrendous, life-threatening, crippling, horrific
not serious = minor

Section 7: Education

education 52

Ex 1: 1. gave 2. get 3. returning 4. pay 5. invest
Ex 2: 1. nursery 2. private 3. higher 4. religious 5. sex 6. good 7. secondary
Ex 3: 1. standard 2. right 3. aim 4. Access

answer key

course 53

Ex 1:   1. runs 2. do 3. complete 4. deals 5. drop 6. consists
Ex 2:   1. demanding 2. crash 3. vocational 4. on-line 5. introductory
Ex 3:   1. requirements 2. place 3. guide 4. completion

lesson 54

Ex 1:   1. giving 2. prepares 3. skipping 4. starts 5. having 6. catch
Ex 2:   1. with 2. in 3. about 4. during
Ex 3:   1. lessons 2. classes 3. lessons 4. class
We use 'class' for the group of people who are taught together.
Ex 4:   1-d 2-a 3-b 4-c

practice and homework 55

Ex 1:   1. had 2. gives 3. need 4. improve 5. comes 6. learned
Ex 2:   1-c 2-d 3-a 4-b
Ex 3:   1. done 2. hand 3. get 4. gave 5. help 6. corrected

exam and mark 56

Ex 1:   1. revising 2. sit 3. passed 4. scrape 5. marked
Ex 2:   1-d 2-c 3-a 4-b
Ex 3:   1. get 2. deducted 3. gave 4. lost
Ex 4:   1. good 2. full 3. top 4. final 5. low

Section 8: Sport and fitness

sport 58

Ex 1:   1. play 2. hated 3. take 4. watching
Ex 2:   1. popular 2. contact 3. dangerous 4. indoor 5. spectator 6. team
Ex 3:   1. events 2. centre 3. equipment 4. coverage 5. facilities

team 59

Ex 1:   1. played 2. made 3. dropped 4. support 5. take 6. lost 7. celebrated
Ex 2:   1. strong 2. defeated 3. matched 4. winning
Ex 3:   1. captain 2. spirit 3. sports 4. mates 5. effort

game 60

Ex 1:   1. play 2. lose 3. making 4. miss 5. abandon
Ex 2:   1. quick 2. physical 3. clean 4. tiring
Ex 3:   1. object 2. coverage 3. rules 4. result 5. preparation
Ex 4:   1. team 2. Board 3. party 4. card 5. computer

race, competition and match 61

Ex 1:   1. won 2. withdraw 3. take 4. finish 5. watch 6. disqualified
Ex 2:   1. Enter 2. knocked 3. holding / running
Ex 3:   1. competition 2. match 3. competitions 4. races 5. match 6. race

victory 62

Ex 1:   1. celebrated 2. robbed 3. led 4. swept
Ex 2:   1-f 2-e 3-d 4-c 5-a 6-b

Key Words for Fluency – Intermediate

answer key

defeat 63
Ex 1: 1. accepted 2. avenge 3. suffered 4. avoided
Ex 2: 1. heavy 2. shock 3. narrow 4. humiliating
Ex 3: 1. revenge 2. possibility 3. jaws 4. string 5. disappointment

prize 64
Ex 1: 1. win 2. accepting 3. shared 4. present 5. claim 6. awarded
Ex 2: 1. first 2. major / top 3. booby 4. fabulous 5. consolation 6. Nobel
Ex 3: 1. winners 2. draw 3. money

strength 65
Ex 1: 1. using 2. underestimate 3. build 4. saving 5. gather / recover
Ex 2: 1. superior 2. full 3. superhuman 4. physical, inner
Ex 3: 1. lack 2. feats 3. reserves

energy and exercise 66
Ex 1: 1. have 2. use 3. sapped 4. saving 5. give 6. running
Ex 2: 1. source 2. deal 3. burst
Ex 3: 1. strenuous 2. warm-up 3. regular 4. light
Ex 4: 1-b 2-c 3-a

Section 9: Health

health 68
Ex 1: 1. deteriorated 2. look 3. nursed 4. improved 5. causing
Ex 2: 1-d 2-c 3-b 4-e 5-a
Ex 3: 1. bad 2. harmful 3. essential 4. wonders

illness 69
Ex 1: 1. suffer 2. causing 3. treated 4. recovered 5. had 6. diagnosing
Ex 2: 1-b 2-c 3-d 4-a
Ex 3: 1. recovery 2. cause 3. symptoms 4. recurrence 5. extent

disease and infection 70
Ex 1: 1. prevent 2. suffers 3. contract / get 4. eradicated
Ex 2: 1. fatal 2. infectious 3. rare 4. incurable
Ex 3: 1-c 2-e 3-d 4-a 5-b
Ex 4: 1. suffering 2. prevent 3. clear 4. spread

stress 71
Ex 1: 1. relieve 2. suffering 3. copes 4. thrive 5. place
Ex 2: 1. moments 2. source 3. effects 4. sign 5. levels

smoking and drugs (illegal) 72
Ex 1: 1. up 2. down 3. from 4. of 5. up
Ex 2: 1. taken / used 2. legalised 3. came 4. supplied 5. seized 6. smuggling
Ex 3: 1. addicts 2. dealer 3. overdose 4. abuse 5. habit 6. trafficking

pain 73
Ex 1: 1. causing 2. bear 3. gets 4. passed 5. complaining
Ex 2: 1. throbbing 2. sudden 3. burning 4. unbearable 5. constant 6. dull
Ex 3: 1-c 2-e 3-d 4-b 5-a

answer key

appointment, symptom and test 74
Ex 1:   1. make 2. get 3. missed 4. cancel 5. wait 6. have 7. keep
Ex 2:   1. go 2. treats 3. include 4. persist 5. show
Ex 3:   1. repeat 2. take 3. do 4. have to have

treatment and cure 75
Ex 1:   1. given 2. responding 3. undergoing 4. needed 5. begin
Ex 2:   1. new 2. effective 3. various 4. urgent 5. free
Ex 3:   1. known 2. complete 3. instant

operation and drug 76
Ex 1:   1. performing 2. had 3. need 4. surviving 5. go 6. gone
Ex 2:   1. take 2. prescribe 3. injected 4. withdrawn 5. approved 6. tested
Ex 3:   1. Powerful 2. fast-acting 3. safe 4. wonder

Section 10: Money

money and cash 78
Ex 1:   1. raise 2. paid 3. refund 4. lend, borrow 5. inherit 6. run 7. earn 8. save
Ex 2:   1. spending 2. extra 3. pocket 4. missing
Ex 3:   1. accept / take 2. have 3. carry 4. pay

savings, fortune and debt 79
Ex 1:   1. spent 2. fall 3. cheating 4. build 5. put
Ex 2:   1. cost 2. came 3. lost 4. save 5. made 6. spends
Ex 3:   1. pay 2. get 3. run 4. Faced 5. write

price 80
Ex 1:   1. risen 2. includes 3. haggle 4. agree 5. afford
Ex 2:   1-I 2-D 3-D 4-I 5-D 6-I
Ex 3:   1. half 2. full 3. competitive 4. fixed 5. extortionate

fee and charge 81
Ex 1:   1. pay 2. charge 3. waived 4. increasing / raising
Ex 2:   1. nominal 2. flat 3. normal 4. reasonable 5. highest 6. record 7. additional
Ex 3:   1-b 2-a 3-d 4-c

expense 82
Ex 1:   1. save 2. was 3. spared 4. go 5. justify
Ex 2:   1. medical 2. extra 3. living 4. operating 5. travelling
Ex 3:   1-c 2-a 3-b

Section 11: Food

food 84
Ex 1:   1. waste 2. eats 3. preparing 4. been 5. pick 6. serves
Ex 2:   1. delicious 2. fresh 3. raw 4. disgusting 5. frozen 6. hot / spicy
Ex 3:   1. portions 2. variety 3. shortage 4. consumption

Key Words for Fluency – Intermediate

answer key

drink 85

Ex 1:   1. order 2. spill 3. offer 4. had 5. sipped
Ex 2:   1. farewell 2. quick 3. celebratory 4. free 5. stiff 6. relaxing
Ex 3:   1. hot 2. refreshing 3. soft 4. long

meal and dish 86

Ex 1:   1. had 2. serves 3. made 4. going 5. order 6. miss / skip
Ex 2:   1. proper 2. delicious 3. main 4. ready 5. hot 6. light, heavy
Ex 3:   1. vegetarian 2. expensive 3. rice 4. local 5. national

diet and appetite 87

Ex 1:   1. healthy 2. balanced 3. poor 4. low-fat
Ex 2:   1. go 2. cut 3. follow, stick / keep 4. watch
Ex 3:   1-b 2-a 3-d 4-e 5-c

party 88

Ex 1:   1. invited 2. go 3. planning 4. arrive 5. came 6. threw
Ex 2:   1. surprise 2. fantastic 3. all-night 4. noisy
Ex 3:   1-e 2-a 3-b 4-c 5d

Section 12: Fun and entertainment

fun and entertainment 90

Ex 1:   1. spoil 2. had 3. join 4. get 5. miss
Ex 2:   1-e 2-g 3-d 4-b 5-c 6-a 7-f
Ex 3:   1. in-flight 2. family 3. free 4. popular 5. live

joke 91

Ex 1:   1. heard 2. get 3. laughs 4. telling
Ex 2:   1. hilarious 2. corny 3. dirty 4. private
Ex 3:   1. play 2. gone 3. take
Ex 4:   1-b 2-a 3-d 4-c

television and programme 92

Ex 1:   1. watches 2. turn 3. shown 4. switch
Ex 2:   1. series 2. coverage 3. presenters 4. licence
Ex 3:   1. interrupting 2. record 3. attract 4. shown
Ex 4:   1. favourite 2. live 3. violent 4. following

concert 93

Ex 1:   1. cancel 2. attended 3. give 4. perform 5. putting
Ex 2:   1. brilliant 2. farewell 3. open-air 4. live 5. badly organised
Ex 3:   1. ticket 2. broadcast 3. proceeds 4. venue

fan and audience 94

Ex 1:   1. thank 2. disappoint 3. besieged 4. packed
Ex 2:   1. big 2. rival 3. devoted
Ex 3:   1. clapped 2. attract 3. thrilled 4. played
Ex 4:   1. delighted 2. live 3. target 4. captive 5. family 6. invited

answer key

film 95
Ex 1:   1. see 2. shot 3. watch 4. showing 5. banned 6. appearing / starring 7. released
Ex 2:   1. award-winning 2. an action-packed 3. good 4. low-budget
Ex 3:   1. parts 2. enjoyment 3. screening 4. Reviews

music and song 96
Ex 1:   1. Listening 2. composed / written 3. appeals 4. performs
Ex 2:   1. deafening 2. background 3. live 4. folk 5. classical
Ex 3:   1. beat 2. piece 3. gift 4. taste
Ex 4:   1-e 2-c 3-d 4-a 5-b

Section 13: People

life 98
Ex 1:   1. save 2. prolong 3. took 4. risk 5. lost
Ex 2:   1-b 2-d 3-e 4-c 5-a
Ex 3:   1. rest 2. loss 3. quality 4. pace 5. aspect 6. lease

death 99
Ex 1:   1. hear 2. escaped 3. get 4. causes 5. mourned
Ex 2:   1-f 2-d 3-e 4-b 5-a 6-c
Ex 3:   1. sudden 2. early 3. certain 4. horrible 5. violent
Ex 4:   1. point 2. cause 3. event

age 100
Ex 1:   1. get 2. look 3. feel 4. lying 5. guess
Ex 2:   1. early 2. old 3. impressionable 4. average 5. mental
Ex 3:   1. at 2. over 3. for 4. from 5. of
Ex 4:   1-c 2-a 3-b

character. 101
Ex 1:   1. transformed 2. blacken 3. reveals
Ex 2:   1. judge 2. strength 3. flaw 4. stain 5. defamation
Ex 3:   1-b 2-a 3-d 4-c

clothes and fashion 102
Ex 1:   1. wear 2. pack 3. makes 4. taking 5. fit 6. put
Ex 2:   1. loose 2. warm 3. clean 4. casual
Ex 3:   1. up 2. in 3. out, into

appearance 103
Ex 1:   1. improve 2. worrying 3. neglect 4. judge 5. changing
Ex 2:   1. untidy 2. youthful 3. deceptive 4. outward 5. physical
Ex 3:   1. similar 2. self-conscious 3. despite 4. pride 5. change

habit and routine 104
Ex 1:   1-E 2-D 3-E 4-E 5-D 6-E
Ex 2:   1. good 2. annoying 3. disgusting 4. anti-social
Ex 3:   1. have 2. upset 3. changing 4. get 5. stick
Ex 4:   1-c 2-a 3-b

Key Words for Fluency – Intermediate

answer key

Section 14: Relationships

friend 106

Ex 1: 1. meeting 2. remain 3. became 4. visiting 5. bring 6. make 7. with 8. of 9. on 10. out
Ex 2: 1. good 2. best 3. old 4. close 5. work 6. mutual
Ex 3: 1-c 2-a 3-b

enemy 107

Ex 1: 1. have 2. made 3. face
Ex 2: 1-e 2-a 3-b 4-c 5-d
Ex 3: 1. attack 2. defeated 3. kill 4. retreat

marriage 108

Ex 1: 1. save 2. broke 3. rush 4. disapprove 5. believe
Ex 2: 1. previous 2. happy 3. arranged 4. perfect
Ex 3: 1. by 2. before 3. by 4. at
Ex 4: 1. break-up 2. basis 3. announcement 4. years 5. offers

divorce 109

Ex 1: 1. get 2. go 3. ends 4. granted 5. wants 6. came
Ex 2: 1-c 2-a 3-b 4-d

love 110

Ex 1: 1. fell 2. feels 3. need 4. declared 5. sends 6. grown
Ex 2: 1. affair 2. song 3. letters 4. life 5. child
Ex 3: 1-e 2-a 3-c 4-f 5-b 6-d

respect 111

Ex 1: 1. have 2. lose 3. treated 4. show 5. gained
Ex 2: 1-d 2-a 3-c 4-b

family 112

Ex 1: 1. have 2. come 3. bringing 4. start 5. support
Ex 2: 1. close 2. immediate 3. respectable 4. extended 5. whole 6. single-parent
Ex 3: 1. friend 2. member 3. opposition 4. addition 5. interests 6. baby, brains

Section 15: The body and the senses

head 114

Ex 1: 1. nodded 2. shook 3. banged / hit 4. aching 5. turned 6. hung
Ex 2: 1. clear 2. big 3. bald 4. level
Ex 3: 1-b 2-a 3-d 4-c

hand 115

Ex 1: 1. shook 2. Raise / Put up 3. wash 4. held 5. tied 6. waved 7. joined
Ex 2: 1-c 2-a 3-b 4-f 5-d 6-e
Ex 3: 1. with 2. by 3. on 4. off 5. over

answer key

heart 116
Ex 1:   1. beating 2. broke 3. sank 4. leapt 5. transplanted
Ex 2:   1. kind 2. heavy 3. broken 4. cold
Ex 3:   1. from 2. with 3. by 4. from, of 5. of 6. of

eye 117
Ex 1:   1. strain 2. protect 3. watering 4. keep 5. take 6. have 7. making
Ex 2:   1-d 2-a 3-b 4-c
Ex 3:   1. with 2. to 3. into 4. under 5. in

sight 118
Ex 1:   1. disappeared 2. came 3. let 4. hidden 5. keeping
Ex 2:   1. welcome 2. terrifying 3. beautiful 4. pathetic 5. pretty 6. common, rare
Ex 3:   1. by sight 2. in sight 3. out of sight 4. on sight 5. at first sight 6. within sight

view 119
Ex 1:   1. blocking 2. get 3. came into 4. admired 5. spoil 6. hidden
Ex 2:   1. poor 2. panoramic 3. clear 4. full 5. sea 6. bird's eye

smell 120
Ex 1:   1. have 2. get 3. fills 4. love 5. getting 6. detect
Ex 2:   1-d 2-e 3-h 4-a 5-b 6-g 7-c 8-f

taste 121
Ex 1:   1. leaves 2. spoil 3. improve 4. lose 5. take
Ex 2:   1. bitter 2. metallic 3. fresh 4. authentic 5. strange 6. strong
Ex 3:   1-b 2-c 3-d 4-a

voice 122
Ex 1:   1. raise 2. recognise 3. shook 4. hear 5. lose 6. lower
Ex 2:   1. deep 2. soft, loudest 3. whining 4. muffled
Ex 3:   1-d 2-c 3-a 4-b

breath 123
Ex 1:   1. hold 2. catch 3. take 4. smelled / smelt 5. struggling
Ex 2:   1. on 2. under 3. in 4. out
Ex 3:   1-d 2-a 3-e 4-b 5-c

sleep and dream 124
Ex 1:   1. get 2. catch 3. disturbed 4. sends 5. get 6. goes 7. get
Ex 2:   1. deep 2. good night's 3. light 4. broken
Ex 3:   1. had 2. appear 3. woke
Ex 4:   1. bad 2. vivid 3. sweet 4. recurring

Section 16: Feeling and mood

feeling 126
Ex 1:   1. hurt 2. show 3. hide 4. suppress 5. control
Ex 2:   1. true 2. mixed 3. sinking 4. bad 5. mutual
Ex 3:   1. guilt 2. well-being 3. apprehension 4. dissatisfaction 5. loneliness

answer key

mood 127
Ex 1:   1. changed 2. lighten / lift 3. affect 4. depends
Ex 2:   1. confident 2. bad 3. defiant 4. lazy 5. festive 6. good
Ex 3:   1-d 2-c 3-e 4-a 5-b

happiness and pleasure 128
Ex 1:   1. found 2. wish 3. brings
Ex 2:   1. key 2. pursuit 3. guarantee
Ex 3:   1. get 2. give 3. combine 4. is 5. read
Ex 4:   1. simple 2. few 3. unexpected 4. endless 5. great

anger. 129
Ex 1:   1. express 2. control 3. aroused 4. subside 5. feel
Ex 2:   1. moment 2. surge 3. outburst
Ex 3:   1-b 2-c 3-d 4-a

fear and anxiety. 130
Ex 1:   1. confront 2. Showing 3. have 4. live 5. overcome
Ex 2:   1. irrational 2. constant 3. sudden 4. worst 5. deep
Ex 3:   1. hide 2. caused 3. reduce 4. increased
Ex 4:   1-b 2-c 3-a

worry 131
Ex 1:   1. forget 2. causing 3. added to 4. discuss
Ex 2:   1. nagging 2. unnecessary 3. main 4 constant
Ex 3:   1-b 2-c 3-d 4-a

confidence 132
Ex 1:   1. lose 2. gained 3. boost 4. lacks 5. destroyed 6. have
Ex 2:   1. lack 2. blow 3. boost 4. air
Ex 3:   1-b 2-d 3-a 4-c

disappointment and relief 133
Ex 1:   1. expressed 2. avoid 3. hide 4. get 5. was 6. ended
Ex 2:   1. look 2. sense 3. string
Ex 3:   1. felt 2. came 3. sighed

surprise and shock 134
Ex 1:   1. have 2. got 3. expressed 4. took 5. springing
Ex 2:   1. pleasant 2. complete 3. possible
Ex 3:   1. got 2. died 3. wore 4. get 5. came
Ex 4:   1-b 2-c 3-a

Section 17: Society

government and election. 136
Ex 1:   1. elected 2. bring 3. led 4. criticised 5. resign 6. form
Ex 2:   1. hold 2. won 3. boycott 4. stand 5. rigged
Ex 3:   1. issues 2. seats 3. gains 4. turnout 5. candidate

answer key

vote 137
Ex 1:   1. counted 2. have 3. winning 4. casting
Ex 2:   1. casting 2. unanimous 3. popular 4. single
Ex 3:   1. majority 2. thousands 3. result 4. share
Ex 4:   1-c 2-a 3-b

society 138
Ex 1:   1. live 2. dropped 3. destroying 4. create 5. integrate
Ex 2:   1. civilised 2. multicultural 3. affluent 4. open 5. industrial
Ex 3:   1. members 2. role 3. danger 4. cross-section

justice 139
Ex 1:   1. fight 2. escape 3. bring 4. denied 5. uphold 6. demanding
Ex 2:   1. sense 2. miscarriage 3. fight 4. travesty

law 140
Ex 1:   1. enforce 2. breaking 3. obey 4. introducing 5. change
Ex 2:   1. prohibits 2. apply 3. states 4. requires
Ex 3:   1. by 2. above 3. against 4. under 5. within
Ex 4:   1-b 2-a 3-d 4-c

Section 18: Crime and punishment

crime and criminal 142
Ex 1:   1. committed 2. cut 3. fight 4. convicted 5. charged 6. solve
Ex 2:   1. Violent 2. petty, serious 3. terrible
Ex 3:   1. war 2. life 3. scene 4. victim
Ex 4:   1. hardened 2. common 3. Convicted 4. known

offence, offender and victim 143
Ex 1:   1. committed 2. fined 3. convicted 4. makes 5. charged
Ex 2:   1. minor 2. serious 3. first 4. capital
Ex 3:   1. persistent 2. first-time 3. worst 4. sex
Ex 4:   1-c 2-a 3-b

arrest and charge (criminal) 144
Ex 1:   1. made 2. leading 3. escape 4. resisting
Ex 2:   1. house 2. close 3. wrongful
Ex 3:   1. face 2. deny 3. prove 4. pressing
Ex 4:   1. pleaded 2. cleared 3. arrested 4. appear

evidence 145
Ex 1:   1. have 2. give 3. withholding 4. gathering 5. destroy
Ex 2:   1. false 2. overwhelming 3. circumstantial
Ex 3:   1-b 2-c 3-a
Ex 4:   1-b 2-c 3-d 4-a

trial and verdict 146
Ex 1:   1. receive 2. brought 3. stand 4. awaiting 5. guaranteed 6. gone
Ex 2:   1. right 2. conduct 3. costs
Ex 3:   1-c 2-d 3-a 4-b
Ex 4:   1. reached 2. appeal 3. returned

answer key

sentence and fine 147

Ex 1:   1. serving 2. received 3. reduce 4. deferred 5. pass
Ex 2:   1. suspended 2. life 3. light 4. stiffer, lenient
Ex 3:   1. gets 2. carries 3. pay 4. imposed 5. got 6. face

punishment and prison 148

Ex 1:   1. deserves 2. receive 3. escape
Ex 2:   1. capital 2. barbaric 3. harsh, lenient
Ex 3:   1. sent 2. go 3. released 4. escaped
Ex 4:   1. sentence 2. conditions, cells 3. population, service

Section 19: Conflict

war 150

Ex 1:   1. declared 2. prevent 3. won 4. prepares 5. were 6. broke
Ex 2:   1. full-scale 2. civil 3. futile 4. conventional, nuclear
Ex 3:   1-d 2-b 3-c 4-a

peace 151

Ex 1:   1. keep / preserve 2. worked 3. bring 4. live 5. made 6. threaten
Ex 2:   1. talks 2. treaty 3. process 4. campaign
Ex 3:   1. period 2. threat 3. symbol 4. plea 5. commitment 6. hopes

attack 152

Ex 1:   1. come 2. carried 3. protect 4. repel, launch 5. claimed
Ex 2:   1. surprise 2. savage 3. unprovoked 4. devastating
Ex 3:   1. possibility 2. target 3. ferocity
Ex 4:   1-c 2-d 3-b 4-e 5-a

defence 153

Ex 1:   1. strengthening 2. broke 3. overwhelmed 4. came
Ex 2:   1. strong 2. vigorous 3. effective
Ex 3:   1-d 2-c 3-b 4-e 5-a

bomb and explosion 154

Ex 1:   1. planted 2. exploded / gone off 3. dropped 4. detonate 5. threw 6. make
Ex 2:   1-b 2-c 3-a
Ex 3:   1. shook, shattered 2. caused 3. heard
Ex 4:   1. time 2. series 3. force 4. reports

casualty 155

Ex 1:   1. suffered 2. resulting 3. reduce 4. inflicted
Ex 2:   1. civilian 2. road 3. heavy
Ex 3:   1-b 2-c 3-a

weapon and gun 156

Ex 1:   1. supplying 2. banned 3. Lay 4. develop
Ex 2:   1. murder 2. superior 3. offensive 4. hidden 5. lethal
Ex 3:   1. fired 2. carry 3. went 4. loaded
Ex 4:   1. with 2. out 3. to 4. at 5. down

answer key

dispute and strike 157
Ex 1:　1. settled　2. handled　3. involved　4. intervene
Ex 2:　1-b　2-c　3-e　4-a　5-d
Ex 3:　1. avert　2. hold　3. lead　4. break　5. disrupted

campaign and demonstration 158
Ex 1:　1. support　2. conducted　3. launched　4. led
Ex 2:　1. advertising　2. election　3. publicity　4. anti-obesity
Ex 3:　1. held　2. took　3. led　4. break

Section 20: Communication

language 160
Ex 1:　1. speak　2. acquire　3. translated　4. mastered
Ex 2:　1-c　2-a　3-e　4-b　5-d
Ex 3:　1. in　2. for　3. of　4. in

conversation 161
Ex 1:　1. interrupted　2. carry　3. monopolised　4. got　5. overheard
Ex 2:　1. private　2. sensible　3. polite　4. civilised
Ex 3:　1. topic　2. art　3. middle　4. tone　5. lull / break　6. snatches

discussion 162
Ex 1:　1. have　2. take　3. generated　4. widen
Ex 2:　1. heated　2. lengthy　3. full, frank　4. detailed　5. fruitful
Ex 3:　1. item　2. level　3. deal
Ex 4:　1-c　2-d　3-a　4-b

speech. 163
Ex 1:　1. made　2. prepared　3. devoted　4. interrupted　5. avoid
Ex 2:　1-c　2-e　3-g　4-d　5-f　6-a　7-b

secret, rumour and lie 164
Ex 1:　1. keep　2. tell　3. have
Ex 2:　1. dark　2. closely-guarded　3. open　4. best-kept
Ex 3:　1. heard　2. confirmed　3. going　4. started　5. denied
Ex 4:　1. telling　2. believe　3. spreading

Section 21: Information

news 166
Ex 1:　1. tell　2. waited　3. heard　4. celebrate　5. catching　6. made　7. break
Ex 2:　1. bad, good　2. good　3. latest　4. great
Ex 3:　1-e　2-c　3-f　4-d　5-b　6-a

message 167
Ex 1:　1. take　2. sent　3. got　4. give　5. pass　6. leave
Ex 2:　1. good-luck　2. new　3. garbled　4. urgent
Ex 3:　1-b　2-c　3-a　4-d

answer key

document 168
Ex 1:   1. signed 2. deliver 3. e-mail 4. shred 5. checked 6. produce
Ex 2:   1. original 2. enclosed 3. important 4. forged 5. confidential
Ex 3:   1. saving 2. create 3. print 4. send, receive 5. edit 6. scroll

article 169
Ex 1:   1. appeared 2. contains 3. covers 4. Read 5. written 6. published 7. criticises
Ex 2:   1. fascinating 2. informative 3. whole 4. critical
Ex 3:   1. end 2. copies 3. series 4. summary

letter 170
Ex 1:   1. got / received 2. addressed 3. signed 4. post 5. wrote, reply
Ex 2:   1-c 2-d 3-a 4-b
Ex 3:   1. sympathy 2. support 3. complaint, apology 4. resignation 5. application 6. recommendation

mail 171
Ex 1:   1. delivered 2. sorted 3. checked 4. forwarded / redirected 5. open 6. answer
Ex 2:   1. junk 2. hate 3. first-class 4. unopened 5. snail 6. fan
Ex 3:   Correct words are 1. mail is 2. letter 3. mail 4. mail 5. letter 6. letter

advert, publicity and reputation 172
Ex 1:   1. scanned 2. placed 3. responded 4. aimed 5. influence 6. appeared
Ex 2:   1-c 2-a 3-d 4-e 5-b
Ex 3:   1. save 2. has 3. gained 4. living 5. lose 6. ruined

Section 22: Technology

machine 174
Ex 1:   1. install 2. operate 3. invented 4. switching 5. repaired / fixed 6. dismantle
Ex 2:   1. performing 2. broke 3. work 4. runs
Ex 3:   1-b 2-a 3-e 4-c 5-d

equipment 175
Ex 1:   1. use 2. tested 3. handled 4. hires 5. invested 6. installed
Ex 2:   1. proper 2. Faulty 3. special 4. fragile 5. latest 6. sensitive
Ex 3:   1. tools 2. instruments 3. stuff 4. appliances 5. apparatus 6. devices

computer and internet 176
Ex 1:   1. shut 2. crash 3. hacking 4. be   5. perform
Ex 2:   1. viruses 2. games 3. software 4. dating 5. screen 6. programs
Ex 3:   1. shop 2. spread, download 3. surfing 4. connected

fault 177
Ex 1:   1. repair 2. discovered 3. report 4. develops 5. check
Ex 2:   1. technical 2. common 3. electrical 4. minor 5. serious, design

repair 178
Ex 1:   1. undergoes 2. cost 3. needs 4. carried, completed
Ex 2:   1. major 2. minor 3. essential 4. simple
Ex 3:   1. worth 2. need 3. programme 4. cost
Ex 4:   1-c 2-d 3-a 4-b

alphabetical list of words

accident	49	earthquake	18	language	160	salary	36
accommodation	14	education	52	law	140	savings	79
advert	172	election	136	lesson	54	secret	164
age	100	enemy	107	letter	170	sentence	147
air	24	energy	66	lie	164	shock	134
anger	129	entertainment	90	life	98	sight	118
anxiety	130	environment	16	light	25	silence	28
appearance	103	equipment	175	love	110	skill	34
appetite	87	evidence	145	luggage	44	sleep	124
appointment	74	exam	56			smell	120
arrest	144	exercise	66	machine	174	smoking	72
article	169	expense	82	mail	171	society	138
attack	152	explosion	154	map	48	song	96
audience	94	eye	117	mark	56	speech	163
				marriage	108	sport	58
bomb	154	family	112	match	61	staff	32
breath	123	fan	94	meal	86	storm	19
building	13	fare	44	message	167	street	47
		fashion	102	money	78	strength	65
campaign	158	fault	177	mood	127	stress	71
career	31	fear	130	music	96	strike	157
cash	78	fee	81			surprise	134
casualty	155	feeling	126	news	166	symptom	74
character	101	film	95	noise	28		
charge	81	fine	147			taste	121
charge (criminal)	144	fire	26	operation	76	team	59
clothes	102	flight	40	offence	143	television	92
competition	61	flood	18	offender	143	temperature	23
computer	176	food	84			test	74
concert	93	fortune	79	pain	73	traffic	46
conversation	161	friend	106	party	88	training	35
confidence	132	fumes	17	passenger	42	treatment	75
country	11	fun	90	passport	43	trial	146
course	53			pay	36	trip	38
crime	142	game	60	peace	151		
criminal	142	government	136	pleasure	128	verdict	146
cure	75	gun	156	pollution	17	victim	143
				practice	55	victory	62
damage	20	habit	104	price	80	view	119
death	99	hand	115	prison	148	visa	43
debt	79	happiness	128	prize	64	voice	122
defeat	63	head	114	programme	92	vote	137
defence	153	health	68	publicity	172		
delay	41	heart	116	punishment	148	wage	36
demonstration	158	heat	23			war	150
destination	41	holiday	39	qualification	33	waste	17
diet	87	home	12			water	27
disease	70	homework	55	race	61	weapon	156
dish	86			relief	133	weather	22
disappointment	133	illness	69	rent	14	world	10
discussion	162	infection	70	repair	178	worry	131
dispute	157	injury	50	reputation	172		
divorce	109	internet	176	respect	111		
document	168	interview	33	route	48		
dream	124			routine	104		
drink	85	job	30	rubbish	17		
drug	76	joke	91	rumour	164		
drugs (illegal)	72	justice	139				
duty	32						

Key Words for Fluency – Intermediate